And When

Written by Wendiann

And When

Book cover design by: Wendiann

Copy edited by: Susan Huebert

And When

I'd like to dedicate my first novel to my best friends who have always been there for me. Laurie, Jacquie, Sandy, Vicki, Margaret, Neil, Jeff, Night, Natalie, Chris, Renee and Karen...I never would've made it this far without your support. Thank you for believing in me.

To Clair Gibson, a fellow writer from Scotland; without your advice and support this book wouldn't be what it is today. Our writing is the reason we met, but the friendship we've built; priceless.

To Jacquie & Renee who helped fine-tune the story to make it the best it could be.

I believe that fate guides us through life and brings us the people we are meant to meet. That is the only thing that truly matters; people who touch our hearts. Memories are the one thing we all get to keep...Love lives forever

And When

Prologue

Wrapped in a cocoon of blankets unable to breath, Jade battled to unwind her body then bolted upright in bed. "Holy crap," she said as she wiped her sweat-matted hair. "Are you here?" She held her breath as if she'd hear the voice confirm its presence. "If you're here, show me a sign that it's you." Again she waited for a signal, the dream too vivid this time, not like the others. Hearing nothing, she glanced at the clock which glared two-thirteen. Moving to her living room, she curled on the loveseat to still her rattled nerves.

"Why tonight?" The question whispered in the dark echoed as a lecture for her brain. "Not now, I've got a plane to catch."

She'd stayed up until midnight writing after she excitedly placed her suitcases at the door for her six a.m. departure to New York. It had taken a year of toil to get to this moment. Once she signed the publisher's contract for her series last year, their endless demands started. She fulfilled their daily requests and to end her nights, she had started the novel that plagued her. As words danced to the page, tears flowed as she exorcised the pain.

"Focus on the series," she lectured herself. "The time is finally here, your time." Exhaling deeply, she closed her eyes to clear her mind and relaxed against the cushions.

Footfalls echoed against the pavement as she walked across the parking lot. At the stairway to the upper balcony of rooms, her heartbeat sounded in her ears, and time slowed to a snail's pace when she gripped the railing to climb. From the top landing, one door stood open a hundred feet away, the light from within filled the darkness of the corridor. Knots formed in her stomach as she walked towards it. She could hear each breath as her pulse drummed louder. Steeling her nerves at the threshold, a rumble started within like the very earth shook underneath her.

Centered on the wall, the lights above the bed were an eerie fluorescent glow, a signal that it was time and a familiar coldness greeted her. Please no, her mind pleaded as she inched towards the bed to stand next to the mass covered with the linen. Reaching for the top hem, she pulled back the cream-colored sheet and the drumming in her ears stopped.

With hair disheveled like straw, his expression told the story of pain. Dragging the sheet down she saw the evidence of his decision, the empty pill bottle lay by his fingertips. Memories flooded, moments shared, the tears began.

"I don't understand." Her words barely a whisper, "You didn't say goodbye." Through her watery gaze, he appeared at the far side of the room.

"I'm here, I'm not going anywhere." She heard his voice, but his lips never moved. Looking down at the still body then back up at the figure before her, a shimmering light surrounded him, his smile so warm and peaceful.

"I didn't want to...I had no choices left," he explained.

Thoughts tumbled as she struggled with the pain. He wasn't taken, he left. Gasping, the pounding began in her chest and the room spun.

Opening her eyes in her darkened room, tears trailed down her face and that familiar ache returned. "Stop it, it was just a nightmare!" She rubbed angrily at her cheeks. Her cell phone on the coffee table taunted her and her finger moved over it to wake the message screen. Gently touching his name, his last words appeared. *'I'll call ya later.'* Scrolling through the history left as her memory of him, a rogue tear escaped.

"Why?" She whispered. His wonderful laughter and voice reverberated through her head. "This is crazy! He's been gone for over a year, damn near fourteen months!" Jade pressed the button and the screen blackened. "I've spent the last year working my ass off and I'll be damned if I'm gonna let you make me feel sad. If only you could see me now, all those years telling me to fight for happiness have paid off, I've done it."

And When

The Art of Relocation

Chapter One

"You can sit up," Dr. Brennon said as he stepped back from the exam table and waited for her to settle again.

"Okay, Doc." Jade slid the paper gown up over her chest then turned to sit as the paper from the table stuck to her behind. It had taken three years to find a physician accepting new patients and this was her first check-up. She was already unnerved enough, then in walked a man with a chiseled jaw, perfect smile and eyes as blue as the summer sky. He didn't look like any doctor she'd ever seen. Her mind wandered as his fingers tapped, pressed and touched her during the breast exam. Look at the ceiling, remember why you're here, she told herself. It's impossible to think straight. Man, he's cute!

"You look tired; is there anything I should know?" He asked with his thighs an inch from her knees while thumbs pressed at the front of her throat.

You should know you're the first man to see my boobs in years, she thought. "I just finished moving, I'm supposed to be tired." Hearing her voice, she cringed. I sound like a nervous twit. Try again. "I got possession of my house last Saturday and I'm trying to get organized." Better, she thought.

"What's going on with your thyroid?" he asked from inches away.

"Maybe it's tired too?" I wonder what it's like for a young educated man to look at my forty-one-year-old hefty body. Don't think there's enough money in the world to do that job, the thoughts played as she watched his expression. I wonder if he thinks I'm attractive. She nearly laughed out loud. Stop it you're being a dork, her brain lectured. He's a doctor, not some man. She squared her wide shoulders trying to shake off the nerdy feeling and it raised her generous chest underneath the flimsy paper. Oh great, now I look like I'm pushing my hooters at him. Stop fidgeting!

When he turned to walk towards the computer, she let her shoulders slump and quickly adjusted only to feel the paper from the table now wedge uncomfortably between her cheeks. Sheesh, barely fitting on the exam table was embarrassing enough, now this?

Tall and more Amazonian with a large hourglass figure, she never felt very feminine. It was her long auburn hair and coppery hazel eyes that people always commented on. Every compliment always sounded like an unfinished sentence. 'You have the most beautiful hair and bedroom eyes....' She expected to hear 'but it's too bad you're big', the exception that would point out her flaw.

"Make sure to book another appointment for the pap and I'll re-check your thyroid at that point," Dr. Brennon reminded her as he typed on the keyboard.

Oh, how she hated that smear. Relax, slide down further, don't tense, further down please...it was like being a frog crunched to its tightest position before a leap with its butt dipped down past its hip joints. And just when you think you'll fall off the table, the doctor looked like a miner going into a cave. It'll be even more uncomfortable with Dr. Wonderful doing one. How uncomfortable will that be? She pictured the future event and blushed.

When he left the exam room, she dressed, then scheduled the next available appointment with the receptionist for a month from now. Hurrying on her way, she thought about her to-do list on the drive back to her little house. She had sold her first home two years ago when her sister, Lisa, and her family moved back to their city. The master plan was to sell and find a home in the same neighborhood, but the housing market had skyrocketed and she couldn't afford the area. She decided to wait it out and moved in with a best friend, Eric.

The first few months had been an uneasy time when the strangest of requests had become a learning process. The dish soap was to remain closed, for fear it would dry on the spout. Dishes needed to be placed in the dishwasher precisely. There were many rules, but thankfully she'd learned from a young age to bite her tongue at the little things. Growing up in a small Canadian town with parents who drank had taught her to choose her battles.

After the first year they had settled into a routine and friends had joked they were like an old married couple. For the past six months, they were an old married couple that should never have been. Things turned ugly with a daily angry dance on the remnants of their friendship. Tired of his constant criticism and name calling, she rushed to buy the first suitable house.

Parking in her gravel driveway, next to the old garage that slanted to the right, she looked intently with a frown at what she owned. The need to escape Eric's had overruled a home inspection, a decision she now regretted. Opening the back door, she was greeted by the foul air. "That is so gross, I'm going to barf," she said, cursing the previous owner for leaving her dog locked downstairs while she moved. The stench was horrid.

She opened the kitchen windows then peered through the wall cut-out into the living room that looked tiny with her over-sized furniture. For the next two hours, she shifted the pieces until the phone rang with a welcomed break.

"What are you working on today?" Lisa asked.

"The living room, but I still hate that ugly feature wall."

"I like it. You just have to find something to tie it all together in the room."

"Like a new can of paint?" Jade chuckled.

"How did it go at the doctor's today; is everything where it should be or is it all heading south?" Lisa snickered.

"I was sitting in that stupid gown and in walked my new doctor who's a fricken hotty! Man, it was uncomfortable. Why can't he be a geek like every other doctor?"

"Eww…and he saw you naked? The poor man must be traumatized. He'll probably tear up his license to practice now."

"He is the luckiest man on the earth and is probably phoning his parents right now to thank them for putting him through medical school."

"Uh huh, keep telling yourself that." Lisa laughed.

All three of her siblings had the genetic disposition from their father's side of being a smart-ass. Her younger brother Jared, and Dane, her older handicapped brother, shared the offbeat sense of humor. Many cousins, aunts and uncles were the same. If there was a smart-mouth comment to be made, they'd find it.

"Do you need me to come help you with anything after work?" Lisa offered.

"Nah, I'm just going to go through boxes. I gotta figure out where to put everything since this house has no storage room. How much can I stuff into one tiny hall closet?"

"What's on the agenda for tomorrow?"

"I rented a carpet cleaner, so I'll head downstairs to try to get rid of the smell, then maybe paint the bathroom."

At the end of her night she reviewed the plan to tackle the repairs. The insulation in the attic was Wednesday's project, the new window installation, Thursday's. With only one week of holidays, she'd need to work steadily having spent her limited cash on the priorities. If today was any example, she wouldn't get far and barely kept awake during her shower, then collapsed exhausted into her sheets, having made only a small dent in the list.

Waking at eight fifteen the next morning, she instantly felt the effects of yesterday's accomplishments in her muscles. She stretched, mumbled a few swear words as she stumbled to the kitchen. Half asleep, she rummaged through the cabinets for her coffee maker. "Where the heck would that thing be?" Lisa had unpacked the kitchen, leaving her to guess where anything was. She pulled open every one of the six cupboards in a desperate search. "It's not a big kitchen, so you'd figure that thing would jump out," she grumbled. Aggravated, she started to boil water, deciding to use the teapot she had found instead.

"Where the heck are the filters? Oh ya know!" She pulled open every cupboard once again. "Can this day start any rougher?" Hearing the kettle whistle, she gave up the futile search and settled on paper towel and began the slow process of filtering the mess into the teapot. Water gushed and the paper towel ripped, allowing grounds into the mix, but taking that first sip she let out a sigh. "Mmm, that was worth it."

Walking into her living room she looked around. "Why couldn't I afford a house that didn't need all the work?" She thought of her poor bank account that was already drained dry. The doorbell sounded and not dressed, she grabbed her housecoat then made her way to the back door.

"Morning, I wasn't sure if you'd be up," her dad said.

"Hiya Pops, what brings you here?" This is not a coincidence, she thought. It took forty minutes to drive from his house in the country to her doorstep.

"I was in the area and just thought I'd stop by and see if you needed any help," he said with a grin.

"Sure, I can always use help. Come on in, I'll pour you a cup of coffee. Kinda."

He sat at her kitchen table and watched her struggle with a fresh paper towel and coffee grounds to make him a cup of the sludge she was drinking. When finished, she passed him a full cup.

"Are you sure I can drink that? Maybe you should give me the spoon so I can chew on the grounds later." He smiled mischievously.

"Here you go then." Jade smirked then passed him a spoon, the sugar and milk.

"Thanks. So what do you want to tackle today?"

"I need to clean the poop carpet in the basement," she said with a grimace.

"We'll do it together."

Over six feet tall with a broad husky build and a serious expression, Pops could be intimidating at first sight, but actually was the complete opposite. Never one to express himself seriously, he always threw a joke into conversations. She emulated him in many ways. His dark hair and strong character were part of her genetic make-up. She had inherited his creative approach in problem-solving. Even the great big heart hidden beneath their tough, bulky exteriors was the same. Jade was daddy's girl.

He loved the quiet of the small hometown they grew up in while she left at age seventeen. Life at home wasn't easy and the isolation had stifled her. When she moved to the city, she found people were drawn to her and she quickly became the person to talk to in difficult times for many. Having always landed on her feet, she managed to laugh at life no matter what came her way.

She watched her dad walk slowly behind the carpet machine. He looks happy just to be here, she thought. Pops had worked from the age of thirteen until sixty-five having retired two years ago. He was learning a completely different lifestyle, filling his time with home, yard work and today, poop carpets. He didn't say a word about her dingy basement's dark paneled walls and brown carpet. It was far from the comfortable middle class home she'd grown up in.

Not finding a new partner after her divorce in the eighties, with only one paycheck and no children, she got by with being a flea market/garage sale queen. It was just how her life played out. One day someone would come along and see all she offered, but being stubborn and independent, she wouldn't settle for anything less than an equal. While she waited for him to appear, she'd simply let destiny guide her.

"Well it looks and smells better," her dad said as he shut off the machine.

"I don't think it looks any better and I can't tell if the smell is gone. I'd need to go outside and fill my nose with fresh air first since I'm kinda used to the stench. Next year I'll re-do this room when I can afford it," she said with a smile. "Why don't we go upstairs and have lunch, it's almost eleven."

"I'm not hungry, but how about a drink?" He suggested.

They sat at the kitchen table with the first drink of the day; rye for her dad and she had a beer. "I feel bad you're working on my house. You should be traveling and enjoying your retirement."

"Who can afford to go on constant trips?" He said as he looked at her living room. "I wouldn't mind buying a house and having things to do. We've been in the same house all our lives. Maybe it's time we move to the city. I could see living in a house like this."

She'd heard that before. "Are you coming back tomorrow with the truck to pick up the windows and insulation? Greg is coming to give me a hand in the attic," she asked with a smirk. There's no way he'd miss out on this, she knew him too well.

"I'll be here. It's been a long time since I did any insulating, but I'll give it a try." He smiled, happy to be included. "I'd best be going and see what your mother's up to." Finishing his drink, he stood to leave.

"Thanks for the help, Pops. Are you sure you want to help? There's no telling what we'll find in the attic."

"I'll be here." He smiled warmly and walked out the door.

"What else to accomplish today?" She checked her list of chores stuck on the fridge. "I should call Greg and make sure he's ready for tomorrow morning." He was one of her closest friends and the most unreliable person in the world, but she had a hook to lure him, money. She knew exactly what made people tick. Actually, she knew too much about too many and had the knack to put a new spin on people's way of viewing any situation. Analytical by nature, Jade never saw one option, but a multitude of paths to choose from that lead to many outcomes. She was always great at seeing through the 'what-if' game, except when it came to her life.

The rest of the day she went through boxes. Each one she opened felt like Christmas, since she had forgotten the many possessions left in storage for two years. Her friends phoned and she'd reiterate her trials, but she never expected company. Late afternoon, she opened her door to find Lucky, Tom and Eric standing on her doorstep. Instantly she felt awkward as the past six months of Eric's hurtful behavior played through her mind. Keeping her outer façade in place, she smiled to mask the discomfort.

"Hi guys, come on in."

"I laughed so hard when you told me what you went through to have a cup of coffee that we decided a coffee maker made the perfect housewarming gift." Lucky said passing Jade a brand new machine.

"You didn't have to do that, I'm sure I'll find that thing somewhere."

"This one even has a timer so your coffee will be ready when you wake up." Tom said with a smile.

"Thank you, that's so thoughtful."

"Come in and I'll get us some beers."

The visit lasted an hour and she was thankful when they left. "Well that was uncomfortable," Jade said out loud as she closed the door behind them. Eric was quiet the whole time, so why did he come? "Is it so hard to say I'm sorry for being a jerk?"

Over the next month, she added gravel to the driveway, planted shrubs and built a shed for the yard tools. She was always busy with one thing or another. Friends dropped by to see the progress and quite a few times it turned into an evening of drinks when several showed at the same time. Jade enjoyed having a place to entertain again.

Waking on Thursday morning, she looked at the X with 9:00 a.m. marked on the fridge calendar. "Great," she mumbled and her thoughts went to the appointment ahead. I hope I don't turn into a total dork. Maybe I'll say nothing and that'll save me tripping over my tongue, she lectured herself as she headed out.

"What's going on in your life? You still look tired," Dr. Brennon asked as he pressed on her neck.

Sitting in the flimsy paper gown, buck naked underneath, her nerves were on edge. "I'm still working on the house and my work causes stress. I can't sleep sometimes even though I'm beat, kinda like my mind keeps going, but

I did manage to lose a few pounds in the past couple weeks." The words rattled out and she silently kicked herself. *Why do I sound like such an idiot around him?*

"We'll do your pap today, but if anything changes come see me again."

It's normal to be tired with busting my butt. He only met me a month ago, so how the heck would he know what normal was? She silently questioned.

"I want to keep an eye on your thyroid, it seems slightly bigger," Dr. Brennon said as he sat on the swivel stool and put the miner light on his forehead. "We'll take a blood sample just to check things."

Her hand went to the base of her throat. *What the hell is a thyroid? I never felt one before.* "Great, even that's fat," she mumbled.

"What's that?" Dr. Brennon asked as he extended the metal footholds on each side of the table.

"I guess that's that."

"Alright, you can lie back and put your feet in the stirrups."

Leaving his office bright red in the face after her favorite frog test, she only half listened to what he'd said about her thyroid as she tried to concentrate on other things. *How do you make small talk with someone looking up your wazoo?* She wondered.

And When

Jumping the Hurdles

Chapter Two

During the September long weekend, her family gathered on her sister's patio in celebration of Lisa's birthday when the usual joking was interrupted.

"We've decided to sell our house in the country and move into Jade's basement until we find a home in the city," their dad announced.

"When did you decide this?" Lisa asked looking at Jade's stunned expression.

"We figure it's time for a change. You both live in the city and it would be nice to move closer," he explained. "But it may take some time to find the right place."

Jade thought about her basement. I can't let them live down there, they're used to nice surroundings. "Uh, when are you putting your house on the market, exactly?" She stammered, hoping to hear next spring.

"We've phoned an agent and the sign goes up next week," her mom said. "That is, if we can move into your basement until we find a house?"

"Uh, sure, that'd be fine." Jade managed, not knowing what else to say. Looking at Lisa, this was obviously something she hadn't expected to hear either.

For the past thirty years their Pops had mentioned many times that he'd like to sell and move. It was always one dream or another. Operating a fishing lodge or moving to the east coast, she couldn't keep track of the number of dreams not followed. With a 'For sale' sign going up, this just might happen, she thought. I'll renovate and I won't tell them. My friends will help me, but I got shit for savings. I need to find a cheap way to update it, she began to plan.

"What are you doing next Saturday?" She hesitantly asked Eric the next day, swallowing her pride because she needed his help.

"Why?"

"Tomorrow I'm going to tear down some the walls in the basement and next weekend I need a crew to help me re-build since my parents are moving in."

And When

"What? Why are they moving in with you?"

Hearing the news, he agreed to give her a hand. She called a few close friends who said they'd pitch in. If they sell today, this could happen in as little as two months. If I have to, I'll do most of the work myself, she decided.

Up bright and early the next morning, she called Eric to borrow a larger sledgehammer and crowbar.

"I thought you were going to start this next weekend?" He sounded put off.

"No, I said I'd take down the walls myself. Next weekend is the build." She held her breath and waited for the answer.

"You're crazy, can't you wait?"

"That's okay, don't worry about it. I'll talk to you later." She hung up, aggravated.

Fifteen minutes later, he stood at her door with both tools in hand. When she reached to retrieve them, he pushed her aside and walked down the stairs. His mood warned her not to say anything and she followed in silence. He prowled around the main area as she briefly described what she wanted. At the edge of the center wall he bounced up and down, the sub-floor bending easily under his weight.

"What the fuck is this?"

"A rotted floor maybe," she said sarcastically, his mood rubbing off on her.

Using the crowbar, he hooked the edge of the carpet and tore it several feet away from the wall. Jade grabbed the edge and heaped the ugly carpet in the center of the room. With the plywood exposed, Eric ripped open a joint and lifted a sheet. "For fuck sakes!" he barked.

She moved in for a closer look and what she saw made her breath catch.

"Look at the fucking mold, it's everywhere!" He said as he pulled up more sections. "We have to get this out of here. Call everyone you know, we're going to need help. I'll go home to get masks and gloves."

She followed him back upstairs. How the hell could people live here and not know about this, or did they just cover it up? Her mind tried to comprehend as she dialed her friends' numbers. Lucky and Tom responded to her plea, but unable to reach anyone else, she grudgingly called her parents to ask if they could come by later to prepare dinner to feed her crew.

When Eric left she went down to inspect the nightmare. Huge cauliflower-shaped growths, some black, others white or gray in color, in a path three feet wide, narrowing to inches near the outer wall. She stared at the thick fungus. "What else could go wrong with this place?" Making a trip outside to retrieve a shovel, she started to scrape the mold off the cement into a garbage bag, cursing up until the time her friends appeared downstairs.

"You shouldn't be doing that without protection. Let's wait until Eric gets back." Tom herded them upstairs. "That shit may be toxic. I've never seen such big chunks of mold."

When Eric handed out masks and gloves to the small demolition crew, he delegated the work. "You have to put the wood by the garage, far away from the back door. Only half the basement has mold, but it all has to come out. Tom and I will cut the sub-floor and you two run the pieces out."

Hearing that nothing was salvageable, the dollar signs began to add in Jade's head. Frustrated, her anger fueled her to run up and down the stairs to form the garbage heap. She was out of breath and flushed beet red in the face when her parents arrived and Pops wanted to help. She asked that they just prepare dinner, not wanting to expose him to the hazard. Once the wood was up and gone, she dumped a bottle of bleach over the cement then left the room to join the tired crew for dinner. Damn house! She thought. I haven't even been here two months, it's never gonna stop falling apart.

After dinner, with everyone gone, she made a trip to the corner store to buy three gallons of bleach, a spray bottle and then scrubbed every inch of the basement. At two in the morning with her nose burning from the smell, she called it quits, showered, then crawled into bed. Gone was the stench of dog, replaced by a sickening chlorine smell.

Over the next weeks, during her evenings, she worked on her own and on weekends, friends and family pitched in. With the framing and drywall complete, her friend Chris installed the garage sale carpet she had found and Lisa painted. By the end of November it was finished. It wasn't perfect, but it was ready for her parents when they sold. She suffered many sleepless nights as her brain kept raking over plans to make sure everything got done. Even her weight fluctuated from week to week with not eating right. In no hurry to start any other projects, she took time to relax and settle into normal life.

Watching television a week later, she moved a loose hair tickling her neck to find a lump. "Oh man, now what?" Going to her bathroom mirror, she raised and twisted her head to see a tiny circle the size of a dime. From work the following day she called the doctor's office. Explaining the situation to the receptionist, she was given his next available appointment.

"That's three weeks away!" she said to Monique, her coworker, as she pointed out the strange bump. "That's the earliest they could fit me in."

"What the heck is going on with you? First your weight goes up and down, now this thing is sticking out of ya." Monique, a strong-willed, tell-it-like-it-is personality, measured the lump which seemed to grow like a rotten weed. For three weeks she checked its progress since Jade couldn't see it without twisting her neck. Both worried since the big boss, a real horse's ass, would frown upon any type of health problem, but her direct supervisor Tony, a funny, kind-hearted man, was concerned. She was his favorite project manager and he relied on her constantly.

Waiting the three weeks, she slept little and the smallest of chores became a burden. Shoveling the snow took twice as long with needing to stop and catch her breath. As she brought in groceries or took out the garbage, she'd feel her heart race. I knew I was out of shape, but this is crazy, she thought. Slowly, dark circles appeared under her eyes as testimony to her lack of sleep and her voice began to crackle like a tickle that wouldn't stop. By the time the appointment arrived, the tiny lump was the size of an egg and protruding from the side of her neck.

"So I hear you're having problems." Dr. Brennon started the examination. "Wow, I can't believe how big this got. When did you notice the change?"

"I didn't really notice anything until the day I called for the appointment. I had to wait three weeks and at that time it was the size of a dime. Now it's ballooned to this!"

"It's spreading to this side as well." He probed the left side of her neck and she began to hack.

"Don't press on it. It kinda chokes me when you do that."

"I have to do it again to see just where this thing starts and ends." He pressed again to get the same reaction. "What symptoms have you been experiencing?"

"My heart races for no reason and I'm not sleeping. I feel tired all the time." Her raspy voice was clearly evident, along with the dark circles. The doctor kept his demeanor professional, but Jade read the concern in his eyes. "What is it? Just say what you think."

"I don't know, but we need to find out. I'm going to send you to see a specialist."

"What?"

"This could be a number of things and until we know for sure we're not going to guess at it. We'll do a blood work up here, but we may need to get a biopsy."

"I would like to know what the possibilities are, why it ballooned up and the word biopsy usually means testing for cancer and..."

"Okay," he cut her off. "We're definitely testing you for everything, but until we know we're not going to worry. You'll go to the lab today, but I want a specialist to have a look. We'll figure this out by going through things one at a time."

"What makes you think I'll need a biopsy?"

"Growths that are cancerous tend to grow at a rapid pace, but at times lumps can appear for no reason, it's quite common."

Driving home, she worried at how long she'd have to wait. At least I noticed it right away and got it checked, that's what all the commercials say about finding lumps. Since her friend's breast cancer diagnosis she'd always checked her boobs, but who thinks to look for lumps elsewhere? "A fricken biopsy," she mumbled. The medical system is slow, so I bet it'll be months before I get in. I better talk to Lisa before I tell the folks. Once home she dialed her sister's number.

"What?" Lisa said after Jade explained. "Okay, he said it's probably nothing so don't worry until we know."

"I just wanted to let you know what's happening. We'll wait and see what they say."

When she dialed her parents' she was prepared. Talking to her folks about things was never easy.

"Hi, did I interrupt anything?"

"No, we we're just watching television. What did the doctor say about your neck?" her mom asked.

"He's arranging to see a specialist, but he said these things are quite common."

"Push to see them right away. Demand answers. Tell the doctors you need to know. Dad's been having troubles with a sore shoulder for the past month and he's pushing to get answers."

"Mom, there's no pushing or demanding. I have to wait until I'm scheduled and knowing the system, it'll be a while."

And When

Nightmare of Needles

Chapter Three

At the appointment, Jade hesitantly walked into the doctor's office. It was scheduled much too fast, only three weeks after meeting with Dr. Brennon, which left her uneasy. The lady doctor seemed rushed as they went through questions and answers, poking and prodding and the grand finale would be a scope. Dr. Vittor explained that a long narrow tube with a camera on the end would be inserted down her throat or up her nose to get a clear view of the growths.

"I'm not so good at down the throat. I have a bad gag reflex and I'll barf at the first attempt." She felt queasy just thinking about it.

"We'll try the throat first and see how you do. If that doesn't work we'll go through the nostril."

Going through a nostril is just plain gross. Relax your throat, Jade thought. Try your hardest. As the camera reached the back, the gagging started. "Sorry," she said in apology as her eyes watered.

Frustrated, the doctor grabbed a spray bottle. "This will taste bad, even though its banana flavor. Which nostril feels clearer?"

Just getting over her cold, Jade sniffed. "The right feels better."

"This will sting, but it will freeze the interior to get the scope in." The doctor pressed the button of the nozzle.

The burning reminded Jade of swallowing cola in the middle of a joke only to have it come back out her nose. It stung, but within seconds the taste far outweighed the sensation. You think they'd have found a better way to do this, she vented silently.

"Okay, hold still." Dr. Vittor shoved the tiny camera up then downwards.

Feeling it tap inside on its way down, she closed her eyes remaining still and followed the instructions.

"Swallow, now again. Try to speak."

She did as asked as the end of the camera played inside. Her throat opened and closed around it and once finished, the doctor extracted the contraption and handed her a tissue.

"So what did you see?" That just felt wrong on every count, she wiped her nose, feeling a trickle of liquid racing down, not knowing what part of her that was coming from.

"The thyroid is enlarged so there are masses. We won't know for sure until we schedule a biopsy," Dr. Vittor said in a matter of fact tone.

"When will that be?" The doctor seemed annoyed, almost cold and disconnected. Doesn't she know how this feels?

"I'll have my receptionist check my schedule and we'll get you in as soon as we have an opening."

"Let me know when and what to prepare for." Jade tried to sound relaxed, but it came off snarky, a reflection of the doctor's icy response.

As she was being rushed out of the office, her head filled with questions. She had been a smoker for years and she wondered if this was her due. The 'what ifs' played through her mind on the drive to work and in the evening, her family called to ask what came next. Jade sounded nonchalant, far easier than trying to explain her worry, having researched 'biopsy' on the computer.

Two days later she received the call from the hospital. "You need to report to the outpatient ward tomorrow at ten o'clock," they advised.

"Is there anything I need to do, like no food or drink?"

"No, just show up. You can eat and drink as normal."

She told her supervisor she'd need the day off and Tony asked if she'd need a couple more days. Jade didn't know what to say, she forgot to ask.

She telephoned her family and then asked Greg to drive her to the hospital. Since a biopsy was taking a piece of tissue to analyze, she assumed she'd have a small cut on her neck, making turning her head difficult while driving.

"Morning Darlin', you ready for this?" Greg got in the car and leaned over to kiss her cheek the next morning at nine.

"Ready as I'll ever be, I suppose."

When they arrived at the outpatient ward, she was handed a form. Taking their seats, Greg sat back while Jade filled in the blanks. She looked around the room at several people doing the same, some had a look of tension, while others appeared totally at ease. Returning the form to the nurse, she sat beside Greg who chattered away, but she barely heard a word. He didn't seem to notice the people called one by one to the back area, but Jade was ever mindful of who, where, when, and kept watch on the clock as they'd come out with bandages or gauze on various parts of their bodies. None look worse for wear, so that's good, she analyzed each person.

"Jade Prency," a nurse called her name.

"See you later."

"I'll be here," Greg said quietly.

Going into a small room no larger than a doctor's office, she took in her surroundings. The nurse placed her chart on the door and said the doctor would be in momentarily. Alone, she noticed a tray sitting only a few feet away with a white cloth covering the contents and imagined the instruments. Half of her wanted to lift the material to take a peek, but the other half was scared. As she was about to reach over, the door opened and in walked Dr. Vittor, the nose lady.

"I'll get you to jump up here and sit facing me." Dr. Vittor pointed to the exam table with a cool smile and pushed aside the tray Jade was eyeing. A nurse came into the room to unveil a tray of several large syringes with long thick needles and empty labeled test tubes in a plastic tray.

"I thought a biopsy was an incision and removal of part of the growth?" That wasn't on the website, what is she doing with those? Her head quickly recalled her research.

"It depends on the location of the growth. Since they're in your thyroid, we're going to do a needle biopsy to take samples. There's no freezing the area so there will be some discomfort, but nothing major," Dr. Vittor advised.

No freezing? Great, I hate needles! As far back as she could remember she couldn't watch as they were inserted. It was common sense. Come at me with something sharp, I'm gonna pull away.

The doctor's gloved hands picked up a needle and placed it over the syringe. "Lift your head. There that's good. Now hold still."

The doctor gripped it in her fist and in one thrusting jab the needle pierced Jade's neck. Frozen in place, afraid to move, as the plunger was slowly pulled back, Jade watched the doctor's hands move in a circular motion. Within seconds it was out and gauze was taped on the pierce wound. The nurse took the syringe and emptied the thick pinkish red substance into the test tube. Whew, thank god that is over. That kinda hurt.

"I'll prepare the next." Dr. Vittor picked up a second syringe. "Okay, turn your head upwards and to the left. Okay good. Now hold still." The doctor plunged the second needle into her right growth at a different angle.

With the same pattern of swirled motions, Jade sat silent as parts of her body filled the tube. The quick pinch from the initial pierce of the needle was the worst, followed by a pressure.

"One more time on the other side, turn your head slightly to the right…there that's good."

Jade felt like a pincushion when they were done, having three pieces of tape on her neck. As the doctor removed her gloves, Jade took the opportunity to ask one of the million questions running through her mind. "So when do you think you'll know what this is?"

"We took a good sample from the two visible tumors so in eight to ten days we should know more. These types of biopsies are like looking for a needle in a haystack so the results may not be conclusive," Dr. Vittor said.

"This may not tell us anything?" I can't fathom going through this for nothing, she thought.

"You have to understand that a cancer cell is tiny. It's possible they weren't in the area we took the samples from."

How stupid of an answer is that! "So if we didn't get enough or missed the cell, how is someone supposed to know if other parts of the growths are cancerous? I thought early detection was the key."

"There are other ways we monitor like growth rate, cell counts, ultrasounds or MRI's."

"Let me get this straight. These growths may have a cancer cell, but we may have missed getting it into a test-tube, so what happens now?" This is just stupid. In this day and age of technology that doesn't make sense.

"I'll send the results to your doctor and he'll advise you of the next steps. You have a good day and try not to worry." The doctor left the room leaving Jade to stare at the door.

Hopping off the table, she went to the waiting room, put her coat on and grabbed her purse, completely pissed off with the doctor not taking the time to explain anything.

"So how'd it go?"

"Let's get out of here, I'll tell you on the way home."

"Your voice sounds better."

She hadn't even noticed she could talk clearly, the raspy feeling in the base of her throat lessened. "I guess that's a good thing. What a bunch of mixed-up answers. They said this may not even tell me anything!" She recounted her experience as they walked to the car, suddenly realizing she no longer had growths, the doctor called them tumors. That word stuck. Everyone she'd known with tumors had ended up having cancer. Her cousin with a brain tumor had undergone years of treatment, then died. Another cousin with a tumor in her leg had died at age thirty-four after seven months battling cancer. Her uncle had died from cancer last year. 'Tumor' is not a word I'm ready for. Why me? Because you smoke and you're a dork, you have the shittiest luck at the best of times, the words whizzed around her brain as she kept explaining the situation.

Stopping for lunch at the local greasy spoon, Greg chatted away while her mind kept going back to the word. What should I tell the family? What do I tell anyone? Work would want answers and her friends want to know. She nearly jumped when she felt Greg's hand on hers.

"I'm not letting you go down that road, don't you even think about the cancer word."

"I'm okay, I must've zoned out. I'm just tired, that's all." They finished their meal and left.

Once home, she listened to the messages left on her machine, taking a deep breath she returned the calls. Lisa got quiet at the word. Using a positive encouraging voice she said there's probably nothing to worry about, but uncertainty came through in her tone.

They were close as two sisters could be and Jade felt guilty having to worry her. "What do I say to mom and dad?"

"Better they know right from the start what comes next. I know they're gonna go off the deep end, but you gotta tell them all of it." Lisa was adamant.

Jade dialed their number. "Hi, what were you doing?"

"We just walked in the door from getting Dad's shoulder checked. The doctor thinks he sprained a muscle in his back. He's been in pain for almost two months and it took the doctor this long to say a sprained muscle? It's ridiculous! But what about you, how did it go today?" her mom asked.

"It went well and I won't know until they get the results in a couple weeks. They took three samples of both tumors and they'll send the results to my doctor." She slipped the word into the conversation.

"They're tumors?" Her mom's voice changed an octave as she relayed the news to Pops in the background.

"Mom, they use 'tumor' when they find any kind of unexplained bump." They reacted exactly how she expected.

What Jade didn't expect was the reactions from her closest friends.

"Jeffy, it's me and I have to tell ya something. I'm just gonna come out and say it, so don't interrupt until I tell you it all, okay?"

Jeff, a close friend for nine years was a little A.D.H.D. and could take a subject in a million different directions. Frustrated by the doctor's coldness today, she didn't think she could handle jumping from subject to subject.

"Okay, I'm ready," he responded hesitantly.

"I went for a biopsy today and they took samples of two tumors in my neck. This may not show anything or it may show something, but the doctor couldn't say for sure. I just gotta wait and see." She paused and waited for his questions. "Jeff?" The line was quiet. "Jeff?" she asked then realized he was sobbing quietly at the other end. "Jeff, are you okay?"

He cleared his throat. "I can't...I don't know what to say. I'm scared I could lose my friend."

"Heck no, I'm not going anywhere. This is just the beginning and I's a fighter, ya know that!" She tried for humor to lift his dark thoughts. Her comical antics throughout the call did little and she could tell he was still upset when they ended the conversation.

Calls to Lucky, Karen and Chris were much the same. It must be the fear of the unknown. Lord knows I'm scared, but she needed to comfort her friends, not wanting this to bring them down. The word 'tumor' seemed to shake everyone since many had lost someone after hearing it.

Not wanting to upset anyone else, she flipped on her answering machine and put on music. The doctor had said, "Don't worry." Tumors, biopsy, cancer cells, what to expect, how did this happen, she couldn't stop the internal voice that came out of nowhere. How do I just stop thinking?

At work the next day, Jade told Monique the news and discussed her worry of keeping up with the mortgage and bills if she ended up sick. They researched the company disability plan to find it paid only sixty-five percent and that wouldn't be enough to keep her house. Jade slept little the next nights, waking more tired from over-thinking things. At work she functioned as best she could, fuzzy from the lack of sleep. Three days later when the phone rang at work, her world stopped.

"Dad's in emergency!" her mother said in a rush. "He coughed up blood and we're waiting to see the doctors."

"What do you mean 'coughed up blood'? What hospital?" A twisted panic gripped the pit of her stomach. Jade didn't hear the phones or her co-workers, just the quiet voice on the end of the line.

"He started this morning and it didn't stop so we're at St. Nick emergency. The doctors took some x-rays and we're waiting for them to talk to us."

"I'm on my way. I'll be there right away."

"Okay, see you soon."

She hung up and turned to her boss. "I gotta go, it's my Dad!" she said, bolting through the door with little explanation. Running on autopilot, the drive passed in a flash and she arrived breathless at the emergency desk. She gave the nurse his name to hear he was down the hall and took off in that direction before hearing the end of her sentence. Pops was lying on a gurney with her mom and Lisa by his side.

"What's going on?" She tried to calm her racing heart as she searched his face for some clue.

"Well, they took some x-rays and it seems there's something in my chest. They aren't sure, but they say it's a mass and think it may be cancer," he calmly explained.

She didn't know what had hit her. "What do you mean they think it might be cancer?"

"Tomorrow, they want me to go see a specialist to run some more tests."

Lisa and Jade looked at one another, both trying to absorb what they'd just heard, a frightened look mirrored in each other's eyes.

"Oh man," Lisa said. "This is crazy! What time do you go tomorrow?"

"First thing in the morning," their mother said.

"We wait until tomorrow. You never know, maybe it was bad film, maybe they're wrong." Jade tried to sound positive, but felt scared beyond belief.

She lay in bed that night with all thought of sleep long gone. Silent tears ran down her face that seemed to have no end as she talked to the man above. "Please don't let this be happening. Let it all be a big mistake," she whispered. "God, you know my dad, he's a good man and worked hard his whole life. He never did nothing wrong to no one. He's a good guy and just retired. They're going to sell and move in and start a new life." She pleaded with the powers that be, hoping someone was listening.

And When

When Nothing Else Matters

Chapter Four

Jade showed up at work looking like something the cat dragged in. Her swollen eyes, along with underlying black circles she'd accumulated since December, radiated a 'look at me I look like crap' statement. Monique immediately came to ask what happened, worried her health turned for the worse.

"They think my dad has cancer." She could barely say the words. "He goes this morning for more tests."

"What the hell? Like you don't have enough to handle right now, when will they know?"

"I'm waiting for the call."

Jade waded robotically through her work. Her normal cheerful voice was gone, replaced by a distant tone as she picked up the phone lines and constantly checked the clock, willing it to move faster.

"It's me, are you sitting down?" her mom asked in a faint voice.

"What's going on, what did they say?"

"Well…" Her mom began to sob. "They say its terminal lung cancer and he has two weeks to four months." She sobbed in between shortened breaths.

The tiny wheel in Jade's head, stopped. "What? Two weeks to four months! How do they know that?" Angry at the words, "What can they do, what about chemo or radiation, there has to be something?"

"We're on our way to Dr. Sith's who's supposed to prescribe medications to ease things."

"I'm on my way I'll meet you at his office. Don't leave until I get there!" Hanging up she turned to Tony with tears in her eyes. Sobs and guttural sounds escaped and she could barely breathe. "I gotta…"

"Go," he said. "Don't worry about anything. Go be with your dad."

She ran out of the building, thankful he'd overheard the conversation. Starting the car, her cell phone rang with Lisa in the same state; in shock, crying and trying to find words for what just turned their lives upside down. She'd pick Jade up at home and they'd race to the doctor's office together, both girls needing to see their dad this very minute.

Jade parked in her garage as Lisa pulled in behind her. Her neighbor said "hello," but it didn't even register. Getting into her sister's van, with one look at each other, both girls began sobbing.

"Oh my God, what just happened?" Lisa said. "What are we gonna do?"

"We're going to lose our Dad." The words seemed to explode out of her and once Jade said them she wished she could take them back, they sounded more evil than when they were in her head.

On the drive they talked of options, cures and treatments, anything to help them try to find a solution. Turning into the doctor's parking lot, they saw their parents' car with their dad in the driver's seat, the passenger seat empty. Wiping their tears away they walked to the vehicle.

"Pops," Jade paused. "This is crazy. I'm not ready for this." She searched her dad's eyes for some kind of punch line, for him to tell her this was some sick joke. He looks ten years older, she thought.

"I'm not ready for this either." The tears welled in his eyes as they stared at each other for a long moment.

"Where's Mom?"

"She's in the pharmacy buying prescriptions for me."

A quiet response, not the strong, tough guy she'd always known. Leaving Lisa with dad she went inside to find her mom by a counter. "How are you doing?"

"Isn't this something? I can't believe what they're telling us. Two weeks to four months. It's in his upper right lung and it's a huge mass already. They're talking of radiation and finding a way to slow the growth," her mom spoke as if in a daze.

The pharmacist called her name and Jade welcomed the break from the devastating news. Wandering back outside, she stood silently at the driver side window and looked at her father's face. This isn't right. How the hell does this happen? Damn doctors! Sprained shoulder my ass, she vented silently at the health system.

The girls followed them to the homestead and neither spoke. Jade prayed silently to the man above that the chemo would work and they'd caught it in time. As they pulled into the driveway she'd come to a thousand times, the guilt flooded over her for not using it ten thousand times more. Why was life so hard? Is it like this for everyone?

They gathered around the kitchen table where many discussions took place over the years. This was where they had grown up, in the kitchen with dark cupboards, beige linoleum floors with everything traditional from the decorative mirror and needlepoint pictures, to the displayed china in the cabinets.

"I can't believe this is happening. What did the doctors say exactly?" Jade asked.

Their dad went into detail about x-rays and CT scans, then the specialists' best advice. "They're going to try to slow the cancer, but don't feel there is much chance to survive. They said two weeks to four months at most," he said in a quiet voice.

Again that deadline! Like an expiry date stamped on his body somewhere. "How could they possibly know it's only that amount of time? Every person is different. They didn't even diagnose this until you were in emergency, so what do they know?" Jade vented.

"What about chemo, is that an option?" Lisa interjected.

"They talked about it, but said it was sort of like closing a barn door after the horse ran away. They'll start with radiation and see what happens. I really don't think I want to go through chemo," their dad said it as casually as talking about not wanting to cut the grass.

"Why wouldn't you try if it means you have a chance of getting rid of the cancer?" Jade piped in.

"I saw what Uncle Jake and my brother went through. The quality of life just isn't there. It's awful, you get sick and you just don't have a life."

"Dad, when my friend Nancy in Houston got cancer I took her to the appointments. I'd sit with her while she got the chemo and she rarely got sick from it, just tired. Nancy beat the cancer. She's still alive!" Jade wanted her dad to fight, needed him to fight.

"I'm going to do research on the computer for alternatives too," her mother added.

"We'll find a way to beat this," Jade added. Please give us a burst of hope...please God?

"What about you, what have the doctors said? Any news on the biopsy?" he asked.

"I'm not worried about me, I'm worried about you!" How could he even worry, it was simple test and he was just told he was going to die?

In late afternoon the girls headed back to the city, her sister's family would be home soon. Their parents would phone Jared, their youngest brother who lived away, to tell him the outcome. The drive was quiet, both lost in the reality. Why is it when I cry I could sleep for days?

The hurry up and wait game had just begun for their entire family. Jade had played that game since her own growths had first appeared. We can send a man to the moon, but we can't get proper medical treatment, she thought. How could the medical profession drag their asses when they're dealing with people's lives? Don't they know patients aren't just numbers? Dad went to emergency to get a diagnosis, his own doctor oblivious and never looking further. Why hadn't he investigated? Dad was in pain for two months, for crying out loud. If they'd found this earlier, maybe it could be different. He had his appendix removed two years ago and was told he was healthy as a horse. The damn health care system was crap! If it wasn't government- controlled, people would be in charge and could pay for what they need. Her internal voice ran steady as she stared out the passenger window.

Over the next days, she spoke to friends who had dealt with cancer in their lives. Greg had lost his father to cancer and she listened intently as he recounted the experience.

"My father drifted in and out of reality and didn't recognize people. The worst was the incredible pain. He'd lived with that brain tumor for a year before it was ever discovered. I'm warning you, there will come a time when your father yelps in pain from a sheet being placed on him," Greg said with care.

She didn't want to hear it, yet needed to understand and it left her shaken. Before bed, she used her computer to research lung cancer and read posts of others who had suffered.

A new routine began with working during the day and heading to the country every night. Since she wasn't sleeping well, it was a difficult pace to maintain. When nine o'clock came, she drove back to the city and went to bed to get ready for the next day.

During the weekend visit, Lisa asked their dad if there was anything he'd like.

"I'm fine just sitting here," he said, the sparkle gone from his eyes.

"Come on Dad, if you could do anything or have anything, what would you like?" Lisa prodded. "You've worked your butt off your whole life, there's got to be something?"

He thought for a few moments and looked from one daughter to the other. "Well I would like one of those big-screen televisions they have. A more comfortable recliner would be nice since this one hurts my neck." It'd been two weeks since his diagnosis and they wanted their dad to enjoy what time was left.

The next Saturday they all met at the furniture store and walked around the showroom looking at chairs. Sales-people would ask if they needed anything and they'd say no, hoping to be left alone. A sales woman approached once again and began a sales pitch, the second to come up to them. Jade was aggravated as the woman continued her spiel of warranty and workmanship. When her eyes caught Jade's, she nodded to say leave us alone. With a look of disdain the woman promptly went off. Sneaking away from the family, Jade wanted to have a word with this ditz.

"Excuse me. Can you ease up on the big sell? Just so you know that man is my Dad and he's got terminal cancer, so mind your manners and back off." She said with such a blunt demeanor that within seconds, a flicker of I'm sorry appeared across the sales-person's face. "Just know that sometimes you don't know what's going on in another's life, so it's not always about a sale." She turned and walked back to her family where Lisa found an oversized, plush recliner, built for a man the size of Pops.

"Hey Dad, this looks good." Lisa pointed to the chair.

He took his time lowering himself into it. They watched his hands slowly slide up and down the arms and his head lean back into the soft pillow top.

A third sales woman appeared. "Can I help you?"

They're like vultures circling, Jade thought.

"How does this recline?" Their dad inquired and the lady pointed to the lever on the side.

"I think this is one I can be comfortable in, how much?" Her dad asked and hearing the $1100.00 mark, he cringed. "That's too much!"

To have terminal cancer and still worry about a price tag wasn't right in Jade's thinking. She'd be racking up the Visa with trips and gifts. To heck with it, let them try to collect. "Woo hoo Pops, we found the chair and now for the television. Let's go next door and have a look." Comfort would mean everything in the coming months, according to Greg.

Walking through the rows at the big box store they looked at the big-screens. Not wanting to go through the sales pitch the other store offered, Jade took over. "I'll go get us some help to figure this out."

She cornered a salesman with kind eyes, explained things and as they walked back to her group, he opened up. "I lost my Dad last year to pancreatic cancer so I know exactly where you're coming from. It's not easy," he said as his eyes watered.

"I'm so sorry to hear that. It's just not right, is it?" Jade felt a kinship, but how can I feel a connection with a stranger? Is this going to happen with anyone I meet that's gone through this?

"Afternoon, my name is Peter. I understand you need to know the difference in the big-screens we have," he said with a pleasant smile as he shook her dad's hand. He kept the explanations simple and brief then pointed to one on a stand. "That would be the one I would choose."

Pops was tiring as he stared at the picture and his eyes wandered to the price tag. "Wow, that's a bundle."

"That's not a bad price, Dad. It's a plasma, the newest technology, look at how clear that picture is," Jade prodded.

Her mother spoke up, "We'll have to get a stand and I'd like one of those things that go over it that has bookshelves."

"That's silly, why do you need all that?" Dad became aggravated.

"We can't have this thing just sit on the floor," was her mother's retort.

"Mom, why don't you and Lisa go look at the furniture and we'll come see which ones you pick out," Jade suggested, seeing sadness in his eyes. He's not used to splurging on himself, she thought. He provided for us and never put himself first, so how many other things has he given up? It shouldn't have taken a horrible disease to have things he wanted. The guilt washed over her.

And When

Alternative Thinking

Chapter Five

Trying to find a solution, Jade tucked extra pillows against the headboard in an attempt to remain upright and prevent the coughing that woke her throughout the night. She'd fall asleep wedged between the pillows, yet always woke lying flat on her stomach in her usual position. When she told her friend Chris about the trouble, he brought her to a naturopath who recommended mass doses of vitamins. Chris also suggested an aboriginal friend of his that was in touch with traditional healing. Willing to try anything, she agreed, and Rick arrived at her home that night with a medicine bag and a will so strong she could almost see it.

Lighting sage grass in a large shell, he walked from room to room, wafting the smoke. She watched, fascinated, as he blessed the home. When finished, he took a sacred pipe from its cloth covering to reveal a long carved decorative shaft with a large bowl at its end. Rick puffed while his hands danced in the air, symbolically moving the smoke. Jade felt ridiculous as she tried to mimic the movements at his instruction.

"This is to begin talking to the spirits. The smoke needs to be moved in each direction to ask their help," he explained.

He wanted the elders to meet with her and perhaps take her to a sweat lodge. Readily agreeing to the elders, she asked about the other.

"They're held in a tent where they build a fire so intense that it cleanses the body. Most enjoy the experience, but some get nauseated or pass out. Prayers are done for the people who need them."

"With my crazy heartbeat, I don't think it's something I can risk."

"I'll get you in to see the elders, but it may take some time."

Closing the door after he left, she felt relief that someone was trying to help. I just wish he could do something for Pops or switch things so I would take his place, she thought, remembering his weekly radiation at the cancer treatment center. She met him at every one and walked at his side into the nuclear medicine unit. It scared her the first time he disappeared behind the thick steel doors that barricaded him in. The hazardous markings warned to avoid the area, yet he allowed the poison into his body. Silently staring at that door waiting for it to re-open, she felt sick inside that this was his only option. When he finally came out in his hospital gown and socks her heart ached.

Gazing into her mirror before bed that night, the dark circles were getting puffier each day. "Great. It's bad enough I feel like death warmed over, now I look like it," she mumbled.

The next morning she called the doctor's office to explain her frequent choking, only to hear the receptionist advise her results had arrived last week. Furious, Jade demanded to see Dr. Brennon and was given an appointment for the next day after pleading her case. How could they let me just sit and wait? That's just stupid.

On the drive to the appointment, she thought about what she'd do if suddenly both she and her Pops were dealing with cancer. Would she tell him? Nothing mattered except what he was going through and the last thing he needed was more worry. He frequently asked how she was faring and she'd tell him "fine", hiding her troubles. "What if they found cancer?" Saying it out loud didn't help find an answer.

"How are you feeling? You look exhausted," Dr. Brennon asked with his usual perfect smile in place.

"I'm tired and having a rough time right now. My dad was diagnosed with terminal lung cancer and I need to be there for him. I'm with him for every radiation appointment and spend every waking minute I can. Since you have the biopsy results, maybe you can fix this somehow and I can focus on my family."

"Let's see." He stepped away and searched his computer. "They are inconclusive at this point."

"Doc, this sucks! I have to be there for them. I need to be able to sleep and gain some energy. I wake up choking so bad that I have to sit up to stop and I feel this awful pressure in my throat."

He pressed on her neck lightly to get the result she just described. "I guess you need to learn the difference between choking and emergency choking."

"What does that mean?"

"We've all swallowed something wrong. We cough to clear our airway and usually within a minute we feel it getting better. That's choking. Then there's emergency choking, where no matter what you do you can't clear your airway and may not be able to."

"What the hell? That is the stupidest thing I've ever heard."

"You'd need to call 911 for help and you may not be able to talk at that time," he explained as if talking to a child.

"Well that's great! How the heck am I supposed to call for help in the middle of the night when I live alone?" Doesn't he know that? He's got my damn chart.

"Don't live alone, because you may not be able to talk through the coughing fit well enough to tell them what's happening," he replied in a no-nonsense tone.

Her expression should have said it all, of all the dumb-ass things to tell someone when they don't have the option of a husband, child, or live-in maid. "Find me an expert, I'm done fooling around. I want answers!" she demanded.

"I want you to see Dr. Paul. He's the top in this field. I'll make the arrangements and they'll call you with the appointment, but it could be a couple weeks." Dr. Brennon smiled as if he just solved her problem.

She left his office, dumbfounded. If Dr. Paul was the doctor who'd be able to figure out how to fix this, then why hadn't he sent her there in the first place instead of the snotty doctor? With no real assistance from him, she needed to figure out what to do until the specialist's appointment. I definitely don't want to tell the parents. Not now. I'll ask friends to help me out and see if Rick can find something to fix this, she thought. Although she hated asking for anything, she hated the idea of dying in the middle of the night even more.

Once home, she called Lisa, who was sworn to secrecy and was just as angry as Jade was at the stupidity of the situation. The next calls were to Jeff and Greg. Both were more than ready to be there to watch her while she slept. They'd take up residence on the couch and split the shifts to be her night guardians. Jeff would take the weekends, Greg, the weekdays. They said she should quit working to deal with things, but she couldn't. The only way she knew how to cope was to keep pushing ahead. Her last call of the day reached out to Rick and when he learned of her latest health complication, he immediately called the elders then called her back.

"Okay, we can go tomorrow night. They'll make time to see you."

"I don't get it Rick, why don't they do everything they can at the first appointment? I mean we pay for health care through taxes. It's not like I have a pimple on my butt, I have lumps in my neck! They say early detection is everything and here it's been almost a month. My Dad complained of pain for two months, so why didn't his doctor try to find out what was wrong instead of waiting for him to cough up blood? Maybe they could have saved him." Her mouth ran at full speed, frustrated with it all.

"Why do you think I follow native healings? I think doctors are quick to put you off or prescribe something to make the symptoms go away. I've lost many people because of the system. I think it's better in the U.S. where you make your own arrangements with doctors, but that takes money."

A new chapter began when Greg arrived for the first shift at Jades' house. The next morning he told her that he had heard her cough several times and had sat holding his breath to see if she'd need his help. It scared him every time and he hadn't slept a wink. This won't work, there's no way I can ask people to be scared.

Rick called her at work and said to pick up two pouches of tobacco from a native specialty store on the way home. According to their customs, it was insulting to offer money; tobacco was the acceptable payment.

Picking her up at seven, Rick drove Jade to a small home on a residential street that looked like every other house on the block. Nervously, she followed him to the front door, unsure what to expect, feeling at odds with putting faith in people she'd never met. Stepping into a very small living room where three aboriginal men and two young children were watching television.

Two men sat on the couch, and a younger man sat in a chair off to the right. The children sat squished in a chair at the end of the room until one elder asked them to turn off the television and leave. Invited to sit, Jade chose the floor, while Rick sat in the chair that the children had vacated. The men began talking of different sweat lodges, letting Rick know what was available as she sat quiet, uncomfortable.

Rick introduced her then explained the tumors and side effects. The younger man asked her beliefs of native spirits and faith.

She stumbled as all eyes focused on her. "I believe something is at work in the universe, I just can't say what that is."

When they asked to see the tumors, she raised her head and lightly pushed on the left side to show the right lump, then on the right to show the left. Her eyes watered as she stifled the cough. Nodding, they picked up two pipes from the table and began stuffing tobacco into the bowl ends. The ornately carved instruments were much different from Rick's, slender, with detailed carvings to the ends. The shafts were much longer and a small feather was attached to the bottom of each bowl. Lighting the pipes, taking large puffs, they followed the ritual of wafting the smoke, each moving their hands through the air while mumbling. Several minutes later the man sitting in the chair suddenly thrust a pipe at her and Rick prodded her. She hesitantly puffed lightly as he'd shown her then passed it to Rick, who in turn took a puff before passing it on. The second pipe came around and she repeated the pattern. By the time the first pipe came back, her throat hurt and she signaled by nodding her head from side to side. They skipped over her and continued while mumbling nothing decipherable. During the fourth pass of the pipes, one spoke up.

"She upset Mother Nature and breathed something she wasn't meant to. This is the result."

Rick clued in right away about her basement. Long forgotten in the turmoil she'd been dealing with, the lumps appearing shortly after moving in. How could it have happened so fast? She'd only been there a month before cleaning the mess. Her brain stopped when she realized her dad had helped her rebuild. Did her damn house cause all their problems?

The healers told Rick she needed to drink fireweed. He nodded and then passed the tobacco pouches brought as payment. Finished as quickly as it started, they left the home.

"I'll drop off the first batch tomorrow evening after I make it. I'm off work tomorrow so I can go get what I need." Rick said with a smile.

"Thanks for doing this." Jade wondered at her decision. What the hell is fireweed and what if it tastes really bad, she wondered.

"Anything I can do to help, I will," he assured her.

True to his word, the next evening he appeared at her door with a gallon jug. "You drink one glass first thing every morning. Call me when you have a day left and I'll make a new batch."

"How much of this stuff do I have to drink?" She looked at the murky brown tea-like liquid.

"I guess we'll start with this and see what happens. It will depend on how well you do, but I'll talk to the elders and see what they say." He opened the jug. As he poured it into a glass she noticed small bits and chunks in the liquid then downed it in three gulps.

It tasted similar to cold herbal tea and something she definitely wouldn't choose to drink. Thanking him with a hug, she promised to follow the regimen.

Within two days her voice seemed less raspy and the pressure was easing in her neck. Everyone commented on her sounding clearer and now that her cough lessened, she could do without her night guardians, waking feeling better than she had in a long time.

Her dad noticed the change and with hearing what she tried, he was open to looking at alternative measures. As the disease progressed, he tired easily and visits with the local priest spurred his thoughts into the afterlife, a sign that he wasn't fighting as she'd hoped.

They discussed chemo several times, but his fear of the side effects kept that off the table. Her mom found a drug that claimed it could possibly halt his ever-spreading cancer and he agreed to try. Rarely talking, he seemed to pull away from the world with every day that passed. The family tried to keep life normal as each dealt with their own internal war as things transpired.

Everything in Jade's life slid into a not important category, her thoughts always on her Pops. While doing laundry she'd stare at the shelves he had helped build. The basement, morphed into a welcoming place where her parents would never stay, was a reminder of time spent.

After drinking her swill, nightly she fell asleep as soon as her head hit the pillow from exhaustion, emotion or concoction and would wake only a half dozen times during the nights.

The appointment with the specialist came eleven days after seeing Dr. Brennon and ten days after starting the fireweed. Dr. Paul was a man of few words and even less of a sense of humor. Her smart mouth didn't go over well. After her first few attempts, she kept to the family history and asking questions.

"Could the mold have caused the problems for me and my dad?"

"It is possible, but nobody can say what starts tumors or cancer. In your dad's case, his brother died of cancer last year, plus your father is a smoker. With your problem, there's no way to tell what started this. Thyroid problems are becoming more prevalent and there are many studies being done. Some theories are that dental x-rays may cause them, others believe it's genetic. There is no one answer really."

He scheduled a CT scan for the next day and an appointment with an endocrinologist on Monday. Dr. Paul was serious about her problem and she left his office content feeling he understood and would help. Calling Rick on the way home to let him know the fireweed was running low, he asked her to come by that evening to make another batch.

"You're looking better," he said with a grin.

"And all thanks to you." Jade flashed him a smile.

They stood in his kitchen talking about her latest appointment as they started removing the excess dirt on long narrow sticks with a dark red bark and short roots. On the stove, two large pots of water sat, one had reached the boiling point.

"Okay, it's time. It all goes into the pot," he said taking them from her to set bunches in the water. "If we were to walk into a burnt patch of trees after a forest fire you'd see all these plants poking through, hence the name fireweed. It has a stubborn determination to survive even after devastation." He looked up at the clock. "We boil it for the exact amount of time because if you do it for too long, it becomes poisonous. I won't let it boil one second longer," he said with a smile. "This will have to be the last batch since the elders said you can't drink it for too long. Maybe you won't even need more since you're doing better.

After dinking the fireweed for almost two weeks, Jade noticed the lumps seemed to have stopped growing. Poison or not, it was nothing compared to what her dad was going through.

"We'll be making another drink for you though," Rick announced. "This new one is to be taken along with the fireweed to start your mornings. Don't worry, it's made from dandelions and you can drink as much of this as you want as long as it helps, the elders said."

"I've heard of dandelion tea," she said. "It can't be worse than some of the herbal teas I've had."

At the exact time, Rick removed the twigs from the rolling water then moved the fireweed pot to the counter. After placing the other pot on the large element to bring it to a boil, the two worked side by side. They carefully siphoned the fireweed mix through a large strainer, then again through a fine filter into a container to allow it to cool before filling the jug.

"Okay, now the other one." With the water almost at a boil, he produced a paper bag filled with the longest yellow dandelions she'd ever seen. The roots were thick white with long trails of hair like strands covered in chunks of guck and white nodules.

"These dandelions aren't like the ones in the city. I pulled them from the wild," he said as he smoothed the long roots. "People spray weed killer and poison on these things to kill them, so it wouldn't do to use anything that even grows nearby. I walked a ways into the bush a half hour out of the city. It's where medicine men go to get what they need," he explained as he picked off the larger chunks of muck from between the roots.

Astounded that a man she barely knew would take the time and trouble to do this, she went to her purse. "I want to thank you for doing this for me," Jade said and handed him two pouches of tobacco.

"You didn't need to do that! I'm doing this because you're a good friend of Chris's."

Shit, she'd done the wrong thing. "Rick, anything you do to help me will always be repaid, it's just who I am. I'm kinda stubborn that way." She smiled and he shook his head as he accepted her gift.

"It's time to put them in, the water's at a full boil."

Jade watched in sickened amazement as he picked up handfuls of the bright flowers by their heads and slowly sank the mucky roots into the raging water. Instantly, the water turned murky as chunks of slime churned through the rolling water, turning it to a hazy black green.

Leaving the mix to boil, they smoked the pipe and by the time the mixture was done, what they poured through the strainer made her stomach churn. The putrid smell filled her nostrils as lumps of limp stems and pieces of the flower thumped into the strainer. Stopping frequently to dump the strainer's contents into the garbage, they filtered it a second time to eliminate chunky bits. The oily liquid had a slimy look much like car oil mixed with antifreeze. Holy crap, how am I going to drink that, she questioned silently.

After filling the three jugs, it was eleven o'clock and definitely time for her to get some sleep. Rick repeated the instructions as she walked out the door with one gallon of fireweed and two of the other.

The next morning she looked hesitantly at the jug. "It looks like pond scum," she said as she analyzed the layers that had settled through the night. The top was a hazy brown, then a layer of green silt that got darker in its layers. At the bottom, a two-inch black layer formed she couldn't see through at all. It took a long while staring at it to gain the will to drink a glass. After shaking the container she removed the cap to smell it. "Oh my God…that's a mistake!" She gagged as she poured the designated amount into a cup. Pinching her nose, she held her breath and raised it to her lips, swallowing the contents in three gulps.

Standing next to the kitchen sink, she quickly bent over as the last gulp came racing back up and out, in objection. She coughed and gagged until she nearly threw up, her stomach rolled and twisted. Blindly she reached to turn on the water to sip directly from the stream. Turning her head, she looked at the fireweed container and her stomach growled. When the taste lessened, she stood and poured the glass full once again.

Later as she was getting ready for work, she looked long and hard at herself in the mirror. "How did I get into this mess?" she asked herself.

And When

I'm Okay But You're Not

Chapter Six

She reported to the hospital for her first C.T. scan the next day. Given a cotton blue hospital gown and matching robe, she was told to strip to the waist then ushered into a small office where they inserted a shunt into her right bicep. The needle, which she looked away from, left a tube taped to her shoulder. The nurse handed her a cup with a liquid and said to finish it within fifteen minutes when they'd be ready for her.

"Don't worry," she said with a smile. "You won't feel a thing until they give you an injection right before the scan. At that point it will feel like you're peeing your pants, but you won't."

"Wow, pee my pants, that's funny." What kind of drug would do that to a person?

Once finished the tasteless liquid, she was brought to a large room with a table that looked like it was from mars. The C.T. machine is huge, but will my butt fit on that little table? The thought played through her mind.

She removed the robe and lie down. Once comfortable, the nurse pulled her gown open to just above the swell of her breasts then instructed to remain still and follow the instructions she'd hear.

"This is easy, don't worry," the nurse said as she inserted a needle into the shunt to push a clear liquid through.

Just as warned, the wave of heat started at the tips of her toes, moved through her legs then to her groin. It startled her how accurately they described the sensation.

"Okay, hold still and don't breathe."

Jade held her breath as the large circular part of the machine passed over her head and chest.

"Okay, you can breathe again," said the microphone voice which sounded like a drive-thru window. Would you like fries with that? She almost laughed.

"One more time, don't breathe."

When the machine stopped moving the nurse came to check on her, "Everything okay?"

"No problems."

"They're checking to make sure they got everything or they might do one more."

"Okay, it's good," the microphone voice announced.

"You're done, you can go get dressed."

She walked out the door to collect her belongings, hoping that next week's appointment would give her some answers. Finishing the day at work, she told Tony she'd be late on Monday, needing time for the endocrinologist.

After visiting her parents first, she got home and soon friends called to check up on her, but the conversations were becoming awkward. When this started she had tried to explain, but had since given up. Jade couldn't articulate what she felt and no matter how much friends said they understood they didn't. She couldn't even understand it. Watching her dad was hard. Going through cancer testing only mixed her thoughts even more. Once she started changing the subject to safer topics, with not voicing her thoughts, friends started to drop by unannounced. Never one to let anyone see her struggle, she tried various beauty products to try to reduce the circles beneath her eyes. With little success, she used layers of concealer to hide things, but her once sparkling hazel eyes were dull and listless. Nothing hid that problem.

Friends discussed their problems, looking for her input and then turned the questions on her. Jade was sick of the "how are you feeling" line. There was no answer. "I'm fine," she'd respond. Some asked about the concoctions sitting on her counter, wanting to try them. She'd pour a mouthful of the fireweed, which most didn't like, followed with the pond scum. As they brought it to their mouths a few declined, but others downed it. Jade watched them retch, hoping they'd understood why she dealt with things in private. Still up-chucking the last mouthful of the foul swill daily and she didn't feel any benefit taking it. Her brain argued and her body would convulse, voicing its own objection.

After she got home from the parents' Saturday night, Greg stopped by to fill her in on the latest news. Jade had been refusing every invitation for social gatherings, but he reminded her of their friend Karen's wedding in a couple weeks. Karen had been a friend for years, one of the people who didn't try to pry or push her to answer anything and Jade had already promised her she'd attend.

"Eric stopped by my place the other day and said you lied about having tumors," Greg said after he sipped his coffee.

"I haven't seen him since the basement renovation, so how did he hear about things?" She looked suspiciously at Greg and a door closed inside her. "Never mind all the other comments I forgave him for while I lived there, this one takes the cake! Who the hell are these people to discuss my life?" I don't want to be the topic of gossip. That's it, I'm staying away from people, she silently decided, appalled by the situation.

"I told him I went to the biopsy with you and you should've seen his face. He was shocked and looked hurt almost. I think it scared him to hear it wasn't bullshit. I wish I had a camera so I could show you." He chuckled then went on in detail as Jade fumed inside.

Biting her tongue, she waited until she heard about all the other tidbits about her life being discussed by others. "I really would appreciate it if you kept things you know about me to yourself. I don't want anyone talking about things they can't understand," she said with a fake smile.

"People ask about you and I tell them the truth. It's no big deal really. I just tell them what tests you're going through and that you're having a hard time. I haven't said anything about your dad and I wasn't sure if I should."

Suddenly she felt distinctly different. No one understood her frustration with not being physically able anymore. They didn't understand what she felt as she watched her dad. "Greg, the last thing I need is people talking about me." I'll stop answering the phone and the door, she promised herself.

After the visit, she stood at the door as he gave her his usual hug. "I promise I won't say anything else as long as you take me to Karen's wedding. Can I catch a ride?"

"Okay."

"No excuses. We're going and that's that," he said kissing her cheek as he left.

Spending the next day at her parents, she told them she needed time to get caught up at home. Since she was only managing to shovel the snow when needed and do necessary laundry, the past two months of upkeep had been pushed aside and was starting to show. She'd stay home after work this week with a promise to spend next weekend with them.

Monday morning, the endocrinologist's appointment was more of a total physical and one she wasn't prepared for. Poked, prodded, measured, scaled, she found herself standing fully naked in front of Dr. Richard, who closely examined the skin color on all parts of her body by pushing lightly on different areas.

"If I'd known what to expect, I would've shaved my legs," Jade said, embarrassed. "I researched endocrinology on the computer and it said it was a blood specialist." It's not blood under the microscope at the moment, she cursed herself.

"Don't worry," Dr. Richard said with a smirk. "I want to run some tests to see what we're dealing with." She bent her head while writing on a chart and her shoulder-length blonde hair hid her face.

I bet she's laughing at me, Jade thought. "What kind of tests? There is nothing left. You've pretty much seen it all." Her humor kicked in to diffuse the anxiety.

"We'll get a full set of blood work and I'd like to see you two weeks from now. We'll do this all again at that point." Dr. Richards smiled warmly.

"What are you looking for when you look at my skin?"

"We look for pigmentation or discoloration, things that may be signals of other things to look for."

"And did I pass the test, anything to worry about?" Jade asked still standing there in the buff.

"I don't see anything of concern, but we'll send you to the lab to get a full work-up. So far everything looks good. You can get dressed."

"How anyone can see me fully naked and say everything looks good is beyond me." The doctor chuckled and Jade thought about how Lisa would have fun with this. Getting her clothes back in place she headed to work.

Lisa couldn't stop laughing that night as Jade described the appointment. "I tell ya the hair on my legs is almost long enough to braid!" she said.

Lisa would visit their parents while Jade stayed home. She called nightly to give her updates, but here wasn't much change lately other than their dad being tired and withdrawn. This wasn't the first crisis the family had endured their mom fought her own battle six short years ago when her liver gave out.

It'd been twenty years of trying to get the drinking to stop and the months leading up to her liver shutting down, the biggest fight of all. The sisters had phoned daily back then since Lisa lived away. When their mom was admitted to hospital, the doctors had warned the family they may lose her. Lisa and Jared came home for two weeks, but for Jade, there were many months of going back and forth to a hospital. Their mom never drank again and things finally changed.

Their parents had started with dreams and hopes, just like every other young couple. Lisa came first, then a year later, Dane, followed by Jade. Three small children within three years and when health problems with Dane became evident, by the time the doctors discovered the hole in his heart he was left mentally and physically handicapped. Jared, the baby of the family, came along a few years later.

The alcoholism had started soon after that and it had taken her many years to understand. Now with her parents finally enjoying life, to face another horrible situation just wasn't fair. I shouldn't have been so tough on them all those years ago. If only I knew this is where life would lead, she thought. She regretted her rebel teen years, a result of the confusion the alcoholism brought and how it left her questioning and guarded most of her life. Constant fights and arguing were a part of everyday life back then and she left home at seventeen. Married at twenty, she tried to follow normal life, but walking down that aisle seemed like the proper thing to do. After knowing the man a total of five years, going through a divorce was difficult, but it was by her choice.

Since that first mistake, she formed a kind of shopping list of what she wanted in a partner and it grew longer with every date. For the past seventeen years her expectations were impossible to fulfill, with Jade seeing flaws in almost every man. She told herself she'd rather be alone than end up in a wrong relationship. Dealing with all this now, she would do anything to have someone to see her through. Believing a perfect man would show up one day didn't make sense. It never did. She saw life very differently and that stupid list had disappeared. The years she'd kept safe, afraid of trusting and relying on someone were utterly ridiculous. Why did I act like I could handle the world all on my own, no wonder people don't understand...I never showed them a vulnerable side. Make a joke, laugh, be tough...that's how I lived for twenty years. Right at this very moment, it all came down to a simple heartfelt hug and arms to hold her at night while she wept. Her stubborn tough girl mentality had led to this moment and she'd been such an ass.

No one understood, nor did she expect them to. It was her own damn fault that her life was a series of doing what was needed. Work, shovel, drink the pond scum, fireweed, eat, sleep, go to tests, check on family and start all over the next day. What she faced, she faced alone. How could she offer advice to friends when she needed to fix everything she ever thought? She didn't want to tell friends that she didn't have time to listen anymore, how do you tell a person their worries don't matter to you? That's just wrong. Jade wanted to be left alone until she found her way.

At her desk Thursday morning, she was interrupted by the sound of her dad's voice from behind her. "What brings you here, did you miss me coming out this week?"

"I needed to get out for a drive and went to visit the old workplace. Since you're down the street I thought I'd stop by."

He looked good for all he was going through. His salt and pepper hair neatly combed, his large 270 lb frame was in his usual dress clothes and he wore the overcoat from the company he retired from.

Coming to stand at her desk, he let her know he came to talk to her boss. Her dad had given him his first job years ago, starting his career, but over the years she'd told her father of the type of abuse she'd witnessed at his hands. When he left her desk she was curious and waited for a half hour when he appeared again.

"You still coming for the weekend?" he asked walking up to her with a slight smile after his visit.

"You still want me to?"

"It would be nice, mom is driving me crazy."

She knew he wasn't one to have anyone badger or fuss over him without losing patience. "Okay, I'll be there and stay until Sunday. Anything I should bring?"

With a soft smile and warm eyes he replied, "Just you. Maybe we can watch a movie on the big screen."

And When

Saturday morning, she sauntered into her parent's kitchen with her hair stuck to her head with sweat. Arriving two hours earlier, she had shoveled a better path from the garage to the back door since the snow had only been pushed aside.

"You didn't have to shovel all that," her dad said as if he'd failed to do a good enough job.

"No problem Pops, I was out there and this way you don't have to do it later. We can just relax," she said, afraid to hurt his feelings by saying anything different as her heart thumped wildly in her ears from the exertion.

The three watched TV in the afternoon and talked about life in general. Careful not to touch on sensitive subjects, she asked his opinion about many things, trying to gauge his mind-set. During the conversation he explained the surprise visit to her work and how he had asked her boss to look out for her since he'd help him years ago. Her boss had agreed and shaken his hand, but she doubted his sincerity.

In the evening, they brought out snacks for movie time since both parents had developed a sweet tooth, one their miniature pincer, Felix, enjoyed. Being given the nightly treats of cookies, desserts and sweets, he was spoiled rotten. Dad even built a box on the back of the riding mower so the dog could accompany him mowing the yard last year. With little exercise, Felix looked like a large tube of baloney on four toothpicks.

At the end of the movie and about to use the guest room, Jade learned her dad was going to sleep in the living room. "Why do you sleep out here?"

"I haven't slept in bed for the past month."

"I'll spend the night on the couch then," she said.

It was strange lying in the same room as she listened to his every breath. Pretending to sleep, she stayed awake to check on him. He first fell asleep in a semi-recumbent position and every couple of hours she heard the chair mechanism. She'd wait until she heard the even breathing, then glance silent as a mouse. As the night dragged he'd adjust the chair. In the wee morning hours she looked over to see him sleeping completely upright in a sitting position with his elbows planted on his knees and hands cradling his chin. The silent tears slid down her face. This is awful, she thought.

Exhausted when the daylight arrived, she plastered a smile on and poured her first cup of coffee. "How did you sleep last night?"

"With my eyes closed." His smart-ass personality resurfaced.

"The chair does look cozy."

"I just can't lie down. It feels like there is a big weight on top of my chest when I do."

"As long as you're comfortable, thank God you have that new chair."

After breakfast her uncle and aunt dropped by. This was her dad's older brother, the only brother left, having lost their younger to cancer the year before.

"Have the doctors said anything?" Her uncle put it point blank. It was a chance to discuss the medical side of things since she was careful not to touch on the subject.

"Nothing new," her dad said. "They'll check next week to see what the radiation is doing, but I don't think it's helping much."

Her uncle struggled with the news as much as she did. The two brothers had grown much closer this past year, spending time together daily. Her uncle drove Pops into the city for his radiation treatments. He was a Godsend, and without him, it would've been difficult to try to schedule time from work to take Pops for treatments.

The visit lasted a couple hours and touched on many subjects. Laughter, joking, and serious all wrapped into one, the Prency genes were at work today. It was good to see her dad laugh.

And When

Her Hero's Final Battle

Chapter Seven

She stood before her mirror and used layers of make-up to camouflage the puffy circles as she got ready for Karen's wedding. Skipping the dinner, she took a nap in order to make it through the evening. True to her word, she'd be at the reception. With one final check, Jade left the house to pick up Greg.

They arrived at the large hall crowded with the supper guests. Hidden away for seven months, this was her first public appearance, tumors and all. Deliberately leaving her hair down and swooped to the front, she tried to hide the bumps.

"I am so glad you're here. You don't have to hide anything, we love you the way you are," her friend Nancy said as she moved Jade's hair to the back.

"There's nothing I can do about them." Instantly uncomfortable, she saw Karen headed her way in her dazzling wedding dress. "Wow, that dress is incredible! You look amazing,"

"No, you look amazing." Karen gave her a hug. "I'm so glad you came. I kept watching the door, worried you wouldn't make it."

"I gave you my word and I wouldn't miss this day for anything."

Many old friends were glad to see her and some asked to see or feel her neck, since the rumor mill had spread the news. They'd asked how she was faring, then reiterate stories of people they'd known who dealt with tumors. Her trials opened the floodgates of stories of cancer and loss. Few knew of her dad's health and she bit her tongue and politely listened.

"Eric just walked in." Greg leaned down to whisper the warning as they stood in a group of friends.

His comments still stung and she nearly jumped when Eric's arm appeared around her shoulder, his voice friendly in greeting them all. Nancy gave him a hug and with that distraction, Jade took the opportunity to escape to the bar. Buying two vodkas to settle her rattled nerves, as the bartender passed her the drinks, Greg appeared at her side.

"I figured you'd need a drink," he said with a smirk.

"I haven't had one in seven months so it may only take these two. Look, I don't want to deal with him. You know he's going to ask, so not a word, promise me." She drank the first glass completely empty and set it aside, giving him a warning look.

Greg placed his arm around her shoulder. "I can tell this isn't easy, I'm here for you."

Suddenly, Eric pushed his way between the two and forced Greg's arm away.

"How are ya?" Eric asked.

Excusing herself, she found her coat and went outside for a cigarette then stood in the crowd of smokers in the frigid temperatures until both men appeared at her side.

"How are you doing?" Eric looked directly at her neck.

She gathered her collar trying to hide the evidence. "I'm fine."

"I heard you went for a biopsy, did they say anything?"

"I'm fine. I'm going in." She walked away not wanting to waste time with fair-weather friends. Life was too short and she fully understood that age-old saying now.

At the reception's end, Jade was cajoled by several to go for last call at their old stomping grounds. Greg wanted to attend to find an all night after party, but her last trip to the ladies room showed the black bags under her eyes becoming more prominent. She hesitantly agreed to a quick stop since she was starting to fade.

Pulling into the parking lot packed with vehicles she found a spot at the far end of the lot. Barely stopping the car, Greg jumped out heading for the door. Slowly she shuffled in her heels across the ice when an arm came around her waist and a hand grabbed hers. Eric followed them. Once at the door, she thanked him then headed towards her friends, hoping to create distance. Packed beyond capacity, they needed to constantly step aside to allow people by. Nancy had asked about her father and in mid-conversation Jade turned to allow people to pass to find Eric right behind her, eavesdropping.

Seeing the discomfort, Nancy pulled her onto the dance floor. Hesitantly, Jade moved to the music. So far so good, my heart is calm, she thought. As the next song began, her favorite from years long forgotten, she couldn't help but stay. It's been too long since I enjoyed anything, she reasoned. The heavy metal song, irresistible, she closed her eyes and threw caution to the wind. For a second she was the person she used to be, dancing surrounded by friends, enjoying the freedom she used to have, but when the music finished she realized her mistake.

"A quick drink and we'll be right back out there, dancing all night like we used to. I've really missed you coming out," Nancy said with a warm smile as they walked back to the table.

"I gotta go," Jade said as her pulse echoed in her ears, her heart thumping dangerously fast. Several asked her to stay when she said her goodbyes, but it wasn't an option, already she worried about making it home safely.

Curled up in her much-needed bed, Jade replayed the evening. Watching everyone enjoy normal life had only reminded her how different she was. Shifting in the empty queen-sized bed, wishing for someone next to her to say it would all be okay, she felt even more alone. Just before she closed her eyes, the guilt struck for not being with her dad tonight.

The following Thursday, dressed in a hospital gown, Jade was ushered into a room with a man outfitted from head to toe in a white protective suit. With face protector and gloves in place, he opened a canister with a radio-active label and poured a clear liquid into a test tube, then added water by using a squeeze bottle. "Just sip it through the straw," he instructed.

It rattled her. Here is a person completely protected, telling me to suck this into my body. What if I don't want to? Hesitantly she put her lips to the straw and followed like a sheep to a shearing. Once she emptied the tube, he filled it repeatedly and she ingested the contents.

Brought to a room and placed on a table, they asked her to lie completely still for twenty minutes. A machine was placed directly on her neck to read the harmful liquid pumping through her system, creating a picture the specialist requested.

How do I stay completely motionless? It's like when your hands are full and an itchy nose strikes, she thought. Keeping her breathing slow, Jade stared at the ceiling and her head took over. How does one end up swallowing radio-active materials willingly? I haven't even had an aspirin for twenty years and today I gulped a hazardous material. Suck it up! Dad goes for weekly radiation and lately he needs a wheelchair, so quit whining.

And When

Last Tuesday at the endocrinologist's we weighed and measured again. Life is a series of crap. How much damage can drinking this stuff cause? They haven't found a cancer cell, so would this create one or make a hidden one get worse? Instead of going from department to department, why don't they just take these things out? "'We want to be sure what we're dealing with,'" they'd said. CT scans, ultrasounds, radioactive drinks, even the fireweed…is this good for a body? Then again, smoking and drinking in my twenties and thirties, I've done damage, she thought. Still, these things aren't normal so just take them out, problem solved.

When finished, they told her to stay away from people and animals for twenty-four hours until the mixture cleared her system. Lying on her couch that night, the thoughts tossed through her mind until the phone rang.

"Hi, it's me," Eric said. "I really want to say I'm sorry to hear about your dad. I know we don't talk anymore, but I wanted to tell you I'm thinking about you and I'm here if you need me."

The tears started down her face. "That's nice of you," she said in a monotone voice, angry about today's test, angry at life. He used to be the one to see me through rough patches, but he's been such a horse's ass I can't talk to him anymore.

"It was hard seeing you at the wedding and I know you hate me, but I do care about you."

"Eric, we just don't mix well. It's not that I hate you…it's just we always fight. We've always butted heads and it's time to stop," she said in a clear voice.

"That's not true! Sure we fight, but we just think differently. That doesn't mean we don't care or can't be friends!"

"I don't even have the time or energy to hate anyone. I just don't care anymore. Our disagreements don't even rate in the big picture. I have other things to worry about and I don't want to talk right now." She hung up the phone.

A week later her grandmother passed away after having Alzheimer's for over ten years. Her grandfather had died several years ago and would be joined by his wife. At least, she hoped that's what happened. Some said every soul that died had a chance to come back. Others said there was a heaven for the good and hell for the bad, with the chance to meet up with loved ones. Maybe there was nothing after death and it was nature running its course. So how do ghosts fit into it all? With dad not doing well, her own health in question, she wanted to try to find the answers. With time alone at home, she researched lung cancer, thyroid disease, religious beliefs, miracle healings...anything to help sort out her thoughts.

The day of the funeral, her dad sat surrounded by people, many knowing he was losing his battle. At the wake, Jade watched as family and friends sat to talk with him, but he looked defeated. As much as he tried to prepare he was terrified, she could see that clearly in his eyes. Today brought a reality and it hurt her heart to see his face at the end of the day.

In bed the tears rolled down the face of a lost woman. Afraid to lose her dad, scared about her tests, she couldn't understand why life had done this to them. She wanted to be her Dad's support and strength, but how could she tell him not to be afraid? She was the go-to person, for fuck sakes, but she didn't know the words. Barely holding it together any more, it became a juggling act she was starting to lose. Lately, the tears came at all times of the day. At work she'd take frequent walks to hide. Her few remaining friends heard the difference in her tone and she stopped trying to tell them she was fine. "I can't talk," she'd say and end the phone calls. Exhausted, she drifted into a troubled sleep.

The following Saturday Greg showed up after being cut short on the phone. Annoyed by his invasion, she was even more irritated when her doorbell sounded again. Lucky, Tom, and Eric, stood at her doorstep with a case of beer.

"We figured you could use a beer and a friend," Lucky said with a bashful grin.

Jade eyed Lucky closely, the guilt washed over her face and sadness was written in the group's expressions. Lucky must have told everyone about my emotional state Jade thought as she watched her friend. Well I guess I can't trust saying anything to you anymore, can I? The last thing she wanted was to be forced to sit face to face with anyone when she was at her lowest. Can't I have any privacy, she fumed silently. "Come in," she said out loud and walked to her loveseat, mentally crossing Lucky off the list of people to open up to.

Greg kept up the conversation and Eric watched her from across the room. This visit would definitely put to rest any doubts about how my life is, she thought. The doorbell rang again and she headed to see who it could possibly be, having eliminated almost everyone from her life. Standing there were her mom and dad, his right arm in a sling.

"What happened?"

"Well it seems I broke my collar bone," he said with a weak smile.

"Come in, there are people here, but come in." She needed to hear what happened.

"I didn't do anything. I moved and heard a snap, then pain. We just left the hospital and thought to come by and let you know," her dad said as he sat down in the living room.

"So what are they gonna do about it?"

"Nothing, I just have to be careful with it from here on in, it doesn't hurt too bad." He didn't sound sincere.

The room hushed. Her friends watched for her reaction as she struggled with the news. The quiet lingered like an uncomfortable pause.

"Well, it's starting to get nice out and I was wondering if you could do something for me since I can't really do it because of this." Her dad pointed at the sling. "It seems the eaves trough for the house isn't working. The snow melting off the roof is making the ceiling leak again. I was thinking if we add another trough from the corner, the water would have some place to go. It just might solve that problem once and for all." She could see a plea for help in his eyes as he continued. "And the back yard is covered in dog poop from over the winter. Could you give us a hand getting that cleaned up?"

Greg and Eric jumped in, asking how he wanted the troughs done, both volunteering.

"Tom, what do you say? Want to come out give us a hand next Saturday?" Eric asked.

"We'll all come out and get stuff done," Lucky piped up.

Jade watched her dad relax as he got into conversation about the repair. A little tiny spark appeared in his eyes as he told the men how to fix the problem then turned the conversation to the impending flood in their small town. "The river's claimed only a few roads but we're going to have to watch this." He looked at Jade as if sending a silent message. "Well, we should get going home. I've told you before you really have a great bunch of friends." Jade saw his eyes glisten, he was struggling. It was his warning that he won't be around to take care of things. Biting back tears, she walked them to the door then came to sit in the living room, fighting to hold it together.

"I can't believe he broke a collarbone. I guess the cancer is in his bones." Greg said.

It took everything in her not to explode as he described his dad right before he died. She steeled herself, not wanting the group to see her cry and she was thankful when they left shortly after.

Jade arrived to visit her parents' on Tuesday and found her dad using a walker. The man who'd always been invincible in her eyes now stumbled behind as he made his way from the kitchen to the living room. Following slowly behind, she glanced at Jared who sat watching from the loveseat, his eyes filled with unshed tears. Flying in two weeks ago, Jared was stunned by the change since his last visit. Later in the evening when Lisa arrived, their dad asked them to meet with the priest on Sunday to have a service at home. It was becoming all too real. Family and friends stopped by as news spread of his rapid downward turn.

Saturday morning her group headed to the country to fix everything. After a quick stop at the hardware store for supplies they arrived at her parents'. Jade checked in on her Pops to see an oxygen tube attached to his nostrils, something else new this week. Not wanting to disturb him, she joined the crew outside. Quietly the men worked at re-routing the trough while the women cleaned the yard. Going back inside to warm the lunch she'd brought, she glanced into the living room to see her dad awake, looking tired and drowsy.

"I brought Shepherd's Pie. As soon as we're done, we'll come in to have lunch with you," she said warmly.

"I'm not hungry really."

An hour later, when her friends came in and took seats at the kitchen table, Jade peeked into the living room. "Lunch is served. If you're not hungry that's fine, you can just stay here and rest. Everything is fixed and we tested the trough."

"I watched for a bit out the patio window. I'm happy to see it done." Slowly he rose and bent over the walker, using both elbows on the front bar. The tiny front wheels helped him shuffle awkwardly to the kitchen using the device to stabilize his shaking legs.

Jade watched her friend's faces as he made his way. It was only seven days ago when he walked into her living room and now, they watched in shock.

"We got it all done so I hope it fixes the problem," Greg said with a smile.

He took his seat at the head of the table and looked out the patio door at the work done with love and care. "I want to thank you all for doing this and I also want thank you for being such a good friend to my daughter all these years by being there for her." He smiled, as if making sure her friends knew how much she was going to need them in the near future.

Pops ate a small helping as her friends made conversation. He said it tasted good, but Jade knew everything tasted like cardboard to him, one of the many side effects of the medications. As of two days ago the cancer was in his liver, bones, lungs, kidneys and ever-spreading. There was no stopping. No miracles. No wishful thinking.

They stayed only a short time, then Jade hugged him goodbye and was quiet the entire ride back to the city as she stared out the side window. The memories of the trips he'd taken them on, teaching her how to fish and drive, every second with her dad replayed in her mind until they finally pulled into her driveway.

"Do you want us to come in and keep you company? We've all got time," Eric offered and everyone nodded their head in agreement.

"Thank you for helping today. I really appreciate it, but I just want to be alone," she said then waved them off as she climbed the back stairs.

I have to find a way to say goodbye, all of the family needs to find a way, she thought. The workers from Dane's institution brought him twice a week to help him understand. Jared was in shock at seeing dad in the late stages and he was trying to come to terms. Lisa and Jade witnessed the slow progression, like watching a rose slowly wither and fall apart to leave petals lying on a table. For each petal, something soft, gentle and beautiful was ripped away leaving a stem and a shriveled bud.

The four siblings gathered on Sunday at their parents' place and the priest began with a talk about faith, offering to answer their questions. Jade remained quiet, wondering how any God could allow this type of pain. After the short mass, their dad was blessed and the priest left, leaving the family to discuss matters.

Their dad announced he would go into the respite hospital a week from Tuesday. The last visit with the doctors had revealed his heart could stop at any time with what his body was going through. She dreaded hearing the inevitable news. He asked for a week alone with their mother to say goodbye in private, then divided the things he held dear, handing them each one of his prized possessions and an envelope. He'd written something and they were to open it only after he was gone, a gift for being his children. He calmly discussed his funeral, having chosen most of the arrangements and leaving the small details to his children. As he made peace with his impending reality, he saw the difficulty each of his children had in accepting it, the afternoon filled with tears.

Leaving their house at the end of the day, Jade was completely devastated. Crying most of the way back to the city, she needed to pull over frequently not able to see through her tears. Cars would honk or slow, but she didn't give a damn.

On the day her father went into the respite facility, Jade talked with Tony to book off the next two weeks after explaining the situation. Getting to the hospital, Jade sent her mother home since she'd been there all morning. After she left, Pops asked Jade to take him outside for the cigarette he craved. The doctors saw no point in putting his body through the strain of quitting.

They sat in the sun on a warm spring day, his favorite time of year. Pops in a wheelchair covered with a blanket and Jade on a bench.

"How are things with your tumors, any news?" he asked softly.

"They're still working on it, but I'm doing okay."

"I'm worried you won't take care of yourself after I'm gone. You've been so busy with me and I see how tired you are. I need to know you'll do everything you can to get better." His eyes peered at her through his glasses, watching her closely with his sideways glance.

"I'll do whatever it takes, I promise."

"I need you to," he said then looked straight ahead again as if focused on something interesting miles away. "There are some things you'll have to do for me. Mom isn't young anymore and she'll need help once I'm gone. You'll have to help with the things I used to do." He took a long puff of the cigarette before continuing. "She's not good at driving, so maybe try to teach her and show her how to look after the truck. You need to look after Dane and be the one to handle things since it's too hard for mom to do, she's getting too old." He paused for a few moments. "Make sure the grandkids remember me. Tell them I'm proud of them and I love them. I didn't get much time since Lisa only moved back a few years ago and Jared's boy doesn't visit that often." He took a few moments before continuing. "Remember to shut off the water valve before it freezes and you'll have to remind mom to put proper fluids in the truck for winter. The lawnmower is supposed to be serviced in May too." He took a break for several minutes and Jade remained quiet, waiting to hear every word as she fought the urge to cry. He looked directly at her. "I need you to look out for the family. I'll be watching, so don't think I won't know." He smiled weakly.

After he voiced his worries they sat in silence until he finished his cigarette. As much as she didn't want this moment to ever end, it was time to take him to his room, he looked exhausted. The hospital brought a recliner from the waiting room to make him more comfortable. Arriving back, the nurse said she'd get help to move him into it when her dad spoke up. "It's okay, Jade will do it."

They carefully took either side under his arms. Trying not to hurt his broken collar bone, she mimicked the nurse, learning to hold her father's now delicate frame as they eased him into the chair. When he told the nurse the seat hurt him, she left the room to return with a two-inch thick piece of brownish rubber.

"This is designed to feel like skin and you'll be far more comfortable sitting on it." They carefully lifted him again while the nurse set the large rubbery thing under him.

Her mother arrived with Felix. Since animals were welcome, both planned to spend the night in the room, both lost without Pops at home. Lisa came by after work and Jared dropped by at supper time. Uncles, aunts and cousins slowly made appearances throughout visiting hours and at ten o'clock his children kissed him goodnight and left.

The days continued, with the family sitting vigil at his side. At times in shifts or sometimes together, there was no set schedule, everyone did as they needed. Jade stayed ten to twelve hours a day. From the moment she woke until bedtime, all she wanted was time with him and she'd send her mother home to give her a break. It was taking its toll, the signs clearly visible on her mom's face.

The family sheltered Dane from the technical side of cancer, but on Wednesday when Jared wheeled him into the room, he instantly grasped what was happening. Jade watched closely as Dane's eyes took in the sight of his dad in a hospital bed, looking older and tired. When the workers arrived to pick him up in the evening Dane was quiet and somber, his thoughts clear as day on his face. The sisters walked him outside to meet the institution personnel and spoke to him gently about what would happen the next time he visited.

"Dane, you know Dad is really sick," Jade started. "You know soon he will die and we won't see him, right?" Dane looked intently at them both. His limited vocabulary had two words and his 'Yah' was soft and quiet.

"You know that its better Dad doesn't hurt anymore and he wouldn't leave if he didn't have to," Lisa continued the explanation.

"Yah"

"The next time you come in, you'll have to dress up and we'll need to go to Dad's funeral together in a church to say goodbye." Jade started tearing as Lisa said the words. "We'll have to be strong for Mom, because she'll need us to be there for her." Lisa barely got the words out when Dane's loud reply of "mama" came, his way of saying he worried. "That's right, we'll have to look out for Mom now," Lisa continued. "You're the oldest son and she's going to need you to be the man in the family."

Dane giggled then got quiet as thoughts played over his face. Together they prepared him for what was to come and asked the staff to help to be his support. They were more than ready and would send people to help with Dane for the funeral.

At the end of the week, sitting quietly alone with him in his hospital room, Jade finally was brave enough to voice what she needed most answered by her hero. "Dad," she started then paused to make sure the words all came out right. "We've talked a lot this week about everything and what you need me to do when you're gone." She stumbled, trying to voice the hardest words of her life. "I was just wondering if you had anything you wanted to say to me about my life and how I live. What advice or wishes you have of me." She'd gotten it out, the words that would need to last a lifetime.

"You know I'm proud of you and I want you to be happy." Said in a soft voice, he too stumbled for the words. "You are most like me you know and you have that side of you that always dreams of things." He paused as if thinking back over his life. "I was afraid to try for things and afraid to change things, but you live trying. I'm proud you have the courage I didn't and I understand your need to chase life. There is nothing I can tell you that you don't already know. Just be happy and never lose who you are." His eyes welled as her tears spilled over, staring at one another both scared, knowing their time was almost done.

"I won't, Dad. I love you." The tears that crept down her face said it all. They sat quietly together for the next hour, not saying a word.

Lisa arrived later in the afternoon and his girls carefully shifted him into the recliner as if handling a porcelain doll. The nurse appeared shortly after, needing to take blood samples.

"Okay Mr. Prency, it'll just be a little prick," the nurse said as she finished tying the rubber piece around his bicep.

"How did she know?" Pops said looking at his daughters with a devilish smile.

They couldn't contain themselves and stepped to the hall to stop laughing. Their good old dad came shining through, one they hadn't seen in awhile resurfaced as a gift to them. After staying until ten they headed home to sleep.

Arriving at the hospital Saturday morning, Lisa and Jared greeted her as she walked off the elevator heading towards his room. There was something horribly wrong by the looks on their faces, her heart stopped beating for a moment. I was here last night and there hadn't been any change. "What happened?" she asked, instinctively wanting to run into the room, but slowed her pulse long enough to listen.

"Dad didn't do so good last night," Lisa softly voiced. "He had a stroke sometime in the night and he's catatonic." Her eyes filled with tears and Mom stood next to her, crying.

"What?" It didn't register and her heart pounded faster as if it would explode out of her chest. "Let me see him."

She heard Lisa say, "Brace yourself", as she pushed open the door to his room. Holding her breath she stopped dead in her tracks. Her dad's face was twisted, his breathing shallow and uneven, the sound scared her. Her uncle sat teary in the corner chair looking back at her. Shocked, she walked to the bedside.

"Hey Pops." She leaned to kiss his forehead, the tears gliding down her cheeks. "I'm here to spend the day with you," she whispered to him. Her siblings were standing on the other side of the bed with tears rolling down their faces. Jade left the room to find a doctor and ask what exactly happened.

"We think your Dad suffered a stroke and all we can do is keep him on pain-killers and wait," he said in a kind way.

Wait for what, she wanted to scream. "Is there anything we can do to make him more comfortable?" Her quiet voice betrayed the inner anxiety.

"There are small sponges and you can help by swabbing the inside of his mouth and lips since we won't be giving him anymore liquids."

"What do you mean not giving him liquids doesn't a body need liquid to sustain itself?" She knew full well why they'd stop.

"We have him on intravenous so he is getting fluids, just not orally. It makes them more comfortable sometimes to have the swabs done."

"Where are the sponges?"

He looked at her with sadness, then turned to the nurse at the desk, who handed her a dozen small wrapped blue swabs on sticks. She needed anything to try to help him.

"Don't give too much liquid. His lungs could fill accidentally since they're badly damaged."

Back in his room, she filled a cup with water and used the swabs for the rest of the afternoon, gently running it over his lips and inside his mouth. At one point, he clamped down and as she extracted it he whispered "More" in a painful helpless plea. Everyone heard the cry and she quickly loaded the sponge again. His breath hot and fiery, she imagined the raging cancer burning in his chest and fought the urge to lift the glass to his lips. For the next twenty minutes she filled the sponge repeatedly, but he didn't utter another word.

The next day, the family took turns swabbing as relatives stopped by and talked about the memories he'd left them. With no change Sunday night, Jade headed home and had just walked in the door when her mother called saying the nurse said it was time. As she was pulling out of the garage, Lisa called asking for a ride and they broke every speed limit on the way to the hospital, afraid they'd be too late.

Crying the entire ride in silence, she barely stopped the vehicle when the sisters ran through the door to the elevator. Their mother was at the doors as it opened on his floor and explained she was about to leave when he took a turn for the worse. The elevator sounded again and Jared exited, running towards them. Quietly they walked into his room.

Jade held her breath and instantly the coldness hit her, a feeling that death itself was here, like a living beast waiting invisibly in the corner. The labored breathing was the only sound and the fluorescent lights above the bed gave the room an eerie, cold, lifeless glow. My heart's not ready, she thought. Her head swam as she stood next to his bed and stared at her Pops. His erratic gasps were a struggle to inhale and exhale, the noise painful and desperate. She felt something switch inside of her and emptiness overwhelmed, as if she were standing alone in the middle of a field as it poured rain. She glanced at Lisa, who ran her fingers through his hair, then at Jared, who held his hand. Jade quietly looked down at her hero from the other side of the bed, next to her mother.

Uncles and aunts soon filled the room, their night disrupted by the call and soon Pops was surrounded by those who loved him most. Looking around the room a hollow feeling gripped her soul and the man who'd become her dad's rock sat with tears flowing. Poor Uncle, the last brother from the family she thought. She wanted to comfort him, but there was nothing left inside of her.

Turning her focus back to her dad, she silently watched the pain he endured trying to stay with them. It's time, the voice whispered eerily in her head and she leaned down close to his ear. "Dad, it's okay, you can go. I'll take care of everything for you." She prayed softly in whisper as she kissed his forehead again. "Please, don't let him hurt anymore. If you're going to take my dad then do it. Let him free from this pain," she softly begged the man above and as she stood she heard her father's voice plain as day.

"Leave me be!" The voice sounded angry and tired. Not knowing if she imagined it, she asked if anyone else heard him.

"What did he say?" Her uncle asked.

Jade repeated the words.

"He doesn't want us here. He wants to die alone in peace," her uncle said.

Pops had reached to her from somewhere beyond this room and she left to go sit in the small kitchen on the ward, shaken. The family soon shuffled in and waited for this nightmare to end. An hour passed with little change and the uncles and aunts headed home, thinking Pops could hang on for days. Jade didn't say a word, but in her heart she knew he was leaving tonight.

Silently, the family entered his room and the moment they stepped through the door his breath quickened, as if he refused to leave them. They again left the room and waited. Checking a half hour later, finding the same result, looking at each other they knew he wanted to find his way alone.

And When

The ride home passed in a haze. Dropping off Lisa, Jade went home, her heart filled with a sorrow she'd never known. Sitting on the edge of her bed, she stared at her closet doors until the phone rang.

"Dad just passed away minutes ago," her Mom's sobbing came through the voice piece. "He waited until we were all at home, safe and sound, then he left us."

"Did you call Lisa and Jared?" she whispered.

"I'm going to right away."

"Okay Mom, try to sleep and call me first thing in the morning." Having no wish to talk, she placed the phone down and sank to the floor by the edge of her bed to pull her knees to her chest. Heart-wrenching sobs escaped, causing her breath to hiccup. Gone were the silent tears, replaced by the guttural noises of a child who can't catch their breath while crying. There would be no sleep. Instead, she played memories of her dad over and over- her life was changed forever.

It was standing room only in his hometown church, as over four hundred people attended his funeral and it passed in a sea of faces. The eulogy, proudly written by his children, would've impressed him. A true telling of who he was and what the world meant to him echoed through the speakers to be greeted with roars of laughter at times. They stood proud at the gravesite when the urn was lowered into the ground. Not able to watch, Jade looked skywards, hoping he was looking down at her. As tears streamed down her face, a hand reached to rest on her shoulder. She turned to see Greg and just behind him, Eric, Lucky, Tom and Maggie. She didn't know who all came until the wake when several more friends showed up as support.

And When

Time to Give Up and Fight

Chapter Eight

Since Jade worked in the same industry as her father, often customers would recognize her as a Prency and ask how her dad was, not having heard the news. Her eyes would water as she explained his passing, fighting the tears. The summer passed in a blur as a haze seemed to surround her family like a dark cloud. A wheel of grief passed from one to the other as little slips in conversations would remind them. A *faux pas* of saying that she was going to Mom and Dad's would bring tears and her mother swayed from depression to denial. A phone call started with everyday life could end in tears at any time. Some mornings, Jade woke on a damp pillow and slivers of a dream she couldn't quite remember. In her quiet moments she felt he was right next to her and at others, she struggled to remember his voice.

Her mother was in the midst of having a sunroom addition built. The sisters knew with being kept busy she didn't have to think about being alone or deal with the emotions hiding within. Every weekend over the summer, one or both went to check on her and tackle the endless to-do list ready at their arrival. One by one they'd work on the requests and for each one removed, two more appeared.

Jade kept up with the specialist's appointments and it was mid-August when she found herself sitting in the doctor's office, waiting to learn results from several more tests. Her health an ongoing series of hurry up and wait, she was accustomed to the limited lifestyle.

"How have you been handling things?" Dr. Brennon smiled in greeting as he entered the exam room.

"I've had enough." There was no sparkle, no hopeful tone in her voice anymore.

"I've got your latest reports," he said as he read the computer screen. "The five tumors have slowed down a bit."

Being told in June there were more lumps to contend with, she could care less and just dealt with more side-effects.

"The three at the back of the throat don't seem to be changing. Let's have a look and see." He began by taking her blood pressure and poking at her neck. "You seem a bit on edge," Dr. Brennon remarked.

"My dad died five months ago of lung cancer so I have to look after my Mom. I'm sick and tired of all these tests, fed up with waiting for results."

"Well your blood pressure is high this time and your last set of blood tests show you're borderline diabetic." His brows furrowed.

"Just fucking great," she said with a sigh.

"Excuse me, I'll be right back." He left the room.

If I can't tell him exactly how I feel then who the hell can I tell? The door opened a few moments later and Dr. Brennon led in another doctor.

"Jade, this is Dr. Adam. I'd like him to take a look at you."

Why another white coat and why is Dr. Brennon leaving the room? She stared at the man before her and instantly her hackles went up. I just told him I'm sick of this and he brings me another doctor?

"Hi Jade," Dr. Adam extended his hand for her to shake. "Dr. Brennon seems to think that maybe you're a little overwhelmed with things. He thought someone like me would be able to help," he said nonchalantly as if they'd known each other forever.

"Are you a shrink or something?" Oh boy, if he is, this is the last thing I need.

"I'm actually a psychologist on staff here. From time to time a doctor feels a patient may need someone to talk to when they're having difficulties and Dr. Brennon feels you could use my help."

Pleasant enough, but he sounds like he's talking to a child. That's just wrong! I'm not a child. I'll tell him exactly just how grown up my life is, Jade thought and took a deep breath.

"Well then let me tell you about my life. Let's see…it's almost a year that I've had growths…and three days after I went for my first biopsy my dad gets lung cancer, then dies seventy days later. That is…three weeks after my grandmother dies. My mother is having a hard time adjusting and I gotta be there to help her along…all while these lumps keep multiplying now to five. I go through test after test with no answer. I have a handicapped brother we're petitioning to have moved to a closer facility to be with family, because he's mourning too. I work a full time job, own a house, have responsibilities and I haven't missed a day of work since this all started, except for my holidays…which I spent at my dad's deathbed, then helping my mom. My heart races out of control, I'm tired, I don't sleep…So you tell me just what part of this you think I should feel somewhat less stressed about and what magic pill you think will make me okay with it all?" She got it all out in a matter of two minutes. Let him analyze that, she thought with satisfaction.

"I can certainly see you've had a lot to cope with. I'm sure this has been a strain on you," he said in a soft spoken voice. "Perhaps it would help you to have someone to talk to about these things with and it might lower your stress level to help with your blood pressure."

He stated his case, basing his thoughts that her life was resolvable by discussion. Jade was annoyed and chose her words carefully. The medical system was ass backwards. It didn't care about people and she was fed up with it all.

"Well doc, I tell ya what…If maybe you could get some answers for me about what they're going to do about my lumps, perhaps that would ease living every day feeling tired and worn down. Let alone that they're still looking for cancer cells. Sometimes I wonder if I'll end up with cancer like my dad. Ya know, they say early detection is key and your profession promotes being pro-active in seeking help right away. Well, it's been ten months! So get me the answers I need and I'll do my best to de-stress!" She kept her voice monotone, punctuating the last words, hoping the doctor would get her point. He quickly stood and said if she changed her mind he would be available.

Dr. Brennon returned five minutes later with a grim expression. "That didn't go as planned."

"Look, I'm doing the best I can with what I have and no amount of talking will make any of this go away. You don't know me or my life and presume I need help when I don't. The only thing I need is answers. I need my health back. Without that, I don't have the energy to do any more than I am."

Her internal voice ranted all the way home. Why should I be so fucking polite when doctors treat me like a number? For every visit, they get paid. Was it from the years of being in practice that they didn't understand how people felt? Did they simply shut down their human side? I thought doctors went to medical school to make a difference, but maybe I'm wrong and they do it for the big fat paycheck. With no answer about cancer cells, could this be a time bomb waiting to silently go off? They affect every part of my life and the doctors don't get it. They're skeptical and I guess to them I'm a big girl, but what they don't know and never bothered to ask, I've always been big. Before this, I went to the gym and could do all types of manual labor. I moved and helped friends with whatever they needed; building, lifting, roofing. Now a walk to the back lane and I feel like I'm going to have a heart attack? I'm done waiting around for life to change.

Walking into her house, she immediately went to the computer website she had heard about from Jeff. A chat room he had visited. "If this is how life is going to be, I might as well move on." She didn't want a partner, just people to talk with who didn't see her dark circles and tired appearance. Keeping the world at arm's length she'd pull herself out of this rut.

At the profile section she filled in the blanks; race, hair color, eye color, occupation, the requirements were endless. At the section for "interests and hobbies," did it mean things she did now or things she would get back to someday? She entered a mix of both. Next was the "what she was looking for." "Where's a box for someone to lean on when life sucks?" she said and checked the "friends" box and hoped for the best. She added a picture pre-tumor and hit send, summarizing her life in less than ten minutes.

Within seconds a box popped up and a man typed, 'How are you?'

"I just joined for crying out loud," she said then typed back. 'I'm okay, and you?'

'What are you doing?' He asked.

'Relaxing,' she responded.

'How big are your boobs?'

"Yikes, right to the boobs?" Closing the window she dialed her friend. "Um…Jeffy, I was on that site you told me about and it seems boobs are important, but they didn't ask for that on the profile?" She smirked.

"Of course they are," he said laughing. "Boobs are always important, but no worries you're more than covered there. It's a dating site and they have a group functions I want to try going to. Come with me this Friday night for a few drinks after work, it'll be fun. No one knows us there and you could be my wing guy. You're not interested in dating, so just come check it out with me. At least I'd know someone there."

She at first agreed, but the week flew by too fast and suddenly Friday was here. Looking in the mirror she worried about being seen. "I don' t know, I don't think I'll fit in," she voiced her thoughts.

"What do you care? If it's uncomfortable we leave and you never have to see these people again. At least you'd be getting out. No one knows about your health and I sure as hell won't say a word. Let's just go have a drink or two," Jeff encouraged.

He was right, no one knew her situation. Still dressed in her work attire, she agreed and followed him in her own car. That way if he was having fun, he could stay.

From the entrance she saw people of all ages and backgrounds, singles coming together to meet one another. Following Jeff through the crowd, they took the extra seats on a bench where five people sat. He made quick work of the introductions and was full of energy. With time, Jeff mingled and Jade got into a conversation with two women at the table. Men would make the rounds and she'd shrink back to let the other ladies have the spotlight, telling the men she wasn't looking. She stayed three hours, then said goodbye to the ladies and went looking for Jeff, the social butterfly. He stood near the entrance with several women and she made her way over.

"Jeffy, just to let you know I'm getting tired and need to leave." She waited for a pause in the conversation to interrupt.

"Okay, I'll call you tomorrow." He said with a hug.

The women glared at her with him showing her that affection. If only they knew, they wouldn't be jealous of my life, she nearly laughed out loud.

Jade signed onto the site the next morning to find several emails from men who spotted her over the evening. Again, she politely declined their invitations to chat, but over the next week some persisted and instant message boxes popped open when she'd sign on. Gentlemanly at first, it didn't take long for the sexual innuendos to start, proving this was more of a hook-up site and not what she needed. She'd purposely say the word tumor and they'd leave her alone. Within a month she quit the site and her life settled back into the daily grind until the call in September. Sitting at work, she answered the phone to hear her mom's urgent tone.

"Dane was rushed to emergency."

"What do you mean rushed to emergency, what happened?"

"They said his bowel twisted internally and his lungs filled. He's in emergency and I'm on my way there."

"I'll meet you there."

Again, she bolted from work after reiterating what happened to her supervisor. On the drive, she realized it was six months to the day since her dad passed and now she raced through the city to get to her brother's side.

Finding a parking space, she looked for her mother's or sister's vehicle as she headed to the entrance. Checking in at the desk, she was immediately led to one of the dozen beds in the triage room. Seeing Dane lying in a bed looking scared, she grabbed his hand. "No worries, I'm here." She read Dane's thoughts by the look in his eyes and right now he was terrified.

A doctor appeared at her side. "Are you family?"

"I'm his sister and guardian."

"Well thank goodness you're here. We need to put a tube in through his nose and down to his lungs to get the liquid out and he doesn't seem to understand."

"Dane doesn't speak," she advised then the doctor explained that he constantly pushed or pulled the tube out. "Dane, I won't let them do anything they aren't supposed to. Some things are going to be uncomfortable or even hurt, but I'll be here with you the whole time. I'll hold your hand while they do this, okay?" Dane stared at her words as they left her mouth. "You need to understand how important this is. You're not going to like it, but I need you to trust me, okay?" She tried again finally getting "Yah" in response.

The doctor signaled a nurse who appeared at the side of the bed with a tray and a long clear tube curled in a dish. The doctor put on gloves and once ready, Jade grabbed her brother's hands. "Ok Dane, look directly at me, just me, not anywhere else." With the first attempt, he began to pull away. "Hold still, don't move, it's almost there. I know it's awful, but they need to do this," she said as she watched his face twist and his eyes water as the tube was slowly shoved up his nostril. She knew that horrible feeling from her own nose doctor.

Dane tried to wrench his hands out of hers to grab the tube, but she held fast. "Dane, you have to be brave. Dad's here watching over you to make sure you'll be okay, just remember he's always looking after us." With that, he calmed.

When finished, the tube was like a piece of spaghetti hanging from his nose which drained into a pouch. The doctor presented documents for her signature because Dane needed emergency surgery. He explained the procedure in detail as she kept looking at the doorway, hoping her family would arrive. The enormity of the situation hit her when the doctor asked what level of resuscitation she'd allow. At that moment, her family walked through the door. The doctor quickly relayed the information and when he repeated the question of resuscitation, she spoke. "You do everything! We are not going to lose another family member this year."

Taking a moment with Dane before he was wheeled off, the family took up residence in the private waiting room.

How could this happen, is God picking us off one at a time? Why are we being put through more, haven't we gone through enough? She silently asked the man above.

Finally news arrived that the surgery was a success and Dane would be in intensive care. It would be another month of daily visits to a hospital.

And When

Glimmer of Understanding

Chapter Nine

It was a beautiful August afternoon and Jade relaxed with a beer on her back step overlooking her new patio. Planned to be fixed long ago, it got lost in the shuffle of the last two years. It was a labor-intensive project as she dug grass, packed gravel and placed cement slabs. Taking holidays the first week of July, she worked at it for short periods to keep her heart rate low. It'd been two years living with the tumors and she decided if her health would forever remain this way, she'd rather die trying to live than do nothing.

Things had been somewhat peaceful since Easter. The last health scare for the family was Dane's, almost a year ago now. Their first holidays with an empty place at the table only magnified the emptiness she felt and her biggest hurdle was the one-year anniversary. Going to the cemetery to visit her Pops she felt strange, like an intruder. Her tears flowed as she recalled their last conversation as she stared at the marble headstone, waiting for a warm feeling like he was truly there. He's probably enjoying being with his family again, she thought. Hey dad, are you proud of me still? I haven't done anything and I'm still waiting for answers. I'm trying to do most of what you asked and the family is okay I guess, but everything feels different. The conversation played out in her head over the hour and then she drove home feeling like the color black. No seeing forward and no looking back, like a light had been missing in life. It was in that moment she decided to change things.

She had pushed to see the specialist twice since April only to hear the same-"nothing has changed and we'll keep monitoring." Jeff still attended the date site outings and she went along on occasion. Tired of her solitude, she just wanted to laugh again and be the person her dad wanted her to be. At mixers, Jeff introduced her to the men he'd made friends with, but one mention of her health and they'd vanish. Although she felt awkward, she didn't hold back anymore. "It is what it is" she'd tell them. It was hard enough living day to day, pretending to be normal she couldn't pull off. She wanted to feel like a part of life again and put herself out there.

One man came along in June and lasted only a month. In the end her health was too much for Randy to deal with. "How can I plan a future with you when you may not have one?" His words brought her a new reality. "I think you're amazing and I admire your strength dealing with it all, but I just don't want to risk falling for someone when they may not be here." Randy said as he looked at the picture she had hanging on her living room wall then asked if she'd ever look like that again. The next day she removed it, not recognizing that woman anymore. He looked so disappointed when she said, "I'll never be that person again."

He helped her finish this patio, taking two days holidays of his own. She had struggled the first four days on her own when he pulled into her driveway. "Do you honestly think I was going to let you do this by yourself?" He said with a smile and a kiss hello. "You're so bloody stubborn you'll end up killing yourself."

Working side by side for two days, he panicked when she shook from the exertion. Placing his hand on her chest to feel the speed of her pulse had scared him terribly. Two weeks later, he said goodbye. Randy was honest in his thoughts and she couldn't find fault in his decision. He was right that she had to accept how men viewed her. Day to day, she didn't know how she'd feel, so how could she ask anyone deal with this? To make plans then cancel, sometimes at the last minute, feeling too tired. Her weight fluctuated back and forth in three sizes, her hourglass having multiple versions.

Accepting what she couldn't change, she joined a new computer site that catered to bigger people in the world. Entering her information, she created a profile she would proudly display. Using current pictures, she'd constantly update them eliminating any doubt this is who she was. Hesitantly, she entered the chat-room that first time and was instantly greeted by a multitude of hellos and welcomes. It took a while to learn, but she found her footing as she went along. In this safe haven no one judged anyone by what society deemed perfect and everyone lived far away so she'd never have to worry about meeting them.

Honest right from the start about her tumors, she said it was only one of her life's many hurdles and her candid personality and quick wit gained her friends from everywhere. Over time, close friendships developed as the chat-room screen whirled by so fast she could barely keep up. She'd scroll back and forth to catch the comments or disagreements and when asked, she offered her unbiased opinion, not having anything to lose. She found a place where nothing else mattered except being herself. The black circles, bumps and extra padding didn't make a difference to anyone here. It was the support she needed and a way for her to discover who this new woman could be.

Everyone had a story here, and with many people all on one screen there was always drama of some sort. It took careful listening and sorting through to gain a sense of who was real. She knew life was a series of events that brought everyone to this room. Some events were good and some were crap lessons. Many got lost along life's highway, veering away from who they were supposed to be and others wore a mask to cover their struggles. No one was perfect here, she herself on an unexpected path and she wasn't who she had started out as.

To end her days she'd sign on, and on weekends she'd check in here and there. It became an addiction as her friendships grew. Exchanging phone numbers, she got to know her girlfriends by putting a voice to the picture on the screen. She'd hear about their dating ventures as they met with men from the room. If she couldn't be with anyone until her health got sorted out she'd live vicariously through others. Her close friends shared every facet of life and they helped each other through daily trials. For ongoing tests she received emails and phone calls. The connection to the outside world gave her comfort without ever having to see sadness in anyone's eyes.

The emails from men were far more than she anticipated and it'd been a long time since she felt anything near attractive. Heck, it'd been two years since she'd exuded any type of confidence in her appearance. Since the onset of the growths she didn't know who she was anymore. Lumpy, tired, sleepy, chunky...she sounded like a new set of the seven dwarfs.

In the chat-room, she'd turn heads with her little picture proclaiming 'Jadey' is here, her online handle. Friends used the private function, a feature that kept them in the chat-room with everyone, yet allowed a separate window to speak privately. She'd listen to their updates while ensuring her fun personality kept up in main room. Here she could be her smart-ass self and everyone laughed with her.

Over the summer she finished the work on her yard. With the patio done she got busy with the to-do list started two years ago and even hosted one party for Rob, a friend who came to town after moving away years ago. It was the first time the old gang made time to be together and the first time they'd seen her since her seclusion. Rob used her guest suite and the following morning, Eric dropped by to join them for breakfast.

As she served the meal she gathered her handful of vitamins and sat down to join them. They watched her routine of a few mouthfuls of food, vitamins and so on. After her small meal, she stood to prepare the protein shake the naturopath said she needed. Filling the blender with milk, fruit, chlorophyll and protein powder, she poured a glass and rejoined them.

"What the fuck?" Eric asked.

"What?" She looked from one to the other, their mouths agape.

"What's with all the pills and the drink, what are you doing?"

"I do this to get energy." She blushed, embarrassed.

"You do this every time you eat?" Rob asked with concern.

"It's no big deal, I'm used to it," she smiled, fully aware she was still a misfit.

The men exchanged a look since neither had watched her life morph into this. Rob had called once a month to check on her and this was Eric's first time seeing what she went through since they hadn't spoken in two years. Their reactions confirmed what she knew inside. Her friends tried to be kind, but she just didn't fit in any more. Eric dropped in occasionally after that, but she spent most of her time with family and computer friends, preferring to talk with people who couldn't see her.

By mid-October, the chill in the air meant winter was around the corner. Living on the flat open prairies definitely brought a bite to the temperature. Another fall done, it was time to break out the shovels and snow tires to prepare for the next six months of cold. She prayed the snow would hold off another while. Every day without was a blessing.

Jade looked forward to the end of the year two months from now since it would mark the first year with no medical emergencies for her immediate family. Only a few more months and they'd have made it. The year had been relatively quiet, other than losing an aunt to old age and a cousin to cancer. She had attended each funeral and watched those left behind struggle with the pain, thinking of her Pops every time. Sensitive and vulnerable, she wasn't the same woman who thought she could handle the world anymore. Even heartfelt movies would find her in tears, unable to stop the emotions.

Attending regular visits with the specialist, her vitamins and concoctions helped her function, but did little to remove the emptiness. At first, she had still tried to be the go-to person, but seeing life in its entirety and with new eyes, it was hard listening to people's problems which seemed so solvable.. She'd patiently listen and offer what she could, but it began to feel insincere. How did people get so messed up over little issues? Her brain couldn't comprehend their drama over such solvable problems; troubles with a friend not doing as they wished, a boyfriend forgetting a birthday, or their struggles with work demands. Rather than disappoint people, she stopped listening and they moved on. It was she who changed, not them. She didn't mean for it to happen, but analyzing and re-evaluating had been her way of dealing with life since her teens. When troubled, she'd take time to recharge by pulling away into her own thoughts, only to come back out swinging, ready for anything. Like a battery, she needed to plug into the inner workings to boost the power. This was just a much longer unplug and she was waiting for her boost.

She focused on work, home, family and her few remaining friends who understood this new Jade. They gave her a no-nonsense boot in her ass when she'd pull away too far. Even her chat friends helped to keep her on the straight and narrow without knowing it.

At the end of November while talking in the chat room, she received a private *"Hello"* from someone she didn't recognize. Accustomed to the people and goings on in the room, this was a surprise.

"Hello," she typed back.

"How is life in Canada?" 2 Dance wrote.

"Cold and boring, LOL"

That was all that came through the private window, but they shared laughter and quick wit in the room with the others. She clicked on his picture just for the fun it and up popped a photo of a man too good to be true. Handsome and of large stature, he leaned against a car and looked like he worked in a blue collar job. Maybe construction or a farmer, she thought. His hands gloved in leather, he wore a dark hunter green sweatshirt and his light brown hair was covered in a baseball cap. The first thing she thought was, wow, the second was bullshit, it's probably not his real picture since many posted false pictures or photos from years ago.

Every woman in the chat-room flirted outrageously and she watched his response as he skillfully dodged the attention, he was rather entertaining. The room was always nuts when a new man entered. When the frenzy began, she stepped to the sidelines and offered humor here and there.

At ten o'clock, she typed it was time to hit the sheets and received the usual goodnights from the room. Just before signing off, one more private message appeared, *"Sleep well beautiful"* from 2 Dance. *"Night Cutie,"* she typed then shut down her computer.

As was her morning custom, she sipped coffee while reading emails and once done, she signed onto the site to check on Donna, a close friend who started her days early. Up at the crack of stupid, five a.m., she could check out this new chat guy and he'd never even know she looked at his profile.

Going to her inbox she saw an email from the mystery man and hit the open button. It was a smiley face, a tool the site developed for people to make first contact without saying any words.

"Good mornin', cutie!" She typed and sent, then took the opportunity to view his profile since he'd obviously checked hers. "Let's see what you're all about, shall we?" She said aloud as the page opened before her.

Name: 2 Dance
Age: 40
Height: 6'4"
Weight: little extra
Occupation: Government
Status: Divorced
From: Virginia/ Washington
Looking For: Relationship

His write-up didn't say much, just his viewpoint on life and people as he saw them getting along in the world. No long list of expectations, no big wishes, just a normal guy. At least he's genuine and not a scammer, she thought. Most fake profiles were easily spotted by their insincerity and pleading for love.

Getting home that evening, she signed on to check in on the day's activities to see another message in her inbox.

--Brady wrote:

Talk about captivating! Think you would be having me melt, Hon. Do hope you have a great day.

Brady

"Hon, how charming," Jade said with a giggle, almost hearing an American accent. "Captivating? I've never been called that before, I'm more of a captive. You'll disappear like everyone else, but I guess there's no harm in chatting for a bit Mr. Brady."

--Jade wrote:

Well, Brady, that was sweet so thank you. Why are all the charming men far away? Bet you even have a real southern accent too. I would be in trouble if we lived close. I tell ya, you are one I think I would bend my rules for. And my day, well it was cold being winter up here, minus 10 going to minus 30 tonight brrrr.

Keep smiling,
Jade

She sent the response and continued to the room to speak with her friends. Kendra had gone on a date and Sarah was dealing a family problem, Jade wanted to be sure both went okay. Entering the room she saw that her close friends weren't signed on so she excused herself to call Lisa and her mom. Just before bed, she signed on to see if her friends had arrived.

--Brady wrote:

Hmmmm Jade...you're welcome, just telling it like I see it. I agree that all the ones that I could consider myself to be with are on the other side of the world-especially up North! Think I would be the one in trouble and thinking of bending some rules. Day here was good and finally over with. Started off in the 60's and went down to the 40's. If it is gonna be that cold or colder, I would at least like some snow, a nice fire, blanket, couch and you to snuggle up with to keep warm. Can do without the first, but would definitely take the last part. Do hope your day goes well for you tomorrow and hope to catch up with you later.

ttfn,
Brady

"He must be playing," she said. Maybe he was curious about her. Deciding not to respond, she'd take her time to figure out what to say. It was always a hard conversation to start, sad she'd have to explain things, again.

What a way to start my morning, she thought with a smile as she sipped her first cup of coffee and read the message.

--Brady wrote:

You're hot!

The message was sent at eight his time, with one hour difference in time zones, he must've just left the message, she thought. Best respond and see what you come up with next. These little remarks tied to a smiley face were a collection of cliché lines from the past twenty years.

--Jade wrote:

Ah, you're way too charming. Well we have snow here if you're missing seeing some...can even frolic with a shovel if it would make ya happy? Just trying to look out for you LOL

And funny we have the same rules I guess. But alas you are in Virginia and that is a long ways off. We can talk, nothing wrong with that, but ya just know we're never gonna meet.

Keep smiling, handsome!

Jade

  Disappointed to not see a response after work, she realized it was the world of online and he'd probably found another woman to charm, or in his case, ten. She took up laughing with her friends in chat for the next hour and said goodnight at eleven, then curled up in bed with a book.

"Hello again young man," she said the next morning, seeing his note.

--Brady wrote:

What a smoothie. LOL! Wouldn't mind frolicking in the snow, but probably would have to add you in and next thing ya know...ummmm...there goes that imagination. Yep, do believe the possibilities would be endless if we were both closer. You'd be in trouble, that's for sure. And yes we can chat, really nothing wrong with it at all. Though the likelihood of us really meeting in person is slim and all, I never say never. Just know with you Hon, it would always start with a hug. Just picturing my arms wrapped around you, holding you tight, leaning into you and nibbling on your ear...
Hope your day is awesome!

Brady

  She hadn't seen him in chat since the first private hello. "Let's find out what you're all about, shall we?" she said out loud.

--Jade wrote:

I'm adding you to my favorites, you just make me smile with one lil' old picture.

--Brady wrote:

Gonna have to get more pics so I can make you smile more...*grins*

He responded immediately? Online before the sun even comes up, it's not even five here, that's six his time. Perhaps he'd just got home and checked his email. She had no idea what this man did for a living, for all she knew he could have been out having fun and just crawled in the door. Her curiosity got the best of her.

--Jade wrote:

Did you pick the name 2 Dance because you are a stripper in your spare time? LOL

She couldn't resist the humor. Although a big guy, he was good looking and it was strange someone like him would be on a site at all. In her way of thinking, if you're beautiful or handsome, you'd probably have a line-up of people trying to get to know you. She continued getting ready for work and got through the day.

The storm that'd started this morning left a pile of snow to remove before she could even get into the house. The wind curled around the top step and always left a snowdrift. She spent the next two hours slowly digging out her driveway then the front and back of her house. It should've taken only a half hour, but with needing to calm her heartbeat, she'd take a few shovelfuls then pause before continuing. She had always disliked winter and the cold, but now, she despised it. With such cold, unbearable temperatures at times, she hated being outside longer. Taking her coat off at the door, chilled to the bone, she quickly started the oven for dinner and when it reached its temperature she opened the door to put the pan in, allowing herself to suck in the heat. Content, she signed onto the computer while dinner cooked.

--Brady wrote:

Nope...wasn't picked and not a stripper in my spare time...LOL. I got the name because I love to dance, so when it came to figure out an ID for the Site, I thought it was perfect. Hope all is well with you. Getting cold here now, actually supposed to snow tomorrow. I's getting excited that it is and have finally got my skis out and ready to hit the slopes.

Xoxoxo, Brady

--Jade wrote:

Snow-heck, I just shoveled for 2 hours...and in minus 30! Gotta love Canada, from 90 degrees in summer to bitter cold only a few months later, so I'm doing great I think, well if ya call working and shoveling great. Are you ready to move north yet? (LOL) And just so you know the name 2 Dance still brings up images, so that's what I'm keeping in my head about you, why ruin the visual-LOL. Well off to a hot bath then bedtime.

Jade

She had to admit that she enjoyed figuring out who he was through the bits and pieces he'd share. So far he skied and signed on at all times of the day. No questions about boobs or anything overly personal, but it'll end once I tell you the truth, she thought. The reality, he lived 2000 miles away and he'd find someone local, so this was just a passing fancy until that happened. She'll tell him the truth and he'll disappear soon enough.

--Brady wrote:

Hmmm-Hot bath and bedtime...now there's a fantasy mixing you in with that combo (talk about melting all the snow in Canada!) Hope all is well and I hope to catch you later on tonight....should be online if you have to have time...

Xoxoxo
Brady

"Here we go," she said the next morning after reading his email. "At least it's not the boob question." He'd flirted in an off-handed way, but it was there. Although it was fun, her circumstance couldn't allow her to dabble in thoughts of relationship. She'd go to work and think about how to respond.

Monique stood at her desk and listened intently as Jade talked about the site she was on and the emails she'd been receiving. Monique, who'd been married for years, didn't get the whole draw to the online world. "I got enough talking with the people I gotta talk to everyday, never mind going on a computer at night. When I get home, I feed the animals, relax and talk to nobody," she said

Monique and husband lived on a small farm with dogs, cats and horses. It was a life Jade admired and her childhood dream to raise horses, settle down and have a dozen children. In her teens she rode her friend's horses and loved the freedom. No stranger to barn work, she helped with cleaning the stalls, brushing and tending the animals. There was nothing more wonderful than being around the horses. At home in a saddle, she believed she must have been reincarnated and imagined the simplicity of life in the western days. A three-day ride to the nearest town, a person's word was their honor, a handshake sealed the deal, and if someone wronged you, you shot them. She imagined herself walking around with a six shooter, how many bullets would I need? As with all dreams of a child, they changed when she got older and reality set in.

On her drive home from work she stopped to start her Christmas shopping. This would be their second without her father, a difficult reminder. Buying two gifts and after the quick shovel of the dusting of snow, she settled in for the evening joining the already rambunctious chat-room. Catching up with friends using the private feature, she kept a watchful eye on Brady's playful flirting. He hadn't spotted her name on the board yet and this gave her the opportunity to see him in action. He'd make a few flirtatious comments then totally back off. It wasn't what she expected, thinking any man would certainly suck in all the attention and pursue. The phone interrupted and it was her mother wanting to compare Christmas gift lists, so she typed in her usual *"phone-bbl"* (be back later) and picked up the receiver as the *"hb"* (hurry back), *"ttyl"* (talk to you later) popped up on her screen. Not realizing she'd been in the room the past while, 2 Dance private messaged. *"Hey, I was looking for you!"* She responded with, *"be right back"* then closed the chat window. A half hour later, he was gone.

--Jade wrote:

I came back and you weren't here...so off to read in bed. It's cold up here, minus 30 again all day, so just want to curl up stay warm and fall deep into sleep.

Later,
Jade

--Brady wrote:

*Was looking around for you last night, but didn't see you. Hope your day is going well, Hon–Miss ya! xoxoxo...Wish you were here to snuggle...guess only in my dreams...*long deep kiss**

Ttyl
Brady

The next morning she read his response with a frown. "I guess it's time to just tell you the truth and get it over with," she said with a sigh. That long deep kiss line made her think he might be hoping for more. "Time to cut him loose," she said, hating this part, always. It didn't seem right to use the whole spiel she'd usually send off. This man had taken time and sent emails for almost two weeks, so she'd give him the honest version. It took her less than five minutes to let it completely spill out, true to the very emotion she wrote it with. No thinking or planning, just full on from her very core.

--Jade wrote:

Just so you know I would love to snuggle. It's been a long time since I've felt arms around me. Aw, Brady...ya know I wonder about it all. We get up, go to work, come home, take care of house, life...and try to keep doing it over and over. To have that hug when I get home and arms around me as I drift to sleep, that's what is missing in my world. Knowing someone looks forward to me, to have a connection so strong that I cannot wait to see and talk to him. His voice brightens the toughest days...that he is my strength and compassion when life gets tough. Yep, I need that right about now.

I have been living with tumors for two years and this week I went to the specialist to arrange to have them removed. I cried the night before and thought of all the things I have gone through. Losing my dad and then two years of tests, poking, prodding...yep, was feeling weak about it all. Yet I found the courage to be tough and face it all and ask the hard questions. I told a close friend that it would've been nice to have someone to go through all this with to which he responded...'you have friends who worry'...yet it is not the same as having a partner to lean on. I do not open up my thoughts to people any more since they can't possibly understand the fear. At times I feel a need to be held, but it's not to be.

Well, I have told you too much. I am okay–I just have moments where I feel lost...that is something I don't show anyone. But you are miles away and therefore safe to reveal my honest thoughts. Thank you for starting my day off right and letting me imagine a long deep kiss. It's been nice chatting, I wish you well and hope you find what you're looking for.

Jade

Her nerves were on edge since the visit two weeks ago with the specialist. He told her it would be her decision to undergo the surgery. She'd become accustomed to living half a life the past two years and she needed time to make up her mind. Two days ago was decision day.

Dr. Paul explained he wouldn't know the extent of what he needed to do until he was inside. Confident he'd be able to remove the mass without complication, as always, he warned of all possibilities. The worst was losing or affecting her voice. With all things he discussed, the thought of having no voice stuck in her mind. To actually not talk or worse, have some garbled voice left. She cleaned house singing along to music and when younger, she and Lisa sang together many times harmonizing with each other. Music was part of her. She even sang daily at work in her joking manner to make people laugh. Losing her voice would end all that. She tried to imagine life without being able to say a word. Her family and close site family listened to her concern then voted for the removal to be done. To all it was a no-brainer since it would answer the question once and for all. Is this cancer?

--Brady wrote:

It just is funny, well maybe not, but how I can relate to what you say. I understand that moment you stop and need that other person there to hold, embrace and touch. Many times I have gone through the motions of wondering what it is all about. Getting up in the morning, working, returning home to start it all again, knowing there is this void in my life, but continuing on without stopping and really doing something about it. Then on the other side, knowing what I have experienced and been through, sometimes I wonder if I really want to try it again.

Sorry to hear about the tumors, Hon, I hope all went well with that and you are done with them. It always takes some life-threatening or real hardship to wake us up to realize how short life really is. It gets us to start reorganizing or restructuring our lives. I don't really have many people around me that I really call friend, I am mostly one who sticks to himself. Not a loner, just live in a loner world for now. I do have people I see and talk to, so I'm not anti-social.

You haven't told me too much, never will, Hon. I have seen that it's easier to talk to some complete stranger now-a-days than someone who you know. This world has changed so much that sometimes I don't know if I still exist in it. It seems that people are not much into communicating with each other one-on-one rather than text or email. Hope your day at work goes well, that *you go to and from, safely. Thanks for emailing back, wish I could be there to meet you when you get home; would be so very nice to have someone warm, caring and captivating around. Imagine what you want, but I see it clearly in my eyes. *Long deep kiss**

Brady
Xoxoxo

  After re-reading his email, she looked at the site card he sent with flowers on the front to boost her spirits. Could he sense she was pushing him away? It was very thoughtful, but it didn't allow her to cut the tie. His response wasn't what she expected and it showed a glimpse into his thoughts, both thinking the world moved too fast and left people behind in the rat race. What made him feel this way, had he struggled? Did someone finally understand what it was like for her? She could hope, but maybe he'd heard her frustration and wanted to offer a shoulder.

--Jade wrote:

You are so sweet ya know...thanks for the card. I am surprised you wrote back, thank you. The days are long and all I can do is run around trying to get everything for the holidays and look forward to the couple days off.

Jade

--Brady wrote:

Hey there, sexy! I know how the days seem to get long. Also know how there just seems to be no time to do anything or at least get things that you want done. Been busy getting stuff together for the holidays, think I need at least a week off to recover. Been sick the last couple of days and just back into work today, it sucks being home and not getting anything done. We need to catch up with each other and get some time in, but I know how it is when you're so darn cute and everyone wants time with ya! Hope you're doing well...

Xoxoxo tffn,
Brady

With getting ready for Christmas, she usually signed onto the computer late at night. Brady became a regular face and always made some special comment as she entered, *bows to Jadey* or *hey you gorgeous Canadian*, anything to make her smile. They'd chat privately and comment on the room's shenanigans while getting to know each other. She learned he worked in a government job, enjoyed golfing, biking, bowling, skiing and dancing. He planned to visit his parents in Wyoming for the holidays and would be gone for about a week. His outrageous sense of humor kept her laughing, something she had missed for a long time. His first questions were always how she was doing, what her thoughts were and how she was feeling when they met up in chat every night around ten.

And When

Ducks in a Row

Chapter Ten

Lisa's family would spend Christmas day at her in-laws', so Christmas Eve was the Prency family gathering. Arriving at the care facility, she found Dane sitting at the door in his wheelchair, parka and snow boots. His eyes lit up and his vocal noises the nurse translated as his way of giving her shit for making him wait so long. He laughed hearing the explanation.

After she loaded Dane and his wheelchair, he pointed to the car radio. He loved to sing and would mumble sounds where the words belonged. Arriving at their mom's, the family met them in the garage and helped with the wheelchair. The nephews, always anxious to see the stash of gifts, volunteered their services, but not before giving both their aunt and uncle a hug.

The house was laced with red and gold, the living room hosting the six-foot Christmas tree heaped with gifts. Candles lit all corners of the room, bowls of candy, nuts and chocolate sat on every side table. Through the front window the lit up reindeers stood in the yard, their mom went all out with the décor.

As the family settled into the living room, they'd communicate with Dane by asking a series of questions and he'd laugh, sharing in their joking manner. With everyone comfortable, the tradition began of unwrapping the gifts one at a time. The nephews would hand a gift to each person and all would watch the surprises revealed.

Afterwards, the women made ready the meal and by the time they were done, the table laden with food would be enough to feed twenty. With Dane wheeled to sit at the head of the table, they said grace, feasted, then called Jared and his son to share holiday wishes. At nine, they'd load the vehicles to head back to the city, having spent eight hours together. Their mom was always sad when they left, definitely not the same as when Pops was here. After dropping off Dane, Jade settled in for the rest of the night. Used to spending the holidays alone, she curled up with a movie.

Christmas morning, she grabbed her first cup of coffee and headed for the computer to spend time with her chat family. Brady was in Casper with family. His online appearance sporadic, getting booted frequently being on a dial-up network at his parents' home.

Jade,

I do hope that your Holiday is full of warmth and love, that the New Year finds you wanting to fulfill another year with excitement and learning about each other. Here's to you, Hon, and wishing I was under your tree!

xoxoxo
Brady

The card with a big white and gold present on the front made her smile. It was a pleasant thought, Brady under her tree. She pictured a big red bow and a tag with "Just for Jade" on it. He wasn't like the others; their communication had continued after the news of her health instead of dwindling.

--Jade wrote:

Thanks for the card! I saw you in chat yesterday but was running late for work. Hope you didn't think I was ignoring you. Seems a lot of the ladies find you attractive and rightfully so. I wish you lived closer. I just know we'd hit it off and I can definitely picture you under the tree. Are ya sure ya don't want to move? LOL

Hope Santa was good to you and that you enjoyed the time with family and friends. Now what's up for New Year's Eve, any plans?

Talk to you soon,

Jade

--Brady wrote:

Hey you! No, I didn't think you were ignoring me. Yep, I was bouncing around and having fun in chat. There are only a couple people that I have fun with, that I know I can have fun with and they won't take me the wrong way. Don't know if it's an attraction or a desperate thing, you know how some of those people can get.

Wished you were closer too. Do not doubt that we would hit it off real well. At this point our personality and thoughts seem to *go real well together, at least to my viewpoint. Wish I could move, but as it goes right now it wouldn't be for a year or so; have a contract on the place, but who knows *winks**

Seems like Christmas isn't all that big anymore but not complaining. I've been at my parents for the week and returning back on Sunday. Don't know what plans are for New Years, just looking forward to getting home. Hope all is well with you. Stay beautiful as always and look forward to our talking again.

kisses
Brady

Another few days and it would be a new year. Her sister was having company and invited her, and Jade also received an invitation to her friend's annual party, but declined both. This holiday was her least favorite. Every year she hoped her life would change, but she'd find she was exactly where she started, to celebrate it didn't make sense. This year had been quiet and with her surgery coming up, she wondered if it would remain that way. It played in her mind as she thought of all the possible things to deal with should something go wrong. The only resolution she was making was to get her ducks in row.

She wanted to write a letter to the people who were a part of her life. To anyone else it seemed morbid, but she always planned for the worst and hoped for the best. She'd take the time to handwrite the letter that said all she needed to, just like her Pops did. With the tumors being in her for so long, who knows what it could mean once they cut her open. She'd heard many stories of cancer spreading after a surgery. Whether an old wives tale or fact, this thinking she didn't share with anyone, having learned just how fast life changed from watching her dad.

--Jade wrote:

Well it's New Year's Eve, have you made any plans to celebrate? I will stay in curled up on the couch. I figure no sense in going out...when the clock strikes midnight, I'd rather be home. I will raise my glass and toast ya at midnight Mr. Virginia-Happy New Year!

Jade
PS: Here's wishing I were kissing you when the year starts

--Brady wrote:

*Sorry to hear someone like you is staying home, but know sometimes it can be the best solution-I can relate to that. Don't have any plans, I'll just turn in early, but will look at the stars and hopefully know you are doing the same and raise my glass to one beautiful lady up North. Happy New Year! *hugs and kisses**

Brady

He wasn't doing anything and it gave her comfort that he'd be home. Unsure if she believed him, she figured someone that good-looking would probably head to the nearest singles bar and tie one on.

--Jade wrote:

See, if you were here we could cuddle on the couch watching a few movies. At midnight...well that would start a whole bunch of trouble LOL. Probably best since we'd start the year off very tired. If you get bored you could always call me, my number is 413-555-3579

Thinking of you,
Jade

--Brady wrote:

Don't really see anything wrong with that picture. Tired, exhausted or wiped out, just wouldn't matter if I could be there in the morning looking into your eyes and see that smile of yours. Thank you for your number, I look forward to hearing your voice.

Brady
xoxoxo

At five to midnight she switched the channel to Times Square to watch the ball drop. The cameras scanned the crowds as couples huddled together in the cold. People bunched together, drinking, laughing and starting the year together. She imagined what it would be like to be standing there with someone special. Did it make a difference to be right at the heart of things?

She'd probably opt for a warmer place, having to pee every time her feet got cold. As the countdown finished she said a silent thank you that this year was done and gone. Up past her usual bedtime, the black bags under her eyes said it was time to sleep.

Her phone rang several times the next morning with family and friends wishing a Happy New Year and her cell beeped constantly with texts. She hoped this year would bring happiness.

At eleven, Eric called looking for help, needing to cut through plaster to run wiring and she agreed to help. She had held the vacuum wherever the blade went, eliminating most of the fine powder, but by the time she got home her hair was matted in white dust. Cozy and clean after her shower, she relaxed since tomorrow it was back to work. The flashing button on the answering machine caught her eye. Pressing "play", she turned on the television as she waited for the messages.

"Hello Jade, this is Brady from Virginia calling to say I hope you had a good New Years. I guess you're busy so I will call back at another time."

Hitting the "play" button again, she smiled. The sound of that southern American accent was exactly what she pictured. The call display showed his number and tempted to call, she decided to send an email, leaving it up to him.

--*Jade wrote:*

I'm so sorry I wasn't home to take your call, but your accent can make me melt. I was helping a friend with drywall all day, so by the time I got home I was covered in white. Not exactly a way to enjoy a day off and back to work tomorrow. Thank you for calling; it made my day to hear your voice!

Talk soon,
J

--*Brady wrote:*

*Sorry I missed ya...but at least got to hear ya voice *winks*. Hmmmm, would've been nice to of helped ya...errrrr...clean up after ya got home...LOL. Hopefully we can catch up later. Have a great day, ttfn,*

Xoxoxo
Brady

--Jade wrote:

One look at me and ya would have run. Dust was everywhere! My hair was gray with it. Not exactly the first impression I like to give, prefer to be out of the shower fresh and clean with hair blow dried and smelling wonderful. Sorry, I had to tease-LOL. I can't wait until I can actually have a conversation with you. I have no idea of your schedule or when you're available, but I just know we will sit and have a good long chat. Did I mention I love your accent?

Talk to you soon, handsome
Jade

--Brady wrote:

And here I thought you were the one with the accent. *winks* I hope you have a wonderful day Hon!

Xoxoxo
Brady

At work she updated Monique on the man far away and she seemed genuinely happy for the connection. "At least this puts a smile where one hasn't been," she said. "I still don't get the whole online thing, but as long as you're having fun."

That evening, her phone rang a long distance tone. Looking at the number, Jade tried to hide her excitement as she picked up the phone.

"Hello," she said in her regular lumpy, raspy voice.

"Hey Sunshine, how was your day?"

She smiled hearing his accent. "Hello Mr. Virginia, I'm so glad you called again."

"Mr. Virginia, you're so darn cute." He laughed heartily. "How is life in the north, Miss Canada?"

"The usual, cold, shoveling and it's actually minus thirty-four today."

"Whew, that sure is cold, are ya keeping warm?"

"Could be warmer," she replied, her feet like ice at the moment.

"Oh yeah, how much warmer do you want to be?"

"So how's life for you, young man?" She changed the subject not wanting to go any further with the thoughts playing in her mind.

"Life is the usual here, keeping busy with work and all."

"What do you do for work?"

"I am a computer geek for the government." Pride sounded in his voice.

"Geek, I'd hardly call you a geek. I've seen your pictures." She giggled at his attempt to downplay his looks. "I'm pretty sure you have a line-up of women just waiting for a date. You probably need one of those deli signs, the now serving number machine."

His laughter rolled from deep inside. "Line-up, trust me there is no line-up and never has been. I'm just a boring guy with a simple life and no social life. I don't have time for one."

"You just got back from Wyoming, so you do get out once in a while. How was the holiday, was Santa good to you?"

"It's always good to go see the parents and the ranch, but after about three days I was ready to come home." He chuckled like every adult staying with the parents too long. "Santa doesn't stop by anymore, I haven't gotten a gift in years."

"What do you mean, Santa doesn't stop by? Everyone has to have a surprise under the tree."

"I buy for nephews and nieces. Christmas just doesn't feel the same as when we were young. As you get older it loses that excitement."

"Do you have a big family? Did any brothers and sisters make it out there as well?"

"I have two sisters, one older, one younger and a younger brother. We live all over the place and they didn't make it out." His tone was one of disgust.

"That's surprising. Usually family all gets together for the holidays. That must've been disappointing for your parents."

"Yep, it's hard, but my sisters rarely visit and usually only do so when they get something out of it. My brother is overseas in the navy," he said rather quietly.

"What do you mean, "get something out of it"? Isn't spending time with family worth the trip?"

"Oh…it's a long story, but the short of it is my sisters are rather needy and they usually run to Mom and Dad only when they need something."

Hearing the distaste in his tone, she changed hers to playful. "So ya put on your super hero cape and do the right thing…Brady to the rescue on his white horse?" She giggled at the picture it created.

He burst out laughing at her analogy. "Yep, that's me, the super hero. You should see me in the tights, Hon!"

They both laughed, seeing as they met on a big people site.

"I guess I'll have to sew ya a big "S" on the front, huh?"

"You can sew, Sunshine?"

"Heck, I can sew, cook, clean, build, design, upholster, refinish furniture…you're not the only one with superhero capabilities. I just don't wear tights since that's illegal up here in Canada for big women."

He nearly choked when he laughed. "Wow, you can do it all, can't ya?"

"Well, Buttercup, I's not just a pretty face ya know," she said sarcastically.

"No you're not…and what the heck is with Buttercup, Sugarplum?" His voice indignant, yet a playful teasing emerged.

"I think it suits ya. I's a-tell it like it is person, calls 'em as I see's 'em."

"So how you been feeling lately any word on the surgery?"

"I'm the same as always, tired, fed-up and scared. The surgery is in March sometime, but I don't know when. They'll let me know as it gets closer to the date."

And When

"I know you're trying to be brave and you're probably scared, but I get the feeling nothing keeps you down for long. You'll come out of this no problem." He sounded confident, but she didn't feel that way.

She spent the next while explaining what she went through with her dad and the history of cancer in her family to give him an overview. Her pain must've come through in her tone, he listened without interrupting once and when she finished, he spoke tenderly.

"Hon, I'm so sorry you have been through so much. I'm truly sorry you lost your dad. I can only imagine what that was like for you. The fear you feel, well I have felt that myself, so I know how you try to keep it all in and not show anyone, but ya gotta not let that get to you and believe that you will come through this," he finished.

"What happened to you that you thought maybe you wouldn't be okay?" She suddenly felt maybe someone understood her inner voice.

"It was a car accident when I was young. It ripped me up pretty good and I was afraid I wouldn't make it through." His voice was distant, as if re-living the memory.

"I'm sorry you went through that." She offered him comfort, afraid she'd brought back something he tried to forget.

"That was long ago and a longer road to get back to normal. You gotta be positive and think you can do anything. That's what'll get you through this."

"I have to rely on the surgeon and pray no cancer cells are found once these things are out of me. I'm getting my affairs in order like they said and writing a letter to everyone in case something goes wrong."

"I understand you're trying to cover all the bases, but don't stay in that thinking. I think it's courageous of you to try to do it all for everyone just in case, but don't focus on that part."

She changed the subject since she didn't want to hear any words of courage. Inside, she was a fraidy-cat. By the time the two-hour phone call ended, she learned he'd grown up in Wyoming and spent much of his time riding horses. The accident damaged his legs and he had contemplated surgery to correct the problem, but was afraid to undergo it. He used to be in the Navy then ended up in another government position and had lived all over the States. His job was confidential and he said he'd never be able to discuss the details with anyone.

Moving to Virginia fifteen years ago, he worked in Washington and owned horses as a hobby. His marriage had ended in divorce eight years ago and he'd never had children. Since then he hadn't settled down, but he did try one long distance relationship with a woman from Wisconsin. He did most of the traveling back and forth but it ended when it became too hard to maintain the schedule. Brady wasn't about to give up his twenty-year career when the woman wasn't willing to move.

His brother was a navy man and both sisters were housewives. He rarely saw them since one was in New York, the other in Louisiana. He had three nieces and two nephews, but the constant transfers made it hard to be a part of their lives as they grew up. Brady described himself as a lone wolf of sorts, but wanted something different since he was permanently assigned to Washington. He dated on occasion, but couldn't find what fit his life. His ideal partner would be smart, funny, independent, honest, loyal and not materialistic or needy. His first love in college had broken his heart by sleeping with his friend.

"Going through two relationships, are you afraid to settle down again?" Jade asked after hearing about his heartbreak.

He laughed. "I'm not afraid, I'm just smarter, and with what I bring to the table, I'm cautious," he said.

The phone call was incredible fun and they'd shared such an easy banter. Having learned so much about the man, she looked forward to the next call he promised to make.

And When

Recipe for Friendship

Chapter Eleven

The following night Jade picked up the receiver to hear, "Hey Sunshine, how are ya?" in that all-too-cute southern accent.

"I'm okay, how was your day, young man?"

"It's been a long day. Thank God the weekend is here."

"Tough day at work, Buttercup?" she asked.

"Yes it was. I think I'm going to enjoy just taking the weekend to relax and unwind."

"So what makes for a tough day for you?" She couldn't help but probe.

"I work on computers for the government."

"So you're like Homer and push buttons all day?"

"Doh, yep that's me," he said laughing. "So what's up for the weekend-is you're dance card full?"

"Dance card? Heck, my life has no time for a dance card. I can't even tell ya the last time I danced or even when I had a card for that matter." She chuckled.

"Come now, with your good looks and charm, I can't believe you don't have two or three dates lined up."

"Umm…that doesn't happen up here. I haven't had a date in…what year is it?" She hoped he got the point.

"I don't believe for one second that you don't get asked out all the time."

"Honestly, I rarely dated before this all started, so it's not like I was asked out often and with what I'm going through, it's just too much to put on anyone. The last guy said it was hard to deal with me and it was impossible to make plans when I may not have a future. He was right, so I decided not to put anyone else in that situation."

"That's not right! Just because you're going through something doesn't mean you don't deserve to find someone. It doesn't change who you are. You deserve someone to be there for you." He sounded put off.

"I don't think so. Picture if you lived closer and you asked me out. Let's say we hit it off on the first date, what would you think if'n' on the second date I told ya I have tumors and I don't know what's going to happen? Now be honest, you'd run the other way because who the heck wants to take that on? Or if'n' you could get past the initial shock and we go to a movie when suddenly I'm so tuckered-out I have to cut the evening short. No man wants that." She made her case in a playful voice, interjecting stereotypical southern terminology, hoping he'd laugh along.

"Well I tell ya…'if'n' we were to meet," he exaggerated her words. "And I know we'd get along just fine, Hon, and when you tell me about the tumors...well I'd first hug ya, wanting to keep you feeling safe that it didn't matter. And 'if'n' we were out and you 'tuckered out', I'd drive ya home, tuck ya in and hold ya all night long so ya know someone was there looking out for ya."

"Really, Buttercup, ya think that's how it'd be?"

"I can't speak for them Canadian boys, but that's how I'd be."

"When ya moving north?" There was a pause, then a burst of laughter.

This conversation was opposite to the one the night before. Instead of her learning more about him, he asked about her family, work and life in general. She held nothing back, answering openly and honestly. Her family, childhood wishes, her first marriage and the outcome. She detailed her work and the many difficulties she'd gone through.

Brady added to the conversation. When she talked of her divorce, he'd relay his own experience. Her problems with working and maintaining a home, he'd interject, giving details of things he struggled with.

"Talking to you, I don't understand how you could be single. I think you're just not aware of how many men are looking at you."

"Uh-uh, that doesn't happen up here. I think being bigger puts men off." She chuckled as she tried to describe the situation, but he didn't quite understand. "Brady, you live in a metropolis of millions while here it's a much smaller population. The next nearest city is ten hours away and I suppose if there were millions I'd have a full dance card."

"I think there is something wrong with Canadian men if someone like you is still single. You're smart, funny, intelligent and definitely attractive."

She'd give him the simple math version of the situation. "We have, let's say, 800,000 people and at least half are under age or elderly so that narrows it down to 400,000. Of those, three quarters are married so that brings you down to 100,000. Now if you try to figure out the appropriate age group, which for me is forty to forty-six, that would be maybe one percent. So we're down to 1000. Now out of that 1000, probably half are dating someone or gay, so that leaves 500. Of that 500, the chance of finding what I'm looking for may be only a ten percent ratio, that leaves fifty possible options. Trying to find one who doesn't mind that I'm a bigger girl, I'd guess would be around ten percent…so that means there are five possible options. I've dated those five, which explains why I'm single."

The laughter exploded on the end of the receiver. "So you're pretty much saying I gotta move?"

"Yep pretty much, but I should warn you I suck at dating."

"Oh yeah, why's that?" He couldn't stop chuckling at her antics.

"I'm way too shy. It's been far too long since I was in a relationship and I wouldn't know what to do. I's kinda skittish…like a scared rabbit," said in a playful voice. With only the odd two to three month relationship in her life, suddenly to be with someone full time scared the bejesus out of her. "I'm stubbornly independent and I'm a dunce about men. I'm really kinda man stupid."

"I think I'd take control of the situation. I'd pin you against the wall and kiss ya until you're not skittish no more," he said in a comical tough guy voice.

She could almost visualize the cowboy pulling up his jeans by the belt and digging his heels in to break her stubborn ways. "Ya think that would work, is that what I need, man-handling?"

"Yep, I think after that we'd get along the rest of our days. We'd grow old with me keeping ya on ya toes, learnin' ya." His southern accent added to the humor.

"I don't know…it would take a lot of patience." Jade threw him another curve ball.

"No worries, Hon, I got lots of patience and in the end, I'd get to look in them pretty eyes until we're old and gray." He spoke in a sexy drawl.

He was so much fun, she loved his playfulness and a new pattern emerged in her life. Perhaps he was trying to help her think past next couple months, but as the weeks passed, his calls became a daily event. They talked about everything under the sun from everyday life to news events, thinking the same on most subjects. They discussed the goings-on in the chat room, both coming to the same conclusions about people and how they presented themselves. During one of the phone calls, Brady admitted he was approached by one lady when he first joined. He confided they'd cancelled three meetings when she started pushing him.

Aware of the other person's interest, Jade had asked if she was okay with them talking, even though the likelihood of meeting was nil to none. Sheila said she had only started talking with him and she was fine with it.

They kept their personal conversations private, away from the prying eyes of the site. When he did make an appearance in chat, he'd dote on her in a playful manner. Her close friends knew he called every night at ten and when she signed off, it meant her phone was ringing.

--Jade wrote:

Yikes, we're only a 91% match! That means we are going to disagree 9 percent of the time. If you can keep your disagreeing down to a 4 percent, we have an extra 5 percent to make up...LOL. Okay, now that you're smiling...I added a cam like ya asked...so next time we chat I can see you live. That is, if I can figure out how to work the darn thing. Now, I must do my dishes before bed because I like waking up to a tidy house. (I am a bit retentive).

Night Cutie,
J
Xoxoxo

--Brady wrote:

Morning Sexy and hey what do you mean me disagreeing...LOL! Have noticed the 91% match and glad it's not higher. That gives us room to mess up, able to disagree then make up for it. Knowing that, I probably couldn't disagree with them wonderful captivating eyes of yours. Don't really think there would be much of a problem sitting down and working things out with you. Look forward to catching up. I still gotta get a new cam and get it working, so for now, I just enjoy being able to have the time and share our thoughts. It has been really nice. Going to start my day, but thought I'd send you a quick note.

Have a great day Hon,
Xoxoxo
Brady

The site was designed to match you with possible partners and would send profiles of what the computer deemed a perfect fit. It didn't seem to follow any rhyme or reason. When she'd started the profile she was forced to fill in preferences and chose tall and within five years of her age and the matches were nowhere near either request, the site way off in knowing anything.

One morning, she'd opened an email from a man who'd written darn near two pages in an attempt to let her know the computer matched them one hundred percent. An elderly man of eighty, a grandfather and war veteran, wrote from the heart. She forwarded a portion to Brady.

--Jade wrote:

I'm sorry to say, but I'm now taken. Okay, I get the feeling the computer doesn't know me so good (LOL). I sent him a very kind response since he seems like a very lonely man and he's a disabled veteran. Geez...pillow fights/water balloon fights /tickling until we can't stand it? I guess I'm old enough to have grand-children (LOL)...Had to share this with you, don't know about computer sites, but I guess I'm hitched now...LOL.

LOL,
J
xoxox

--Brady wrote:

Hmmmm....don't know...for a guy he sure talks a lot. Some things you should keep to yourself until ya meet. Just so you know the only pillow fighting we'd be doing is trying to get them out of the way. And who waits for balloons? I'll grab the hose and drench ya. Then of course I would have to towel you off...and ummmm...tickling until you can't stand it? Hmm, if'n' I's that close, I'd rather be caressing those soft lips with mine. Hope your day is going well. And Hon,-something is definitely wrong if ya match up a 100%, but we discussed that.

xoxoxo,
Brady

"It's only fair I tease you back," she said as her fingers typed on the keyboard as she pictured a full-on ice cold hose. He was such a brat at times that he'd definitely kept her guessing. When it came to Brady he easily made her imagine things.

--Jade wrote:

Aw, so many wonderful visions you place in my head, things long forgotten. The fantasy starts...to overcome my shyness you'd pin me against the wall kissing until I'm not skittish...we push all pillows aside and my hands feel your chest as I slip off your shirt. My kiss following where my hands lead yet always seeking the heat your mouth ignites. You're right...some things should be kept to yourself until ya meet...LOL

Hope I made you smile,
J Xoxoxo

--Brady wrote:

Smiles at you...you're just simply amazing. If'n' only I'd move north!

Xooxo
Brady

Calling that evening, they shared the day's events then he brought up the email.

"It's been a long time since I've felt that," he admitted. "You know the crazy rush of excitement and the impatience as two people can't get close enough. Don't you miss having that?" he asked.

104

"Umm…I can't say that I ever felt that or maybe it's been such a long time that I don't remember. I can't even imagine it and now, my heart would probably stop if it did." She laughed.

Brady mimicked the voice of an operator, thinking of the 911 call that would have to take place. "911 what is your emergency?" His scratchy voice sounded through the phone. "Well you see I didn't do nothing wrong. We were just getting started and I managed to move the pillows out of the way…and I must be great at this, because her heart just stopped. Yep, I pushed her over the edge, I'm that good!" Brady's voice went from a chuckle to outright laughter by the end of his imitation.

"I can just imagine you bragging to the operator at your bravado," she said giggling.

"They'd be asking for my phone number!" He howled with laughter.

"Oh sure, leave the Canadian's heart stopped while you get women's phone numbers."

"I guess I'll need to buy a set of the paddles and have them handy just in case. CLEAR!" He made the sound of jump-starting her heart. "What's the matter, Sunshine, lost for words?" He broke out in laughter.

Brady would leave her speechless by deliberately making a sexy comment and she'd get flustered in how to respond. He'd set her up and chuckle the entire time as she struggled to find an appropriate answer. It became one of his favorite sayings when she was stumped for too long. He'd make the sound effect of a pop-fly being hit out of the park as a signal that he'd one-upped her, leaving her out in left field.

They discussed using the webcam to see the other's reactions, thinking it would be fun to watch each other as they shared the jabs and quick wit. Brady bought a camera, but had yet to work out a mutual time. It would be difficult with the difference in time zones and schedules. He worked full-time days and in the evenings had a second job. In the winter he'd pick up a shift at the local hardware store and starting in spring it was fastball umpiring. He'd bought a house a couple years back and in order to make life easier he'd taken the second jobs as added income. "'I got free time, so might as well earn money and this way I can pay things off faster,'" he'd said. By the time he'd drive home she'd be in bed reading. She hated she couldn't stay up longer, but after living this way for over two years, it was her routine. Evening phone calls were an hour, just long enough to hear him say "'Sleep well beautiful,'" a nightly hug for her as he pulled in his driveway after his shift.

The first week of February she sat sipping her morning coffee before work when a message box popped onto her screen.

2 Dance: MORNING! xoxox
Jadey: mornin…yawns
2 Dance: how are you, Sunshine?
Jadey: just waking up>>slowly
2 Dance: *grins*…slides ya some coffee
Jadey: thanks
2 Dance: wake up beautiful, I got the cam on.
Jadey: Nope, sitting in a pink fluffy housecoat (so not a morning person)
2 Dance: bet ya still as beautiful as ever
Jadey: ya making me blush
2 Dance: well red would go with the pink coat LOL
Jadey: great…now he's got a visual
2 Dance: always have visual with you
Jadey: the chat room ladies miss ya…I was in there last night and they gossiped about you
2 Dance: me?
Jadey: yep, I wanted to say he isn't in often because he's talking with the Canadian…LOL
2 Dance: should have told them he is packing bags for Canada, eh
Jadey: this is the first time we're both on messenger. No cam though cause I'm a mess
2 Dance: LOL now there's a cute sexy image *nudges*
Jadey: hair not done, no make-up=ick!
2 Dance: whatever…besides ya don't wear hardly any makeup
Jadey: one day I will be looking my best, better than seeing me at my worst
2 Dance: don't think you're worst is all you say it is Hon…ya have that natural look about ya
Jadey: thank you! oh-oh, gotta get ready for work, I's late…
2 Dance: hope your day goes well for you…be safe and careful xoxoxo
Jadey: you too, have a great day cutie

He surprised her later that day when a text brought a smile to her face. *"You more awake yet LOL?"* He kept her wondering what it would be like if they were in the same city. She could imagine him showing up for lunch unannounced, or anytime for that matter. He'd be so much fun to have around.

On Saturday she was insulating behind the basement paneling and struggled lifting the eight-foot panel to ceiling height when his phone call came. Seeing his number, she didn't even say hello.

"I's expecting my doorbell to ring and it'll be a big tall Virginian coming to help me nail the panel back up."

"I'll be right over, Sunshine, what are we working on?"

Brady had learned that she'd tackle any project. As she explained her predicament, she balanced the phone on her ear, hoisted the panel and attempted to hit the nail all at the same time, but the panel kept sliding out of position. "Oh ya know!" She blurted out, frustrated.

Brady wasn't the typical male who'd tell her she did it wrong, he'd poke fun at her then suggest a solution. "Hey, Hon, did ya ever think that maybe if ya got a crowbar and a piece of wood you could wedge it under the panel and step on it to raise it where it needs to be?"

"How'd you know what position I'm doing things in, do you have a camera hidden here?"

"Nope, I just knows ya. You're pretty darn handy, but ya stumble on the last little bit. You got it all down and insulated, didn't ya? You just never thought about the end part."

"Dagnabbit, you's so smart! If'n' you were here, I'd pass you the hammer and let ya shows me." She whipped out in southern drawl.

"Nuh-uh, that would take away from what you're trying to accomplish and I knows ya like to stubbornly do things on your own. Besides, I could sit back and watch. Your hands would be full and I could just smile at you."

Jade started to giggle as she thought about him sitting two feet away. She looked like a fly slapped with a swatter trying to hold all four corners of the panel. Why couldn't he live here? "If only I could see your face right now. It's time to see what you look like I think," she said then held her breath.

"Well how about Thursday after dancing I hook up the camera. I'll come home and we can talk if it's not too late for you." Mindful of how tired she got, a consideration most would have ignored.

"Woo hoo! Thursday it is." She nearly dropped the panel.

"I'm looking forward to seeing them captivating eyes."

"Umm,"

"Yes?"

"You do know I've got lumps on my neck and I have black circles under my eyes like I told ya, don't ya?"

"So?" He paused. "Do you think that makes a difference to me?"

"Sometimes I look real tired since the sparkle is gone from my eyes and the lumps kinda jut…"

He cut her off. "I don't care about any of that, I care about you! It doesn't matter how tired you look or lumps sticking out, I'm looking forward to laying eyes on you."

She felt he wasn't going to cringe at first sight of her or pick apart the things that plagued her. "I just wanted to be sure you're okay with that."

"Do you honestly think I'd still be calling after all this time if that was all I seen in you?" He turned the table.

"Umm…I guess not. I give up trying to figure out why you call daily for nearly two months. By the way, I got the call from the surgical ward with the surgery schedule." It was hard to hear the actual date. She put the panel aside needing to discuss her thoughts. "I go March 9th and I don't know, Brady, now that the date is set I'm kinda rethinking things. I'm wondering if I made the right choice to have them taken out."

"I know you're worried, but you have to look at the pros and cons. You'll know once and for all what you're dealing with. As scary as it may sound, you have to see all the possibilities."

By the time she hung up she was more at ease. Focusing on the present, she finished the paneling using his suggestion.

He called several times over that weekend to check on her, sensing that her inner hamster churned the surgery around in her head. The following week, he repeatedly asked about her confidence level.

During Wednesday's call, he talked about their cam date and they pushed each other playfully, imagining what the other looked like in real life. She even bet he'd chicken out and he refuted the idea.

"Geez, I'm excited Hon. You'll be all dressed up from dancing and I get to see the real cowboy finally."

"Well if I'm gonna dress like you want me to, don't ya think you should dress how I'd like you to?" He teased.

Thursday at eleven, when she finally decided the call wasn't coming, she sat at the edge of her bed wondering why he'd changed his mind. Taking a long look in the bedroom mirror, she saw what a stranger might see. Staring at the dark circles she tried to conceal, her hand gently ran down the sides of her throat over the all-too-familiar lumps. "Humph"' the noise escaped her. She'd seen better days, remembering the woman who looked very different. No sense beating yourself up, he probably got scared and avoided calling, but he is your friend no matter what, she lectured herself. It might be too hard for him to see me and it isn't the first time you've run into that. She sent an email before crawling in bed. If he didn't want to see her, she'd voice her thoughts and never ask again.

--Jade wrote:

Ya know when ya look forward to something, it just makes ya all...ya know...when it doesn't happen. I guess I should learn Mr. Brady may be uncomfortable. I'm not upset. Guess I'll have to just go to sleep with my head filled with visions. I wish he lived closer, that way he could hug me to ease my worries (big wishes I have). Maybe it's not a good idea. I gotta think of what is best for him...it's not all about me. It's been a bad day all around and with what I feel, could use a hug.

Goodnight Hon.
J

She wanted a hug. From 2000 miles away he'd become her phone hug. His caring showed even in the Valentine's Day card he'd sent in his own hand writing.

For Jade on Valentines,

Well, you know we all have them doubts, the "what ifs", the "what fors", and who knows where that road would take us should we ever get the chance to go down it. No matter the high costs of that phone bill, the long conversations or the emails and cards back and forth, 'tis all worth it. I am thankful for what I have, for you do lighten those heavy days and chase them gray clouds away. 'Tis no matter what path we find ourselves on, you will always have a special place deep inside that will exist for all time.

Happy Valentine's Day!
xoxoxo

Maybe it was crazy, but his words eased her fears. With the hope of seeing each other for the first time on camera, he'd dodged her. Maybe his pictures weren't real or he really was afraid of what he'd see. She didn't know why he'd backed out, but she accepted something just went wrong and didn't hear from him until Friday night.

--Brady wrote:

Hey sunshine, I do apologize for not calling you on Thursday. I knew in the back of my head what you were waiting for, but on my way home I just wasn't in the frame of mind. I think you kind of understand that a bit. It's been a hard week and things just haven't let up, at least as of this point. I know that I can talk to you and that you are there for me, but being who I am, the way that I am, yes stubborn, I usually keep to myself and figure them out. Not to worry about the camera-it will happen. I hope you have a wonderful day and that everything is well with you.

Xoxoxo

Brady

She wished he'd come to her with his worries, it would even up the playing field. Friendships were built sharing all parts of life and she'd exposed everything to him. He was always there to lean on, but men were different, she'd seen it before. They needed to figure stuff out on their own. The "man cave" she nicknamed it. When something troubles a man, he goes into hiding for a few days then comes out as if nothing happened. She didn't respond to his email, thinking he needed time to deal. She didn't want to poke the bear or pry.

They'd gotten to really know each other and could almost finish each other's sentences. Some stuff remained a mystery, like the day to day basics. With the miles separating them she wondered about the things you only learn while watching a person go about their business. Did he get angry? Was he ever lonely? Did he ever need someone to be there? Often she wished for someone in the same room. It didn't always take conversation sometimes just having a body sharing the same space was comforting.

Saturday night Brady called. "Hey Sunshine, turn your cam on. I just pulled into the driveway," his southern voice excited.

He was taking the time to meet her face to face, so to speak. She wasn't ready and hadn't hidden her dark circles or put on make-up. He would see her at her worst. "Right now?" said with horror in her voice.

"I'm hanging up and I'll meet you in five minutes," he said, not giving her an option.

She ran to the mirror to look at herself and her stomach turned. Only having time to brush her hair, she sat down in front of her computer, terrified as she booted up the cam.

2 Dance: hold on...hooking up the cam
Jadey: wow Buttercup, you're cute!

He's handsome, exactly like his pictures, better even as he smiled and waved. She sat very still, typing and watched his reactions at the same time. Looking at the image she projected, her cam let her see exactly what he was. If he'd given me ten minutes' warning I could've looked better, she thought.

2 Dance: you're beautiful, love the way you swoosh your long hair as you type
Jadey: it gets in the way sometimes, and thanks
2 Dance: uh huh I'm sure it does
Jadey: huh?
2 Dance: can't give out all my secrets
Jadey: it's only a matter of time until I'll know them, why not just tell me?
2 Dance: can't go too fast now
Jadey: it's been months...stubborn man
2 Dance: uh huh, just as stubborn as you LOL

Her face an open book, he caught her every emotion on the camera.

*2 Dance: *puts that one down in his book**
Jadey: bring it on Buttercup...
2 Dance: careful Sugarplum
Jadey: sheesh!
2 Dance: nice rollin' of the eyes

Knowing him, he'd always have smart-ass names for me. How many times had he said she'd be left scratching her head with him around?

Jadey: I do have expressive eyes
2 Dance: yes ma'am and mouth and lips
Jadey: you don't know the half of it
2 Dance: not yet, just that ya get kissed a lot...LOL

Jadey: it's not my fault
2 Dance: uh huh, right

He teased her about last week's incident when the mechanic who regularly took care of her car suddenly turned and grabbed her by her coat collar, then kissed her. A younger, thirty year-old man she barely knew with a body of steel and piercing blue eyes. It stunned her and when she told Brady, he teased her relentlessly

Jadey: like you wouldn't do the same
2 Dance: will give that excuse to ya, only one thing I would do differently
Jadey: what's that?
2 Dance: wouldn't have stopped...ain't worth stunning someone like that and just pulling out ya know?
Jadey: well I tell ya Brady, whenever you think your ready...LOL
2 Dance: double dog dare, eh? But I already know one of your weaknesses
Jadey: huh?
*2 Dance: keep her off guard *grins**

Jade re-adjusted her position and Brady raised an eyebrow.

Jadey: sorry needed to stretch
2 Dance: let's see your neck. Is it sensitive?
2 Dance: now there's a look!
Jadey: now you know 2 weaknesses...LOL
2 Dance: just gotta get close enough
Jadey: Virginia's a long ways away
*2 Dance: yeppers *sigh**
Jadey: are you okay, ya look sad?
2 Dance: I had some family things happen this week... 'tis why I was kind of out of it
Jadey: anything you want to talk about?
2 Dance: my sis is having issues with her spouse and is leaving...she has a kid
Jadey: aw that's sad
2 Dance: never been real in touch with her and haven't spoken with her in several years. Had to when she showed up on my doorstep
Jadey: she's living with you?
2 Dance: yeah, couldn't say no
Jadey: are ya afraid to talk to her?
2 Dance: just doesn't seem like the right time.
Jadey: ya need a break? Escape>move north LOL
2 Dance: guess she would get the hint when the "for sale" sign is on da door, eh? But she has 8-yr old...adorable
Jadey: things happen for a reason...gotta have faith in that...just talk to her

2 Dance: easier said than done
Jadey: she's probably walking on egg shells, not knowing what the hell to do
2 Dance: thanks...didn't mean to dump that on ya
Jadey: I like knowing and it kinda evens stuff up for me, I've dumped all over you
2 Dance: no such thing as even
Jadey: I know, I owes ya
2 Dance: don't owe me a thing Hon, never have
Jadey: you're holding my hand even if you didn't know that
2 Dance: ' tis what friends are for and don't throw that back at me either
Jadey: I know, but just who I am Brady, you'll learn.
2 Dance: I know...but ya still don't...was wonderful to see ya tonight
Jadey: thank you for doing this
2 Dance: my pleasure, as always
Jadey: this made my night
2 Dance: totally understand Hon
Jadey: do ya?
2 Dance: yeah
Jadey: don't think ya do. It's not just for what I gotta go through...you've been a bright shiny star since November. You're wonderful and more than I expected.
2 Dance: see...do understand...feel the same way about you
Jadey: on the same page?
2 Dance: seems like we always are...we's two peas in a pod
Jadey: thanks for being there for me-I want the best life for you
2 Dance: same goes for you
Jadey: so no more mechanics kissing me then? LOL
2 Dance: no tune-ups or lube jobs...LOL
Jadey: what would a cowboy do? (Best 8 seconds of your life-cocky aren't I?)
2 Dance: nope...just truthful
Jadey: you're so sweet.
2 Dance: time for bed Sunshine, sleep well and we'll talk later
Jadey: night handsome
2 Dance: niters xoxoxo

Seeing him shined a spotlight on what was missing in her life. Somewhere along the way, she gave up. With the mechanic incident, Brady warned that the young man saw her as a challenge to conquer, but she found it hard to believe she'd be looked at as a cougar. Brady's compliments gave hope that someone else would see beauty in her. After seeing him that night, she wanted to try to find someone like Brady closer to home and started talking with local men on a date site. Jade wanted normal, even if it was just until her surgery, realizing she missed out on a big part of life.

Tim, a forty six-year-old divorcee, asked her out after a few emails and they seemed to get along well. She agreed to meet, but being unsure of men, she reiterated things to Brady to get his opinion and he warned her to keep one step ahead of men.

"I knew there was a line-up for you," he joked. "Good luck tomorrow, Hon. I guess I'll have to talk to you on Friday since you'll be out on a date tomorrow."

"I'm supposed to meet him at eight at a lounge. I guess we'll see how it goes."

"I'm surprised you didn't set up dinner on a Friday or Saturday night for your first meet."

"He chose the place and I chose the time. I prefer having it on a weeknight, that way if I'm not comfortable, it's shorter. Who wants to sit through a long dinner if you don't like each other?"

Thursday evening, having done what she could to cover things she nervously headed out. Tim introduced himself when she entered the lounge. He was a tall, dark-haired man with a mustache and beard. Sitting face to face, it seemed they'd gotten along better through email. A good looking man, but clearly older than his stated forty-six years, he appeared well into his fifties. He tried to keep the conversation interesting, but there was no teasing banter or in-depth talks. Instead, he told her of his work, his children and his struggle to rebuild after a very bitter divorce.

She tried to keep an open mind and at the end of the date when she agreed to see him again, she found herself wrapped in a bear hug. It was awkward, and when she was about to turn away to head to her car he embraced her, this time kissing her. She allowed it briefly then pulled away. On the drive home she weighed the pros and cons of the evening, deciding she'd wait and see if the next date would feel any better. I'm out of practice and I have to stop judging, finding fault with every man, she lectured internally. Getting home after eleven she went to bed and was surprised when her phone rang.

"Hey, how'd it go?" Brady asked anxiously.

"This is late for you, how did you know I just got in? The date was…don't know really."

"What do ya mean you don't know? Either you like the man or you don't."

"I don't know." Why does he sound so frustrated, she wondered.

"Are you going to see him again?"

"I told him I would, but can't say for sure," she said. When he didn't respond she continued. "I think he fibbed about his age, he looked over fifty."

"Hon, you gotta do what makes you happy. I know you're always trying to make everyone else happy, but say no if it doesn't feel right for you!" His voice determined. "You have to choose who you want and what works in your life."

"How was your night, what did you do?" She changed the subject. How do I tell him he's not you? She wondered.

"I went by the book store to look for a book I need."

"Did you find it?"

"Nope, they didn't have it." Brady sounded serious and not his usual light-hearted self.

"Were you looking for a book on Canadian women and how to figure us out?" She snickered.

"I was looking for a book on Jade da Canadian."

She heard his smile. "I's a tough one to figure, so maybe start with a book on Canadian women and then everything ya read, disregard…I'm not like anyone."

Hearing his outburst of laughter he sounded like he needed that dose of fun. "Oh I got ya book alright, I knows ya."

There's that confident brat tone she loved. "You may think ya knows me, but ya only know some of me."

"It's only a matter of time, Sunshine."

After they hung up, she lay in bed reviewing the night. If only Tim could've been like Brady, the date fell short of the bar now set by the stranger, miles away. He sounded upset, almost jealous. Maybe it's because I didn't say more about the date. I'll just tell him the truth in an email tomorrow.

Brady

I think of you often during my days. Why am I so intrigued by someone I've never met? Why do I wonder about things? I wonder what your normal daily life is like. If only you were here, I could get to know you. It's that you are so far away that this all gets mixed up. It's like I compare men to what I know of you. That's crazy, because I haven't met you. I'm lost, kinda. I feel a connection, yet here I am trying to find local people who just don't make me feel that inner smile. Kinda weird having these things play out in my head.

Last night's date had an okay sense of humor and I tried to focus on him, but couldn't. The drive home was reflecting on what it is I want in life. Then the phone rings at 11:20 and it's you! Like you knew I was home and my smile returned.

The man from last night called today asking me out again. Although we didn't firm up a time or date, I wasn't excited. What am I doing Brady? Do I want to see this man again? What a mixed-up girl, huh? Just my thoughts,

Xoxox
J

Not hearing from Brady until the following Thursday, she worried she'd been too open. Used to his regular calls, she hated the silent phone. It was like an empty space that only filled again when it rang.

"Hey, how are you?" He sounded happy.

"You sound in a good mood. Did ya dance a lot tonight or something?" He probably went out since she went out on a date, she thought.

"As a matter of fact I did." His tone became somber.

"That's good cutie, so why do you sound sad, no one special to dance with?"

"There was one girl there, but she was near half my age. She couldn't have been more than twenty-one years old!"

"That's a bad thing? Come on, some young girly was smitten with you," she teased.

"It was just a dance!" He got defensive and the line quieted for a moment before he continued. "It got me remembering what it was like to hold someone that close, ya know what I mean? When you can smell their perfume and feel arms wrapped around ya."

"Kinda." She thought about the kiss from her date, wishing it had stirred her.

"Two peas, I tell ya. It seems we always are," his tone soft and melancholy.

"Definitely two peas and I want to say something, is that okay?"

"Sure, lay it on me," he said, half smiling.

"I think I'm confused when it comes to you, I compare men here to how you make me feel, is that normal?" she asked hesitantly, afraid he'd think she was off the deep end.

"Nope, that's not normal," he said seriously, then laughed at hearing her intake of breath.

"I'm not crazy!"

"Ya know I'm kidding. Of course it's normal. You and I seem to understand one another and I think about the 'what ifs' too," his tone heartfelt. "I can't imagine not talking to you and I always look forward to our time."

It's something, at least. Am I becoming a part of his world in a strange way? I've never been in this position. How does one begin to get attached to another without even meeting? Maybe I am going crazy, she thought as the idea swirled in her mind. "I don't understand. It used to be I got up, went about my work and all the little things I did everyday without so much as a thought. Now, I look forward to a ringing phone, text or email. With the joking and laughing we do, I don't know what I'm supposed to feel. I've never met you and I've only seen you once on cam, but I feel so close."

"So you want to cam more?" Brady offered in a serious tone.

"Do you want to cam more?" She asked, wondering if he was trying to build their connection.

"We could do that if that helps."

"Do you think that'll help?" She asked. Help what, get closer? I'm even more confused, does he want me to get closer?

"We can work on that, Hon. We'll figure it out and see if that makes things fall into place more."

Fall in place for whom, what is he trying to say? After they said goodnight, she kept replaying the offer of seeing him more, the man who was becoming her best friend. He was the first to understand her and never pushed her to change her ways. He'd listen then help her sort through her thoughts one at a time. He is exactly as his pictures, so the attraction is there. Knowing him this long, he went from handsome to gorgeous. The inner person matched the outer. His "Sleep well beautiful" was her last thought before she fell asleep.

And When

Ready or Not the Time Has Come

Chapter Twelve

Tim just didn't click after their second try and they decided to go their own ways. Brady seemed relieved it was short-lived, using his "I told ya so" tone.

With the surgery approaching, her emotions played havoc as she took the time to lay her words on paper. Her family had been through enough and she wanted to make sure to make everything easy for them. With the pre-surgery appointment looming, she became edgy, everyone allowed her space, knowing the anxiety was building. Once she finished the letter, she tucked the sealed envelope away. They were things she would want said only if something went wrong.

Lisa volunteered to drive her to the hospital and with the logistics figured out, Jade walked into the hospital for the final run of tests and the counseling of what to expect before, during and after.

The nurse discussed all possible probabilities. Her entire thyroid would be removed, tumors and all. They assumed everything was contained within the gland, now stretched far beyond normal, but reiterated that the surgeon wouldn't be certain until he was inside. The procedure would take four hours, then a few hours in recovery. She'd be moved to a bed overnight where she'd be monitored during her stay and released when ready. She signed the resuscitation order, having asked everything she could think of. All she needed to do was wait the ten days.

She'd had walked through these hospital corridors often this past three years. As she left, she hoped she'd seen the last of them. Having been in the three largest hospitals in the city in many different departments, she could practically guide others to find CT scans, ultra sounds, blood tests and the ever-favorite radioactive drink department. She'd seen far too many white coats over the years, the memory of her dad the last week of his life popped into her head and her eyes welled.

Stepping out into the bright wintry day she took in her surroundings. Snowdrifts were piled along the roadways where sand trucks left the pristine white snow in gray and black heaps. The parking lot was filled to the brim as always, with people here and there scraping their windshields. It's funny how we all visit a place like this. For every car in the lot, someone was ill, dying, visiting, having a baby or getting something done, tested or changed. It reminded her how vulnerable life could be. Five years ago she was invincible in her own mind, never thinking something like this could happen. Man, how life changes. Dad was supposed to be here until his nineties. She looked at life's realities and how they changed in a heartbeat. If these tumors contained any cancer cells, she'd better be prepared.

Later that evening she explained her plan to her family. "I have to be there at six Friday and the surgery is at seven. No food or drink as of six on Thursday and I report into emergency. They'll take me to the prep area and from there I'll be wheeled away for four hours and be in recovery for a bit. You might as well head to work then come back the next day when I'm ready to come home," she told Lisa.

"Uh-uh, I'm staying there until you're out of surgery. I'm not leaving and coming back!"

"Well that's crazy to sit there! I'll be in surgery for hours, then in recovery. I'll sleep most of the day, being drugged." It didn't make sense for Lisa to waste time doing nothing. They'd spent too many hours sitting in hospitals already.

"I've already told Ken and the boys I won't be home until late and then gone Saturday until Sunday morning, so you're stuck with me. Mom will come Sunday at noon and she'll spend the night and that'll give me time to do what I need to get ready for the work week."

Lisa had planned it all. Jade wondered how much of this was to deal with it. With dad, they needed to be doing something in order to handle the stress. "Okay then, but I'm sure I won't be much company and I'll probably be sleeping most of the time." She needed someone to be with her the first few days, according to the surgeon.

"How did it go with the appointment today?" Eric asked. He called right after she hung up from Lisa.

"Well everything's set, I just have to wait until next week then this will be done with once and for all."

"When will they know if it's cancer?"

"I guess once they get this thing out of me and cut it up. Knowing the health care system, probably another ten to fourteen days."

"At least you'll know and then you can get back to normal."

Whatever normal is? It'd been so long since I lived anything near normal. I barely remember how life was before this started. "Well, the only thing I'm worried about is not having a voice, other than that I can deal with whatever happens."

"Even if that happens there's paper, pens or hand signals, it's no big deal to lose your voice," he said in a "come on, get with it" tone.

"Easy for you to say, my job requires me to talk all day so what am I gonna do if I can't? Do I sell my house and stop paying bills?"

"So what, it's a job and you'll find another one or you'll be disabled and you can collect disability."

"How's my puppy?" She changed the subject.

"He's whining at the phone."

Charlie and Jade had bonded while she lived with Eric. When she'd visit, he'd follow her wherever she went and when she'd leave, he'd sit at the door and put his head down to look at her with sorrowful eyes. A cross between a Husky and wolf, he left balls of down-like fluff wherever he went. When Charlie and Eric would come over to her place, Charlie would jump all over her in greeting then settle to curl up on the loveseat over her lap. She'd have to vacuum the moment they left.

"I have to get going, I have stuff to do."

"I'll talk to you later," Eric said and they hung up.

Why does he always downplay my thoughts? It's been like that since the first day ten years ago. With a direct, harsh view of life, he's always quick to point out my flaws. Sure, I'm not perfect and yes, at times I'm too stubborn and over-think things to death. That is a part of who I am, just like my dark hair. Some things just aren't changeable, nor would I want to change them. It got me this far in life and I've done okay. I own a house, a car, have a career, never missed a day of work and was strong, smart and able. I'm not a rocket scientist, but I'm not negative, needy or stupid, the thoughts whirled around in her mind. I made many friends through life and I'm sure I'd be remembered fondly.

She stumbled on that thought. At her funeral, how many people would stand there to say goodbye? With the way she'd been pushing people away, would everyone forgive her? She should write her own eulogy just in case. I'd start with; 'well I guess if this is being read, it's not so good news for me, but great news for everyone I'm leaving my stuff to. My house goes up for sale and the proceeds split between Lisa and Jared. My furniture goes to my friends, because it supported them many times in their drunken moments. The car to whoever can afford to keep up with the gas. The bills left behind…let them try to collect, please give them my forwarding address,' she laughed at the thought.

Funerals were crappy and she'd like hers to be joke after joke until people had tears running down their faces from hilarity, not sorrow. I want to be remembered for who I am, a person who was a shoulder to lean on and who made people see humor through their ordeals. The phone interrupted her train of thought.

"Hi, how are you doing?" Her mother asked in a sad, worry filled voice.

"I'm doing just fine and how are you?" Jade picked it up a notch.

"How did it go at the appointment today, did you find out about next Friday?"

Jade explained all the details and waited for her mother's response.

"I'll be at the hospital Friday and then at your house Sunday. That way Lisa can go get her stuff done and I'll stay the night," she half confirmed and asked in the same sentence.

"No sense you coming on Friday I'll be in surgery and out of it most of the day."

"Of course I'll be there! Lisa and I will wait it out together."

"Well suit yourself, but I'm sure I won't feel up to company though." What is with her family wanting to sit in hospitals?

She made a list of all the stuff she'd need to get done before the date, wanting no fuss or bother for her family. It reminded her of every trip she'd ever taken. Make a list and double check it ten times. Put the airline ticket in a safe place, check that ten times. She laughed as the memory of the first vacation she and Lisa took together came to mind. Asking Lisa several times where her ticket was, by the time they switched planes in Minneapolis, Lisa had enough. "If you ask me about my ticket one more time, I'm going to beat you!" She smiled at the memory, thinking of how she wanted to take time to enjoy life and travel again. She wouldn't ask her family this time to recheck anything; it was up to her to make this easy for them.

The next week passed quickly with Brady increasing his calls to help derail her inner hamster. He created humor at every turn and would send texts throughout her day with little comments that brought a smile to her face. He asked daily how much she slept the night before and was becoming aggravated as the time lessened every day.

Her site family called during the week to wish her well and talked of meeting to celebrate once she was past this. Jade agreed and vowed to hug them for their support. She could never thank them enough for helping her, but she needed to wait to see how things played out, waiting to know if she could talk and of course be cancer-free. If not, she could be in for a busy time ahead.

She had booked Thursday off before the surgery and when she left work Wednesday her stomach was in knots. Last week's conversation with the nurse about scars replayed through her mind. She'd taken the week to mull it over and when her phone rang, she rushed through the day's events, then began to put a voice to the worries she'd been keeping from Brady.

"Umm Hon…last week the nurse said not to worry about swelling and stuff, but the scar would depend on how I heal. Just so you know I could end up looking like Frankenstein with big lines across my neck leaving a hideous scar." She laughed nervously as she said it.

"It wouldn't matter one bit to me if you looked like Frankenstein, I'd still think you're beautiful and I don't want you to even think about that."

"It's not like you're ever going to see it, you don't live down the block, ya know."

"Who says?"

"Well last I checked Virginia is 2000 miles away."

"How do you know I haven't bought a ticket to come see you through this?" He challenged.

"You better not have! I don't even want friends and family to see me all cut up."

"Maybe I'll surprise you," he said in a serious tone.

"I would be so mad if you spent money on a ticket to see me at my worst!" I'll tear him a new one if he shows. I won't open the door.

They resumed their laughter, but she kept redirecting the conversations to serious topics. As much as the fun helped to keep her calm, she had two days to wrap her head around things.

"I decided I'm going to have the surgery on my legs," he said. They're getting worse and I feel it all the time now. The doctors warned me a long time ago I'd need to do this. I didn't want to because I was afraid of being in pain, but without, I could end up using a cane or worse, a wheelchair."

"How bad is it?" She wondered at the severity of his situation. He looked like a healthy, fine young man on cam, but he never stood while they talked. Without living close, she couldn't tell if he limped towards his bed at night. He groans when he gets in or out of his car, but I thought it was exhaustion, but maybe it was pain he endured. She silently accepted any physical scars she might end up with.

"Oh it's enough that I feel it every day. It's just time to suck it up and go for it. I'm getting old, Sunshine."

"Heck if you're old, what does that make me, a dinosaur?" She said with a chuckle. They kept the conversation on neither surgery, instead enjoyed laughing together.

--Jade wrote:

After we talked I felt bad. Here I am bitching about my worries and it hurts you to walk. I should have been a little less selfish. My petty thoughts about my looks just don't compare to what you probably endure all the time. You're right, we're aging...and this is all part of what lies ahead. I guess at times I forget about what others are going through and get all wrapped up in my head. (Darn hamster). I will be there for you when you go for surgery...if'n' you need me...I will be there. My word is gold...I just got lost for a moment with my stress. Sorry. Sleep well handsome,

Jade
xoxoxo

--Brady wrote:

Ya know there's nothing to apologize for. Been there and know what you are sort of going through. We all have certain challenges, tests and ordeals that we have to face in life. From someone else's eyes it can appear to be simple, easy, or not that difficult. But until you see what it looks like from the person that is going through it, well, you just can't really guess.

We all pick our battles, the ones that are worth fighting for and hopefully we can move on afterwards. After a while, as you probably know you kind of get used to the pain. It becomes a routine thing in your daily activities that you don't really notice it that much.

I have dealt with it for a long time, but the last couple years it's gotten to the point where I know I need to do something. But like you, it's the unknown that makes me scared. I have no doubt that you will be there for me, but what you are going through out weighs mine by far.

Hope you have a great day and do hope you were able to rest some. It's important to try and get rest, which I know would be hard for me to do.

Brady
Xoxoxo

Waking to his email, she knew he understood her fear was hard to control. After getting a solid five hours sleep, she cleaned her house top to bottom, then went to the grocery store and chose foods her family would enjoy. She organized her fridge and pantry, then jumped onto the computer to pass the time. The room buzzed and she instinctively knew he was there. Surprised, he asked why she was on mid-day and within seconds her phone rang that familiar long distance tone.

"So you're playing hooky, huh," he said with a smile in his voice.

"Yep, I deserve it."

"Did you sleep at all last night?"

"I slept five hours and feel better than I have in a long time."

"Five hours? That's not enough! You gotta get a full eight hours. Tomorrow is the big day and I know you ain't gonna sleep tonight," he scolded.

"I went to bed early and five hours is better than the three I'm used to."

"Oh ya know!" He used one of her sayings, mimicking it to perfection. "Don't make me come up there to make sure you're getting the sleep ya need."

"I double dog dares ya to make me!" Jade thought if she lived in Virginia, he'd leave work at that very second. There was safety in being miles away.

"Oh…you's so gonna get it. I'm gonna buy a ticket today and come out."

"I bet you twenty bucks you're full of hot air."

Just then her phone beeped. She put Brady on hold to take the call finding the hospital on the line.

"Hon, they changed my surgery time for six. I gotta call my sister and Mom. Can we talk later?"

"I'll call you earlier tonight so you can get your rest."

"That would be wonderful. I'll talk to ya later."

Jade dialed Lisa's number first. "Hey, how's work going?"

"Good and how are you, getting nervous yet?"

"Nah, not too nervous, but the hospital called and rescheduled. Can you pick me up at quarter to five because they changed the surgery to six instead of seven?"

"Six? So you're the first one going under I guess?"

"If you're gonna do something, best be number one at it."

They both laughed.

"No problem. Do you have everything ready for tomorrow?"

"There's nothing to get ready. No jewelry or make-up and I'll wear baggy clothes with no bra since that'll be a pain. So basically I gotta get up, get dressed and we're out the door, I figure."

"I guess you're right. No sense bringing a house coat or slippers. What about your friends? Who is waiting to hear about how this goes?"

"I'll send you an email with a couple friends that wanted to be updated, they can spread the word." Darn it! How did that not get done before now? I thought I planned for everything, she thought.

Lisa said she'd call their mother to let her know about the change in plans and Jade settled in for the rest of the day, comfortably on her loveseat with the remote in hand. As she flipped through the channels, nothing appealed. If this is what I have to do for the next two weeks, I'll go nuts! After dozing twenty minutes she went outside to shovel snow. When back inside, she put on music and spent the rest of her day reading the book she had purchased to take to the hospital.

"Hey you," Brady's voice came over the phone at four on the nose.

"Hey Cutie, how was your day?"

"The usual, and how was your day, did you change all the arrangements for tomorrow and get a hold of your family?"

"Yep, and I cleaned the house, bought groceries, shoveled, and took a twenty-minute snooze this afternoon."

"Wow, a whole twenty minutes, huh. That'll make up for the night won't it?"

"I tried, but the darn hamster just won't rest, I tell ya."

"I do believe I'm going to have to set a trap for that thing and shut it off to make ya do as you're supposed to," he teased.

"At least I got everything done and ready, you know me, plan for everything."

"Yep, I knows ya." He laughed then talked about his day.

"So let me get this straight. The boss asked you to set up the new office which wasn't part of your job in the first place, but she was stuck needing it done. Then when you finished, she came in and didn't like it?" She snickered. I can only imagine him in a mood.

"Pretty much, I had to take it all apart and not once did she say thanks. I tell ya, inside I was pissed. On the outside I was like "Yes ma'am," but in my head was a whole different vocabulary going on."

"Do tell, Buttercup, what vocabulary?"

"On the outside is proper and polite, but I was swearing a whole bunch of names at her. So "Yes ma'am" really meant, 'are you a bitch or what?'"

"So ya saying...if'n' I asked you to arrange the furniture in the living room then I look at it and didn't like it, is it safe to tell you or will you be calling me names inside?" She asked in a playful tone to change his mood.

"First off, I'd be sure to ask you if you were sure, because you're O.C.D." Brady jabbed. "And if'n' you don't like it after I do it, well then I'd just distract the hamster until it don't matter no more." His chuckle that followed was priceless.

"If I didn't like how it was done, I wouldn't say anything, so no need to distract the hamster. I'd say thanks and wait until you went to work and re-do it." Let him think about that! O.C.D. my ass, I'm not that retentive.

"Exactly, so no need to call ya names. I'd be trying to get it done fast, because then I could focus on you the rest of the night, chica-bow-wow." He sang the tune.

"Buttercup."

"Yes Sunshine?"

"So it doesn't matter where I put stuff, or how I do things, because you'd be fine as long as there is chica-bow-wow?" She smiled at him playing the man-card, that red-blooded virile man talk.

"As long as I get to be by you every day until we're old and gray, nothing else matters."

"Aw...I's all blushing," she said in a playful voice.

"'Tis the truth and just how I see it. Well Hon, I gotta get going. I just pulled into the store and I need to get some groceries. I'll call ya later."

It was nice to have someone think of her that way. She started to feel giddy like a teenager at times. It didn't make sense to have feelings about him, but it didn't make sense not to. He called all the time and flirted constantly. What is this? What does he think it is? The attraction and connection was beginning to morph. It probably stems from my years alone. Now I have someone to turn to who didn't judge my situation or look at my flaws. A mixed jumble of feelings spun. He seems to think they'd be together one day. Maybe he's waiting to see if I come out of this fine before saying what he feels.

With her last solid meal finished, she took a long hot bath then sat cozy on the couch in a pink puffy housecoat. Setting her alarm for four-thirty, she looked at the information package from the nurse. Filled with diagrams, it was the after-care information for her family to read about bandages and infections.

The phone rang at eight fifteen.

"What are you doing?" Eric asked.

"Watching TV then I'm off to bed in a half hour."

"What's happening tomorrow?"

"The surgery is at six and I won't be home until the next day."

"Can I come by Saturday? Charlie misses you and wants to check on you."

"I don't know if I can see Charlie. I'm sure I'll be on pain killers, sleeping a lot, and he jumps up all over me so I don't know if that's a good idea." She didn't want a mishap with the oversized, energetic, lap-dog she loved.

"How about I call to check first and we'll see?"

"Maybe call Lisa on Saturday first."

"Okay. Can she call me and let me know how you are?"

"She's sending out an email after the surgery, do you want her to send you one?"

"Yeah, that way I know it's done. I'll see you on Saturday," he said then hung up.

Signing onto the computer, she started typing the email list for her sister when her call display showed Brady was on the phone.

"Wow, this is really early for you. Are ya skipping out of work to call me?"

"Of course, do ya think I was gonna let you go in tomorrow without me talking to you again?"

"I feel so special. This is three times in one day we get to talk and only hours apart. Heck, it's almost like you're here holding my hand."

"Are ya nervous, Sunshine?" he asked in a serious tone.

"Yep," she squeaked out in a quiet voice.

"What are ya worried about? You'll get through this."

Tears started creeping down her cheeks.

"Sunshine, are you there?"

"Oh ya know!" She paused to find her voice. "This hasn't been easy and tomorrow it all comes to an end. I don't know who I'm gonna be when I wake up." She let it out in a voice which began to crackle, a sign that revealed her tears.

"I know you're scared, I would be too. I really wish I was there to help you through. Heck, I'd be terrified, not knowing what's going to happen. You've been through so much and lost so much time that maybe tomorrow will finally set you back to where you want to be. No more tests, no more worries and no more not being who you want."

He was right, but the fear of the outcome just wouldn't go away. "I know, I'm sorry I'm being a girl." She sniffled and none too lady-like.

"You've always been a girl and no need to apologize. I get it, I would be the same way," he said in a loving voice.

"Really, you'd cry like a girl too?" She giggled.

"Well maybe not like a girl." He chuckled.

"I hates crying," she said as she sniffled. "It's so annoying and weak."

"Heck no, you're not weak, far from it. You've been through so much and crying is perfectly normal."

"So ya saying...I'm normal?" Her humor kicked in to deal with the stress.

"Hell no, I never said that! I said crying under this pressure is normal. Nope, you're still crazy." His laughter warmed her soul.

"Hey, now wait just a minute, Buttercup," Jade said in a sniffly indignant voice, then took a deep breath. "Brady...what happens if I wake up tomorrow and I can't talk? I mean you phone and we talk all the time, so what happens if we can't do that anymore? I mean we haven't even met and I kinda like sharing time with you."

"I don't want you to worry about that. Even if you did lose your voice we have email and the cam. I could even buy you one of those phones that talks for ya."

"Oh great, I'll sound like Darth Vader."

"I---am---Canadian." He said in a breathy husky voice mimicking the character.

"How attractive is that?" she whispered. She'd seen those devices held to a neck to make sounds from the voice box.

"You don't even need one of those because I knows ya so well. I know what you're thinking anyways."

"I know you think I'm worrying too much, but it just goes through my mind without me even trying. It's like wow, tomorrow I could maybe not talk anymore. That's where I get stuck."

"Well get unstuck, no matter what happens you'd find a way! You're just that stubborn and nothing keeps you down, so put that in your pipe and smoke it!"

"Put it in my pipe and what? What the heck is that?" She laughed outright.

"I thought it fit the situation," he said with a warm chuckle.

"My sister is emailing my friends once I'm out of surgery, do you want an email or wait until I can contact you myself?" After this conversation, I'd best ask how he wants to communicate.

"Tell her to email me, that way I know how you're doing right away."

They joked many times about how he'd fit in just perfect with her family since they all shared a zany sense of humor. Brady even mentioned how he'd contact her mother, "Hi mom, I'd like you to know what you're daughter said to me…whew, made me blush." He'd tease about life one day, as if the future held a time when he'd be part of her family. It started as a joke with him trying to one up her using a family angle, but he used it frequently. Dad would've really liked him.

"Okay, you're added to the list. I guess I should go to bed and try to sleep. I don't know when we'll talk again, but as soon as I'm up to it I'll let you know." She'd leave it like that. "And Hon, I just want to say thank you for being there for me, it's made this all much easier not being alone." I don't know how to say thanks for being my lifeline.

"Aw shucks, don't get all mushy on me we'll be talking before you know it. You get some sleep and shut that hamster off so ya do. We'll talk once you're okay again."

"Goodnight Hon."

"Goodnight and rest well, beautiful. I'm thinking of you."

That night would be the longest. She lay in bed talking to her Dad, praying he was watching over her. Did you send me Brady? It's funny how a man with your same character traits showed up right before the surgery. They say life unfolds as it should and everything happens for a reason, the thoughts kept tumbling around in her mind. The last time she looked at the clock it was two twenty-one.

And When

Patients and Patience

Chapter Thirteen

Dressed in sweat pants and baggy shirt, Jade followed her normal routine morning routine on the day of the surgery. After brushing her teeth and hair, she sat waiting as the minutes ticked by, then stood outside on the curb minutes before Lisa pulled up. Traffic was non-existent at this hour and with no coffee, it was too early for small talk. Arriving at the hospital, they parked and walked in silence to check in at the emergency desk. Jade turned to Lisa to say goodbye.

"Nope, I'm coming with you," Lisa said.

Going down a corridor to a prep room, the nurse handed her a gown and robe then showed her to a large room with a white sheet hung across its width. Once changed, with all her clothes tucked away in the duffle bag, she and Lisa were led to the pre-op waiting area. The room had rows of empty chairs and a television in the upper corner broadcasted the world news.

Both not quite awake, the sisters took their seats side by side. Over the next half hour other patients of all ages appeared in the room and all dressed in the same snazzy gown Jade wore. Once assembled, the group was led to the pre-op area where each was assigned a bed and asked to disrobe. Jade hopped in then sat naked under the heated blanket waiting for the next set of instructions.

A young man in a green scrubs appeared, his job was to insert the intravenous line, then the anesthesiologist stopped by to introduce himself while checking her chart.

"Have you eaten or drunk anything since last night?"

"Nothing since yesterday," she replied.

"Ever been put under before?"

"Twice, when I was younger," she said with a smile.

"Were there any complications?" He injected a fluid into the intravenous tube. "This will start to relax her," he said to Lisa, who watched every move.

"No complications besides being nauseous when I woke, but that was long ago."

Finally Dr. Paul appeared in surgeon scrubs, his mask pulled underneath his chin. All that was missing were his gloves.

"So you ready to get rid of these things?"

"I'm ready. Do your best," she said, with full confidence in his ability.

"I've done a thousand of these, you're in good hands," said not in arrogance but the simple truth.

"And Doc, remember if you can make that incision really tight so I don't have wrinkles and less of a double chin, I would appreciate it." Jade tried one last time to get him to smile, failing miserably. Lisa laughed, but he was stone-faced serious.

"We'll see you in there," he said while walking away.

The anesthesiologist made another appearance. "We're going to take you in."

She smiled at her sister as she was wheeled away. "See ya later!" She said and then lay down for the ride down the corridor.

The room was a typical operating room with the big overhead light, monitors, gadgets and five people chattering away. While they were going through their check-lists, two young orderlies appeared to slide her to the table underneath the light. Still fully awake, she wondered why they just didn't ask her to change tables, but they were doing it the traditional way…one, two, three…poof, there she was in the headlight.

A needle was inserted into the IV tube and heart monitors were being stuck to her chest, the blanket pulled down to her waist. Oh great, the boobs are out, she thought. I hope they've seen a few boobs my size. Nervous, she quickly said a silent prayer. "Dad, I hope you're here with me, and God, please don't let it be cancer."

Dr. Paul appeared next to her, gloved and ready to go. He nodded to the anesthesiologist just above her head out of sight and the needle's plunger was pressed down, emptying its contents. Her nerves instantly calmed, the room became a blur as she repeated one last thought over and over. "Pops…God…please not cancer…Pops are you…watch…"

Her first recollection was lying in a slightly raised bed with a need to cough. The first attempt to clear her chest was like a knife through her. She held her breath, not wanting to repeat the action, yet it came again, and again. A nurse appeared through the hazy fog and she saw a needle, then immediately fell back asleep.

She opened her eyes the second time. Fuzzy at first, everything slowly started coming into focus. She could see the outline of Lisa and her mom standing next to her. Slowly her eyes adjusted and she could make out their faces.

"How'd it go?" she croaked, wanting to test her voice.

"It's all out," Lisa said. "Everything went well."

The beginnings of a cough started and she cringed. A knife seemed to be jammed in her throat as a constant discomfort. She drifted off not knowing what was said or how long she was awake.

The next thing she knew her family was gone and Dr. Paul appeared at her side asking how she was feeling.

"Did you get them all?" she whispered.

"We got it all and I'm glad we went in. I had no idea how large these things were until we took them out." She could tell by his tone he was proud of his work.

"How big?" she asked.

"The thyroid was the size of my fist and each growth was another half fist off of that main one." He held up both hands, made a fist with a half fist poking out from behind. "With the five masses in there, your windpipe and esophagus was curved like a letter C, trying to accommodate them. I needed to move things around to get it all." His hands showed her a C-shape.

How did it manage to get that size, the question ran through Jade's mind. Stupid doctors, I told them they were giving me lots of problems.

"Is it cancer?"

"We should have the results in a couple days."

"Thanks for getting them out of me," she said softly, then drifted off.

Waking in a darkened room with the need to cough, she slowly sat upright as the first one escaped and pain ripped through her. She grabbed her throat to stifle the cough. Mistake! Damn that was stupid, she thought to herself.

A tray was next to her bed and she shakily reached for the blue jug to pour herself a sip of water. Tipping the cup to her lips, she felt the water slide down the tender area. As it trickled down her throat a cough came upwards. Across the room in the other bed, a woman watched with concern as she struggled.

"Man, that hurts," she said when she finally settled.

"Are you okay, what did you have done?"

"Thyroid removed, you?"

"Breast cancer," she replied straight to the point. "I had what you got done last year. That one really hurts."

"Sure does," she replied. That poor lady, she thought, damn cancer!

A nurse walked into their room at that moment.

"I need to go to the bathroom, is it okay for me to leave my bed?"

"Let me help you get there." She removed the warmth of the blankets and Jade swung her legs off the edge of the bed. Every move hurt her pulsing head. The nurse took the intravenous tube and wrapped it to the portable device as Jade slowly slid her feet to the floor. The pounding was brutal.

When she came out of the bathroom she couldn't wait to crawl under the blankets. She was freezing and the shivering hurt her neck. "Is there anything I can have for pain?" She asked when the nurse came to pull the blankets over her.

"On a scale from one to ten, how bad is it?"

Compared to what a train wreck? Is this how it's supposed to feel? "I feel like my head is going to explode and every time I cough it feels like someone is severing my head from my body, so I guess that would be a…?"

"Oh, it's a ten for sure," the nurse replied. "I can give you morphine or Tylenol 3's, which would you prefer?"

"Tylenols," she said. If the pain got worse she could opt for morphine.

And When

The nurse handed her the pills and she chewed and then swallowed them. Within twenty minutes she was fast asleep. It became the pattern to wake every few hours wanting to hack and she'd press the button for more medication to put her back out.

Daylight filled the room and she was awake only minutes when the nurse disconnected her intravenous and Lisa helped her dress. Dr. Paul appeared in the doorway having signed her release.

"How are we doing today?" he asked.

"I'm okay, I just feel a need to cough and it hurts."

"That's from moving things around and should subside in the next few days," Dr. Paul explained.

Holy crap, a few days of that, Jade wasn't amused.

"Here is your first thyroid replacement and a prescription to get filled. You have to take one of these every day at the same time with one sip of water then wait an hour before taking anything else. No food, no drink for an hour. And here is a prescription for Tylenol 3's. Take them for sure for the first three or four days every four hours, then try to reduce them as the pain lessens. For the next forty-eight hours, if you feel any type of stiffening I want you to come back to emergency and tell them you've just had your thyroid removed."

"Why would I stiffen?" she said in her croaky voice.

"It could mean a depletion of calcium. Any stiffening at all, get her to emergency," he said to Lisa, ensuring his words weren't lost on the pain meds.

"You ready?" Lisa asked after the doctor left.

"Take me home." Jade was moody, sore and tired. She wasn't a good patient ever and this would push her to the limits. Putting on her coat they walked out to Lisa's van and she climbed in.

"Shit!"

"What's wrong?" Lisa asked in tune with her every move.

"I bent my head to get in, fuck that hurt."

The ride home was quiet. Lisa looked at her after every pothole in the road and Jade was annoyed at every pothole they hit. When Lisa parked in her driveway, she tried to slowly get out of the van. "Damn it!" It's amazing how much you move your neck when you don't think about it, she thought. Once inside, she grabbed a glass of water then bee-lined for the recliner in the living room, grateful for the blanket and pillow she left next to it the night before.

"Are you hungry?" Lisa asked.

"No."

"How does it feel?" Lisa sat on the loveseat across from her.

"It feels like a knife is in my throat and my head is pounding. I'm tired. I think I'll snooze."

"Let me know if you need anything. I'll watch TV." They settled in for the long haul.

Jade woke sometime later needing to cough. Gripping the armrests, she felt something coming up and reached for a Kleenex to cover her mouth. Good God, I'm gonna hork up a lung. What the hell is that? Her eyes watered and she glanced at Lisa, who stood at the kitchen wall cut-out watching with a cringed look on her face. As her face contorted, she watched Lisa grasp her own neck. It took several minutes for the horrible pain to pass, then the pounding began from her neck upwards. When she quieted she swallowed two pills with a couple of sips of water. The smell of food cooking wafted through the room, Lisa had been busy.

"What are you cooking?" She tried to show appreciation for her sister taking the time to be here.

"I made some Kraft dinner, mashed potatoes and soup. Do you want anything right now?" A smile graced her sister's face.

This must be hard for her. She has two teenage boys to look after. To disturb her normally busy life to have her play nurse maid feels wrong. "I'll try some soup, but not much." She wasn't hungry and even more afraid of swallowing something thicker than water. She thought it was best to try to eat since she was living on Tylenols.

Lisa brought her a cup of creamy chicken soup. She cautiously took the first sip and it felt strange. It didn't hurt, yet it didn't feel like it was her neck it was going down. The blockage she'd been used to for three years wasn't there and the liquid found the way easily. Finishing the cup, she took the half-filled pillow and rested her head in the middle as the two puffy sides kept her neck still. Reclined and cozy under her blanket, she drifted into oblivion.

She woke with the feeling someone was creeping around her chair. Opening her eyes, she saw Eric looking down at her with a grimace. He smiled and stared, it looked odd to her.

She half-smiled, then the need to cough started. He sat on the couch and watched her grip the chair. Grabbing a Kleenex, she covered her mouth as she struggled with that lump that constantly headed upwards.

"This is awful to watch. She does that every time she wakes up," Lisa explained to him as he sat watching without blinking.

Finally the feeling passed and Jade looked at him with her eyes watering.

"Can you talk?"

"Yes," she replied.

"How does it feel? Does it hurt?"

"Only when coughing, other than that I sleep. I have to pee." She took off the blanket and when she was about to stand, Lisa was at her side to steady her. Jade stood, feeling light-headed, then turned to look at her sister. "Shit! Why did I do that?"

"Bonehead, your neck is slit. You can't turn your head." Lisa said.

"Wasn't thinking," she said and shuffled off to the bathroom.

In the privacy of the room, she carefully lowered herself letting her sweats fall to the floor. She turned to reach the toilet paper holder behind her right shoulder. "Damn it!" The stupid holder was mounted on the same wall as the toilet. Spying the extra rolls on a metal stand across from her, she reached slowly to grab one. "Ouch, ouch…"she mumbled as she leaned forward.

Carefully she stood holding the sides of her sweats which she reached by bending completely in half. Phew, she thought. The last thing I need is to have to call Lisa in because I can't reach my pants. Turning to the sink to wash her hands, she bent her head down as she reached to turn the taps. Silently she gave herself a lecture as she soaped, then rinsed.

139

Standing again, she looked in the mirror. "Oh my God!" she whispered, terrified. "I don't have a neck!" Her reflection startled her. The swelling had removed any sign of the curve from her ears down to her shoulders. She looked like an over-sized blow-up doll with gauze, yellowy stuff, and a bandage six-inches long and two-inches wide. They were to remove it tomorrow and leave the stitches exposed until the follow-up on Wednesday. Her black bags were more prominent than ever, she looked worse than crap.

Shuffling back to her chair she snuggled under the blanket and swallowed more pills. Feeling the pounding begin in her head she wanted to sleep. Eric left after Jade fell into la-la-land. The phone rang on occasion and she'd hear bits and pieces of the one-sided conversations Lisa was having with her kids or husband.

Waking later, she saw Lisa washing the kitchen floor. "You don't have to do that, I did it on Thursday," Jade said edgily.

"I just thought I'd give it a quick wash since there were foot prints."

Eric never removed his shoes, damn it. "You can relax, you know, just watch TV or something." Her gruff tone came through.

"I'm tired of just sitting. I don't mind." Lisa needed to be going 150 mph. They were really rather similar. She bit her tongue, knowing it was a coping skill. Jade stood to head to the bathroom again and Lisa dropped her cleaning supplies to come and assist.

"I can make it," she snapped.

"I was just trying to help," Lisa snapped back.

Tired and grungy, it was Thursday since her last shower, her hair a stringy mess. I'd best watch my attitude, she lectured herself while in the bathroom, she gave up her time for you, so quit being an ass.

"Are you hungry yet?" her sister asked when Jade made her way back to her recliner.

"I don't know if I'm hungry, but I should try something."

If this continues for a couple weeks, I'll take off some of the pounds I gained since the first tumor. Lisa handed her a plate of macaroni, mashed potatoes and gravy. Lisa's plate mirrored her own with the addition of a chicken breast. Tentatively, Jade swallowed to find that strange feeling again.

"I emailed everyone on your list to let them know you're okay and your voice is intact."

"Thanks. I know a few were worried."

"Some have been calling to check on you. You're usually asleep, so I don't know if you want me to wake you up or not to talk to them."

"I'd rather sleep."

They watched a movie and with Jade on the reclining chair, she thought Lisa would take her queen-size bed for the night, but Lisa grabbed a blanket and hunkered down on the sofa only three feet away. It reminded Jade of what she herself had done with Pops, wanting to remain close, regardless of comfort. In the middle of the night, she woke coughing and tried to stifle the noise, afraid she'd wake her sister.

"You okay?" the sleepy, raspy voice came through the darkness.

"I just need to spit or something. This feeling is killing me."

"Well spit, maybe," Lisa sat up watching her.

As unladylike as it was, she tried to force whatever was desperately trying to come up, out of her. Mistake! The knife was cutting her head off again. Taking more pain-killers, she waited for the pounding to ease.

When morning came she took the pill her sister held out to her, having filled her prescription for her thyroid replacement, just as the doctor ordered.

"I'm going to head for a shower," Jade said, not able to take the grunge any longer.

"Do you need my help?"

"I don't know. I'll leave the door open and call if I do."

It'll feel good to change clothes, she thought as she carefully bent to start the water, never once twisting her head. She stepped carefully in the tub and backed into the hot stream of water, not wanting to disrupt the bandage in the front. As the water pulsed, she automatically tilted her head back to wet her hair. Mistake! She stood frozen as the water pounded and her eyes watered with the severity of the move. "How stupid," she said softly as the tears came down. "Of course you can't do that, you dumb ass." Staying still until the throbbing in her neck subsided, she backed into the stream. The next steps of shampoo and conditioner proved an experience. As she gently washed her hair, the suds came down in the waterfall into her eyes.

Refreshed, with her eyes burning from the experience, she left the room with her hair a tangled mess. Using her brush, she began to run it through the wet strands. Mistake! Even at her gentlest, her head would move. She sat at the kitchen table holding her neck in place with both hands as Lisa manipulated the brush through the mass. When she finished, it was time to remove the bandage. Jade stood to allow easy access to her neck since Lisa was five inches shorter.

"This is gonna hurt a bit," Lisa warned.

With going through the pain of hair washing, the thought of a bandage seemed like nothing. "Take it off, I'm ready." She braced.

The moisture from the shower released the bandage, but small bits of glue stubbornly remained in place. Lisa picked at it with tenderness then used the wipes provided to remove the remaining residue.

"There, it's all off and it looks really good." Lisa smiled.

Jade shuffled to look in the bathroom mirror. "I look like Frankenstein!" The actual wound was five inches long at the base of her neck, held every half inch by medical tape. The bruising and swelling around the long cut had formed a bulbous ridge along the incision. "Eww, it looks gross, look how lumpy it is." She pointed it out to her sister.

"It'll be gone before you know it," was her positive forecast.

After breakfast Jade watched TV waiting for their mom to arrive. A kind of dizzy feeling started, not a fall-down one, more being off-kilter. I'll wait until mom arrives at noon and that way Lisa can go home. When it neared twelve-thirty, she finally had to tell her.

"What do you mean you don't feel right?"

"I just feel off, like the room is a long tunnel. I'm at one end and you're at the other," she tried her best to describe what was going on.

"What else do you feel?" Lisa grabbed the literature. "Are your hands stiff?"

"I guess kinda stiff. Not bone-locking, just achy."

"We're going back to emergency. Dr. Paul said if anything weird starts to take you to emergency." Lisa grabbed for her keys, purse and coat.

"Back to hospital," Jade agreed, not knowing what was happening. She barely noticed when Lisa began to fumble in her purse.

As they drove out of her yard, Lisa found her cell phone, flipped it open, and dialed a number. "Where are you?" Lisa demanded over the phone. "What do you mean you're at the store? You were supposed to be at Jade's a half hour ago and were not there."

Jade could hear a mumble from the other side of the phone.

"We're on our way to emergency, Jade doesn't feel okay and she's stiffening, sort of."

Jade clued out at the moment, lost in her tunnel. At emergency, she needed to sit as Lisa explained to the nurse at the desk what was happening. She watched it all transpire as if watching a movie. Escorted to an emergency room bed, a doctor examined her. After five minutes of questions she was asked to disrobe her upper half and they immediately drew blood, while hooking her to an IV. They waited while the doctor disappeared with the sample and within fifteen minutes their mother appeared and Lisa darn near bit her head off.

"I had a few errands to run. I figured while I'm in the city I might as well return a few things," her mother said.

"Running errands?" Lisa snapped. "You could have run errands any other day of the week, but chose the very day you were supposed to be there?"

Jade watched them arguing at the end of the bed, too tired to care. The doctors returned to hook up a drip, saying her calcium had dropped. Since she'd be here awhile, Lisa left since all was well and their mom took over nurse-sitting. They remained in the hospital until the second blood test showed everything was back to normal.

Back in her recliner, the painkillers put her back on her schedule of sleep, wake up, take more pills and go back to sleep. She remained awake at the longest for three hours. They'd talk about a television show or the goings on in the family. Jade woke throughout the night which startled her mother, who slept on the couch next to her. By Monday, she no longer wanted anyone to stay. It didn't make sense. There was no point in anyone looking after her, least of all her elderly mother. She left and Jade resumed the pattern.

Answering the doorbell three times, she was greeted with flowers. One from her work colleagues, one from her cousins, then roses from Mr. Virginia, the beautiful arrangements graced her living room.

"I emailed everyone about the trip back to emergency." Lisa explained when she called to check on her.

"Thanks. I'm just glad I can have my place to myself again. Not that I don't appreciate you and mom being here, it just seems senseless."

"I totally get that and there should be enough food ready to last you the week, but I am going to check on you by phone and stop by after work."

"If you'd like, but I'm okay really," she responded not wanting the fuss and bother. "Thanks for making all the food."

"No problem. If you need anything else just let me know."

"I should be fine, but thanks."

Monday afternoon, Eric phoned after receiving the email about the trip back to the hospital.

"It was no big deal. I sent my mom home too. No sense in anyone staying, I'd rather be alone."

"It's too soon! I'll come by after work to check on you."

"I'm fine really. All I do is sleep."

"Whatever! I'll see that for myself."

Losing the battle, she left the door unlocked, not wanting to be disturbed if she was asleep.

"Slow down. Relax buddy."

From her haze she heard Eric's voice and she heard the patter of four feet. He was at the doorway to the living room with Charlie, who probably wanted to gallop towards her as he normally did.

"Easy, slow down."

The patter came close and Charlie's nose hit her left hand as he sniffed her. "Hey Charlie," she managed in a croaky voice and the dog whimpered.

Eric guided him on the leash to the front of her chair. Charlie stood in her line of vision staring at her, whimpering as if scared. Slowly he climbed up the extended recliner and lie at her side with his head on her right hand. She rubbed his head, but his noises continued softly. Jade glanced at Eric, who watched the two of them, then she drifted back to sleep. Waking later with the hideous cough she reached for a tissue. Charlie's head raised and the whimpering began as Eric watched her struggle until she relaxed back into her chair.

"How was work?" she croaked out.

"Work was work, nothing new." Eric turned his attention back to the TV.

Needing to go to the bathroom, she nudged Charlie who gently got off the chair and followed to lie outside the washroom door. She heard his soft cries and then Eric's loud "Would you shut up," echo from the living room. Charlie stayed until she opened the door. She bent in half to kiss the top of the dog's nose, petting him as she did. He smelled her face, hair and when his nose reached her neck the cries began.

"I'm alright, just not feeling so good," she talked softly to him. "How about a treat?" she asked. His ears shot up, his big fluffy tail wagged and he headed for the cupboard in the kitchen where the stash was kept. She heated some mashed potatoes for her own supper and handed Charlie the rawhide.

"The dog gets a treat, you get food and I get nothing?" Eric's look was indignant, followed by a gleam of teasing.

"Charlie cuddled, so he earned the treat."

"So I gotta cuddle you to get food? Ain't gonna happen," Eric laughed, then headed for the fridge.

After dinner he took their plates to the kitchen. Taking her medication, she settled under her blanket and when she awoke, Charlie was on the recliner right next to her again. They left once she was settled in for the night.

At nine the phone rang and she answered on the second ring, her head still foggy from sleep.

"How's my favorite lady doing?" That familiar voice brought a smile to her face.

"I'm sore and the painkillers keep me drowsy."

And When

"Well how did it go, are they gone? Are ya less lumpy?" Brady teased.

"I wouldn't say I'm lump-free, but the ones in the neck are gone." Jade definitely didn't feel less lumpy as she explained the large continuous ridge across the incision line.

"That will disappear. You gotta remember ya need to heal and let your body rest. At least you're catching up on sleep. Now I know one more way to stop that hamster of yours." He chuckled.

"Oh great, you're gonna keep me drugged to knock me out?"

"Whatever works, I say." Brady broke out in laughter which she tried to join.

"Oh…it hurts to laugh, no making me laugh." It pulled on her stitches. "Did you get my sister's email Saturday?"

"Yep and one this morning about being rushed back. What was that about?" His voice changed from light-hearted to concern.

"It was weird, like I was in a tunnel and watching a movie. I was shaky and stiff."

"Nothing like being stiff, right?" he said, giggling outright.

"It was more awkward than anything."

"Are you always awkward with stiff, Hon?" He wouldn't stop chuckling. "Nice shade of red, Hon?"

"Oh ya know!" She tried her hardest to not laugh. "Geez, I just been through a surgery and what does a man think about? No playing the man-card."

"Ya know I was just teasing, I's here for you," he stated the last words in a pointed way.

She presumed his goal was for her to realize he worried. "Yes you are, always have been and thank you for the flowers."

"You're welcome. I should tell you I think I'm going to undergo the surgery. I need to book it with the doctor back home that way my parents can look after me."

"Are you scared, Buttercup?"

"Hell yes, but I'll just get it done. It's time."

"Hon, ya getting old," she jabbed. He'd be forty-one in May.

"Hey now, who says 40 is old?"

"You're already going in for repairs, aren't ya?" She chuckled, one-upping him. Score! She thought silently to herself as she cringed in pain.

"Sunshine."

"Yes hon."

"Don't forget who went in for repairs first."

He got her good, dang it! "Easy now, be gentle with the Canadian."

"On that note, we'll have plenty of time to talk when you're feeling better. I just wanted to hear your voice."

"Okay Hon, thanks for calling. I am kinda tired."

"Rest well, beautiful."

Up early the next morning, she decided to start her day with coffee and the computer. It was time to check in with everyone. After she had signed into the chat room, Donna, Jill and Kendra made appearances, then she opened many get well cards in her inbox. When about to sign off she noticed Mr. Virginia signed on, but not in chat. It was six his time, what is he up to? Sending an email, he responded immediately.

--Jade wrote:

Shows you on line, but not in the room...Darn it, go to sleep for three days and poof...he replaces the Canadian...darn it...LOL. I'm gonna retire in front of the TV...again...man, I'm bored.

xoxoxo
J

--Brady wrote:

When you leave work in a hurry and forget to log out you end up online all night long.
Ya best take care of yourself! Know it's hard to sit around and do nothing, but ya know if ya don't, ya might have to sit around longer. Don't make me come up there and sit on ya lap just to keep ya still

Brady
xoxoxo

With her existence of sleep and TV, she could imagine what Brady would go through for his surgery. I've been down only four days and I'm already going nuts, she thought. Getting a pad of paper and a pen she settled back in her chair with an idea to make things easier for him.

Her internal programming had kept her safe, alone and in the routine of life. Everyone says 'I'll start tomorrow to make changes,' but sometimes it's too late. Why do we only stop in a bad moment to rethink things? Life steers people and things happen to force their hand. It took losing Pops and going through the surgery to make changes, why? She wondered.

Brady had been in an accident and was about to undergo another hiccup. Was his life all he wanted? She began writing questions about all the things in life that had changed her and would continue daily. Just before he leaves for Wyoming, I'll mail him a book. That'll stop him from going stir crazy. I should test how open he is first. She put down the paper and went to the computer. Opening a blank page, she sat there thinking how to start.

Conversations with him always dabbled into the "what if" category. He always asked if she was living how she wanted and said it was up to her to choose happiness, but what about his life? Now that she'd gotten through this struggle, was he thinking of the possibilities? The old Jade would've never asked, the new Jade wrote point blank questions.

--Jade wrote:

Brady,

We've talked on every subject and I wonder what your thoughts are. The only way for me to know is to ask. If you'd like, you can just answer yes and no to these.

1-You said it's possible to start caring even though you've never met someone. I have to agree. Just because it's never happened to me before, doesn't mean it isn't what it is. So can one person genuinely start to fall for someone without meeting, or is it just who they seem to be and it fills a void in life?

2-You had one long distance relationship with the Wisconsin lady, so were you kinda in love before you met?

3-With only calls/messages/pictures, do you think you can really gauge a person in their everyday life and figure out if they'd fit into yours?

4-With long distance, do you need a set plan about things if you find the one you want?

5-Does it bother you when I tell you you're stuck in my head? I mean, I'm not trying to feel anything, it just kinda happens. Should I maybe not be so open with you about stuff?

6-I'm trying to look at the advice of others who say logically I should date locally. What do you feel about me doing that?

7-I have admitted to being man-stupid when it comes to figuring out what they think and want. I'm not proud of that, but it's time to come right out and ask things I don't know. I guess I'm asking if you have things you can't explain when it comes to me?

Have a great day, Cutie

Jade Xoxoxo

Going back to her writing, the thoughts kept dancing around her head. How did he view her? Why did he call as often as he did? Local men didn't make her laugh or engage her thinking as much. He challenged her stubborn ways. Getting through this, she wanted the missing link in life. Alone wasn't good, she knew that now, but it'd been a long time since she opened that door.

Taking a break later that morning, she went to the chat-room and asked people how they felt about meeting someone this way. Many had been hurt and said it was the one side effect. There were success stories and some ended up together or married, so it was possible if you kept your feet firmly planted in reality, they said. The miles were the difficult part, it wasn't like a local person you met and then decided in person. There were no weekly outings to get to know one another slowly. Nope, with long distance it was talking a lot and then planning a meet which costs a fortune, then more expense if they were on the same page.

What would I willing to risk to build a life with someone? What would hamper a decision? She mulled it over. A house can be bought anywhere so that's not important. Friends and family would always be there across any distance. The career would be tough and having to start all over. What line wouldn't I cross? She'd miss her family, but as they got older they didn't hang out together much. Karen had a long distance relationship at first and they started a new life, got married and found their way.

In chat there was talk of a meet coming up in Chicago and they set a group rate at a hotel. They asked Jade if she would attend and she answered maybe, but it seemed too soon after surgery. She said goodbye to the chatroom to take a nap. I'll ask Brady if he's interested, then I'll decide, she thought. She checked her email just before signing off to find his responses.

--Brady wrote:

Jade,

Was just gonna put...yes, yes, no, yes, no, yes, maybe...just to be a smart ass. I snickered for a moment, but thought it best to answer as well as I could. Hope all is well. These are just some of my thoughts.

Xoxoxo
Brady

1-You know, that is hard to explain, just like the feelings we both have for each other. I seriously don't think it's possible to totally fall for someone without meeting them. You don't have all the answers to really say what that person is about. I believe that our minds fill in the voided parts with the information we have, making it seem all so real to fall for that person. I do know that one can start to get a picture of what the other is like.

2-I wasn't kind of in love with her; to me, you're either in love or not, there's no kindas in life. We both had feelings for each other, but in the end the distance is what burned us out. She had a little one, and her ex wouldn't allow her to take him out of state, so she couldn't visit. The majority of the time we had was me visiting her. I didn't mind at first, but it got to be hard on me physically. We both decided to take a break, but as you can see it really wasn't just a break.

3-Nope, as stated in #1, you only have bits and pieces from the data you hear, learn and process. I believe you can say how one could fit, but until you have seen them in real life you can't really tell if they do.

4-I always wonder about things and how things would work. I never have a set plan, because how can you plan for someone you haven't met? My thought, if you find that person it will work out or you will make it work.

5-I enjoy the time we have sharing our thoughts and giving each other a hard time. All stuff I have missed for a long time. I might not admit it because I's a man-LOL. All in all, we are true friends, working on becoming even closer ones.

6-I don't have issues with you going out with men there. I really can't until I, myself, can actually say that I am a part of you. So when analyzing all the facts and figures, it would not make sense or logic for you not too.

7-You are so fuckin' cute, I am about in the same place that you are, hon. Lots of things have been stirred up and many you just can't put the finger on. Or those that you can and you wonder how can that be? There are several things that are unexplainable and have me stumped. The majority of the time after we talk, I wonder just how it would be if I were local to you and I could just jump in the car and see you. So, yes, there are things I can't explain.

Jade read it again. Yep, he's confused. How did this happen to them both and what's next? Maybe she'd tell him about Chicago on the phone later.

And When

Friends Not More

Chapter Fourteen

Eric took her for her follow up on Wednesday morning. Dr. Paul and his assistant, Janet, removed the tape used as stitches to inspect his handiwork. He rarely smiled, but he did now and couldn't believe it was only five days since surgery. She was top of his speed recovery list. After the inspection, she asked the one question she had waited so long to hear then held her breath as he checked the chart.

"The results of the biopsy show they were all benign," he said with his serious doctor face on again.

She caught sight of Janet, who had a beaming smile, Jade's eyes watered as she held back tears.

"We have to send you downstairs for blood tests. We want to check your TSH levels now that you're on the replacement," Dr. Paul said as he checked off the boxes on the usual form.

"More needles?" She said in a teasing voice, not caring if they poked her a hundred times anymore, done with the worry of cancer.

"Sorry, you'll have to get these done every six months."

She told her family the minute she got home and they breathed a sigh of relief. Spending the next hour calling friends to relay the news, her neck ached by the time she was finished. Taking the pain meds, she curled under her blanket on the recliner and tears started to roll down her face. I made it through. Almost three years of testing, fighting, losing and worrying are over. She tried to think about where she'd go from here. "Dad," she spoke softly, feeling he was sitting right next to her in the room. "I did it, just like I promised you I would. I guess I have a lot of work ahead to get back to who I should be. Thanks for watching out for me." She closed her eyes and drifted off.

"Hey, how is the patient today?" Brady's call came later that evening.

"I went to see the surgeon and he's impressed at how fast I'm healing," she announced with pride.

"That is great news! And you were worried." Brady used his "I told you so' tone," but he sounded relieved.

"I know, I know, you were right and I worried for nothing. My voice works, there is no cancer and I got more Tylenols since I only had four left."

"You should try to slow down on those things, it's not healthy to use too much of them."

If he was here, he'd be watching me like a hawk, she thought. "Thank you, Dr. Brady," she chided him.

"Just saying, so quit rolling your eyes at me."

How he knew her expressions on a phone she'd never know. "I'm doing just fine, young man," she said in a playful tone.

"I am so happy to hear there is no cancer, how did ya celebrate the good news?"

"I cried," she said softly and paused. "I think it was all the years of worry."

"Ah, Hon, that's not a celebration. You should do something fun like go out to dinner, dancing or something."

She wondered what he'd plan if he lived near enough. "Maybe once I'm not in pain I'll do something. They site members are planning a meet in Chicago next month, so that might be a way to celebrate. You know, go for a weekend and get away from it all."

"Oh? I love Chicago. There's a lot to see and they have a great night life."

"I was thinking that if I'm better I may go. It's only six weeks away so I don't know for sure."

"Maybe I could meet you there."

"Really, you'd like to?" She smiled, regardless of how much it hurt.

"I'd love to. Who's all going from the site?"

"I'm not sure yet. There's a wedding coming up of people who'd met on the site and they're planning the ceremony as a meet. Some will choose to go to that instead of Chicago."

"I think it's just plain weird to have a site wedding."

"You think so?"

"That is one of the most sacred days of your life and you're just gonna let whoever walk in off the street. There is no way I'd allow that. I could see if you invited friends, but just to let anyone come, no way!"

"I suppose for you as a Mormon that kinda goes against everything you believe. For me, it's not so much the sacred stuff, but more people you don't know."

"I don't think it has anything to do with my religion. It's the most important day of your life and you shouldn't make it a joke," his conviction coming through.

"The most important day, is that how you saw it on your wedding day?" She tried to imagine a young Brady making the trek up the aisle. Heck, seeing him in a tuxedo would be heart-stopping.

"Hell yes! I knew I was making a commitment before God, my family and friends. Nothing is more important than that in life. Who would you want to share the day with?"

"I think if I were to marry again I'd want a simple ceremony. I don't think I'd want a big celebration. No fancy stuff, just him and me in front of a couple of witnesses."

"Come now…what about having your family and friends there? And what about a fancy wedding dress?"

"I could see family and friends, but does the rest really matter? I wore that white dress once and it was expensive for one day. It seems like a big waste of money."

"So let's say we were to get married, don't you think I'd want to see you in that gown? Even though we've both been married before, I'd still want to make it special, a celebration of us. You know what I mean?"

"I'm surprised you'd go through it all again. Usually weddings are a headache for men." She'd made most of the decisions and her ex had showed no interest at all.

"Nuh-uh, I enjoyed the planning. It was like the first thing you work on together, the beginning of the rest of your lives."

"That's a really sweet way to put it. I never thought of it like that. I just figured with doing it once you wouldn't want to go through the big deal again."

"It is a big deal, whether you did it once or not. A lot of people marry too young and divorce, but it's still the most important thing in life. It's just how I see it. Now about Chicago, I'll have to wait and see if I can make it, but it sure would be great to finally meet you." He sounded excited.

"So far, all I know is they're staying at the same hotel and planning events."

"I think if we go, I'd like to spend most of our time doing our own thing. We could meet up with the group to say "-hi-," but then we could take off and go see the sights, like Wrigley field."

He's already planning an itinerary? "Wow, you're serious."

"Uh-huh. Aren't you?"

"To think we'd finally meet face to face." Her voice softened as images began playing in her mind. She could almost feel the butterflies while standing there looking at him for the first time.

"We'll talk more and figure it all out. First thing is to see where and when. We'll plan from there," Brady suggested.

They talked until she was ready for sleep and he tucked her in with, "Sleep well, beautiful."

Hanging up the phone, she thought it all out. Meeting each other seemed like the next logical step and she envisioned how the weekend could play out. Maybe they'd plan flights to arrive at the same time, that way they'd meet in the airport. People from the site were sharing the hotel to save costs, so maybe he could bunk in with Steve. But can I bunk with one of the girls? That's not good; what if I still have insomnia? I'd disturb a room partner for sure, she thought.

The next day she researched on the computer, looking at places she'd enjoy while trying to figure out what Brady would like to see in Chicago. Wrigley stadium was obviously on the list of musts. She looked for country dance clubs, it'd been years since her days at a local country hot spot, but she wanted to see him dance. At the time she was considered a good dancer, but could I still do it now?

I hope I know soon if can go, looking at the discounts for booking flights weeks in advance. That'll cut down with the expense. The doctor said it would be at least another week before the swelling changed. Going to her mirror, she felt she aged through this, having more gray hairs and a few extra wrinkles. "I wonder if I'll be okay in six weeks." Back at the computer, she joined the chat-room to discuss the event. There were hints of secret meetings between couples and she wondered how many others were like Brady and her? Speak of the devil, he appeared in the room giving his usual *bows to Jadey* upon his entrance.

The women openly flirted as always and she wondered if he talked to others from the site. How many phone calls did he make in his spare time? There was no way to know, but definitely something she kept in mind. Brady's playfulness revealed hints to the room of their interest in one another and none seemed to catch on. She had emailed Sarah, Donna and Kendra earlier and they were ecstatic about her possibly meeting him, but warned that meeting at these things sometimes brought unwanted jealousies.

Her friends wouldn't make Chicago, but suggested they all attend a meet in Atlantic City in fall. Thinking that she would finally be able to hug all her friends, Jade gave them her word she'd be there. Sarah even asked her to stay longer and she agreed.

Life seemed different in the States. Her friends seemed to have a steady stream of dates, while Mary and Jade were the two from the site rarely asked out. Mary lived in England, Jade in Canada. Dating infrequently, they spent their time with friends at dinners or social functions. Life was work, home and a quiet social life. The U.S. people met at these events regularly and clique groups formed, but Jade had only developed a close friendship with chosen handful. They'd kept in contact on a constant basis, sharing plans and building trust over the year.

Feeling dizzy from the computer screen, she said her goodbyes then typed "talk later" to Brady as she left the room. Back in her chair, she picked up her note-pad to continue writing the book for him.

She'd lost track of time when she was summoned by her door bell and opened it to find Maggie standing there with flowers in hand. They'd known each other twenty-two years and Maggie was one of the very few friends who understood her completely.

"How are you? I thought I'd stop by after giving you a couple days to recoup," she said with a smile.

"I'm doing, I guess. Come on in, I'll put on some coffee." They rarely visited, both having busy lives, but kept in touch with phone calls.

"Have you gotten used to daytime television?" Maggie asked with a snicker.

"I've had enough of it so I've taken up writing instead." She showed Maggie the book while she updated her on Mr. Virginia.

"You want to go to Chicago to meet him in six weeks?" she asked, looking surprised.

"I'm thinking about it, but nothing's definite. I guess it depends if I get back to not being Frankenstein." They laughed.

"You've been through hell and back. This might be just the thing to kick off your new life. What's the worst that can happen? You meet and either like or don't like each other. Plus you have a mini-vacation."

They were in the midst of catching up when her phone rang. "Shoot, it's him," said with a smile. Picking up the phone she spoke briefly and asked to call him back later since she had company. He asked what man was over, but once hearing it was her girlfriend he said to call him back.

"You're smiling like a Cheshire cat," Maggie said with a smirk.

"Yep, and loving it!"

It was after ten when Maggie left and Jade left a message for Brady to call her tomorrow. While waiting for sleep to come she thought about how the prospect of meeting seemed to have changed their conversations lately. It wasn't sharing the present, but more looking to the future. The Chicago date was confirmed for the third weekend in April and neither said they'd attend for sure, but they discussed details and wishes for the trip. He had quit the yesterday, but there were always ten women to every man, if not more. She'd be totally dense if she didn't wonder. Brady had been the center of attention for months and she could imagine the private emails he received. Who's to say he's not talking with a multitude of women? The skepticism lingered. She needed to be sure she wasn't one in a long line of women he showed interest in, and wanted to find out before ever going through the expense of Chicago. The next day when he called her back, she began to pry.

"Brady, if we go, are there other people you're interested in meeting?" She asked off-handedly during his nightly call.

"There are some I'd like to meet, but I don't know if they are going to go to Chicago or not."

"Are there some who are closer to you that you've been talking to and find interesting?"

"A couple, but we haven't talked of meeting," he said without hesitation.

"Well we've been talking for five months and if it weren't for Chicago, we wouldn't be thinking of meeting or talking about it either."

"True, but I haven't talked to anyone as long as I've talked to you."

"If Chicago doesn't happen, do you think we'll meet in the future?"

"Sure we'd meet. We just have stuff we have to do, so no telling when that would happen."

What man invests this much time and money in communicating for no reason? That didn't compute, she thought. Most men hated long phone calls or waiting for anything. Then again, meeting on the Net was a whole new ball of wax.

"With the others that you want to meet are sparks flying, kinda? Ya know the feeling thing?"

"I don't know if it's sparks. There is something that makes it interesting to get to know them. Sparks are more of an in person kind of thing. You hardly know a person until you get to meet them."

"How many women have you been getting to know?" Best hear it now, she thought.

"Three," he said easily.

"I guess with me living far away it makes things difficult." I might as well be on the other end of the world, she thought.

"Yep, just like my other long-distance relationship when I'd drive eight hours just to see her. I'd leave work on Friday and by the time I got there we'd have only a day together. I'd be dead tired from the ride then have to head back early Sunday. It was hard to keep up that lifestyle," he said in a soft voice.

"I suppose it would be hard, it would take ya thirty hours to drive here. You'd hit the border then turn around," she laughed as she said it, but her hopes sank.

He began chuckling. "I'd be so darn tired, I would be like...'Hi, nice to see you' and I'd need to go to sleep just to get up and leave again."

They both laughed, but the truth was sinking in. "Ever heard of a plane? You could fly and be here in five hours. That's way smarter and you'd have a whole weekend here."

"Well it would be expensive to do that all year, wouldn't it? A flight has gotta be at least five hundred return. How many times could you afford to come out here in a year? Probably the same amount I could afford to go out there."

Just when she thought she'd found her equal the reality was hard to swallow. "I could only maybe do it three or four times a year. We'd only see each other six or eight times. With my four weeks holidays and your five, some of those could be long stays. Would that be enough?" Saying it out loud didn't seem to bring any solution. Would that be enough time to really make any type of judgment? Most relationships start with once or twice a week.

"What happens if we do get along and want more, then what? You have your career, family and friends. Could you give that up?"

"Family and friends will always be in my life. A career can change. I think I'd be able to. If I didn't, I'd probably question not doing it the rest of my life." She recalled her dad's words about chasing the dream.

They ended with their usual laughter and fun. "I need to go, Hon. I'm ready to sleep. Go get a good night sleep and don't forget to hug that Jade pillow."

"I never do. Sleep well, pretty lady."

She settled in the recliner under her warm blanket. It wasn't fair, dang it! She'd been foolish for hoping he'd thought about the possibility. Now she'd have to keep conversations on safer topics.

--Jade wrote:

Morning handsome,

With the time we spent talking these past five months a bond grew. You seem to possess most of the things I stubbornly spent a lifetime waiting for. But after we talked last night, I stayed awake thinking about it. I'm bad at reading men. I could've held back...but then I wouldn't be me. I prefer to live honestly with myself and others, just way easier. Well, easier until it gets to this embarrassing stage when you realize it's not what you thought.

I knew the distance would be the biggest hurdle and I was trying to figure out a way to jump it. To have what I want I would move mountains. I figured I'd just pick up the shovel and start digging a path, fly and meet you and see from there. If I felt what I do in person, then frequent flyer club here we come. It wouldn't have been easy, but thought we were both stubborn enough to figure it out. But it's not a possibility and that's okay. As you've said, there are three women you wish to meet. I presume they're closer to you and it would be way easier to start a relationship with them. I hope they know how lucky they are. You are a remarkable man, Brady. I can't say my heart won't stop wondering, but I will try to curb that and develop the friendship we have.

Talk soon,
J

Writing the note, she wiped out her crazy ideals. He would pursue other interests and remain her best friend. If she couldn't be happy for him then there was no point in using the term "friend." Life was the luck of the draw and her draw happened to be far away. He'd been there for every difficulty, so what more could she ask? It was the right thing to do. Chicago would be a "-no'" and she'd start saving for Atlantic City. Life carried on, she learned that lesson. Waking after a nap in the afternoon she found a message in her inbox.

--Brady wrote:

shakes head-Ya know! Do believe that hamster of yours will never cease to slow down and relax, but I guess that is how it goes. You're right, the distance is the biggest hurdle between you and me and yes, I did say that it would be hard to travel back and forth and yes, we would both eventually become members of the Mile High Club. There is that fear that maybe if we gave it a go that it would end up like that last one I told you about...but we really can't even say what could, would or might happen, since we haven't met in person to see how things are.

Things are great on the phone and via the net, but as you know in person is different. You can tell a lot more about each other by the way we act and respond. Who knows, I might just be more stubborn and you might not like that-LOL.

Yes, there are three women that I would like to meet and I have considered having a relationship with one of them, but does that mean I am going to meet them or have a relationship? No.

And out the three did you put yourself in there? So, other than you, there are two women I would consider meeting, but only one I would consider having a relationship with *looks at you*. I know you're probably going to be shocked that I actually put together a couple paragraphs. But hey, that's me, finding ways to keep you on your toes.

You know, I enjoy talking to you and hearing how your day has gone...but most of all, to see how much more smoke that hamster is putting out. LOL

More to come,

Brady
xoxoxo

The *looks at you* part poked her in the eye. Out of the three, did I ever put myself in there? One I would consider having a relationship with? Is he starting to care? He does say that he may be more stubborn than I'd like. It also says, does that mean I am going to meet them or have a relationship, with a big fat "no" after it.

She wasn't sure what to make of his email. I guess I move forward and allow whatever is going to happen-happen. Knowing his stubborn streak, she knew that she'd never get a straight answer.

And When

The Six Million Dollar Virginian

Chapter Fifteen

Spring was in the air that morning on her drive to work. Her eyes glistened with tears as she thought of the holiday ahead. Easter just around the corner and Pop had loved this time of year. When the grass slowly peeked from its wintry blanket, it brought the sad memory marking the occasion.

To clear her head, she compared Brady to the man who'd been her hero. He was a bigger man with a wonderful personality that took time to laugh, just like dad used to. He didn't talk about emotions, but played around to get his point across. Dad was the same, never one to say the words. Did you send him to me? She looked over to the empty passenger seat as if Pops was next to her.

Lately Brady's phone calls had become less frequent. From daily, to every second or third day was hard to get used to. He had started his second job as a fastball umpire and she was back at work, getting into normal life. Replaying their last conversation, she remembered that Brady had mentioned a woman was trying to gain his attention at every game. Sonja approached him several times and at first he joked about it, saying she flirted with him then told him she was on anti-depressants. "She seems way more off than a little depressed," he'd said and they both laughed at her unusual approach. Who walks up to someone and tells them they're screwed up? Brady was shocked by that, yet he had spent time with her this past week, talking after his games.

Jade didn't have the luxury of being in person or dropping by, so she tried to see this from a normal viewpoint. Sometimes people just came along during daily life. Brady still made plans for Chicago and he even teased that her nerves would be frazzled once they were face to face. "I'll remain two feet away at all times in order to keep ya hamster functioning," he'd said. Any closer she'd be "kerflufelled," a term she adopted from a childhood movie and the perfect metaphor for how he made her feel.

"Hey there, Sunshine, how are ya?" Brady's voice was full of smiles that evening.

"Hey you, how was fastball, young man?" With the meet three weeks away, she'd best nail down his final decision about Chicago.

"Oh it was the usual…nothing special."

"I found a flight that would get me to the airport at two on Friday. Are you still going to take extra days off to get that cheaper flight?"

"It only makes sense, plus I'd get to spend more time with you."

He sounds positive so maybe this will happen, she thought. "If I can get Friday and Monday off, we would have Saturday and Sunday. I'd fly back Monday."

Their call was interrupted when Brady's line beeped. She waited while he answered then he clicked back to her momentarily.

"Can I call you back? It's my dad."

"Sure," she said. He rarely spoke to his family, so it must be important. He felt his role was as the black-sheep and he confessed the distance only grows as the years passed.

Within ten minutes her phone rang. "That was quick."

"Oh my God, you won't believe this. My dad saw strangers creeping around and said the neighbor's shed door was wide open when usually it's kept locked, so he grabbed his gun and walked over there," Brady said half laughing, half concerned.

"What? That's nuts! Is he okay?"

"Oh, he's okay. But I'm like, what the hell did you think you we're gonna do over there? He's seventy-one."

"What if there were two or three thugs?" She asked.

"Exactly my point, I was like 'Dad, come on, what could you possibly do if there was something really wrong? Call the police or call the neighbors first and see if someone answers.'" He sounded exasperated.

"What's your dad doing with a gun in the first place if he's older and not so steady?" That was unheard of in Canada.

"Hon, we all keep guns down here."

"Really, what kind of arsenal is in the everyday American home?"

"I have a gun or two," he said proudly.

"Like rifles for hunting?" She imagined a rack across his back entrance displaying his collection.

"Well, I do have rifles, but I also have pistols for protection."

"How many times have you used a pistol?"

"I've never used it, but ya never know if someone breaks in or something."

"Wow, you're all nuts. Is your dad okay, what happened at the neighbors?" She pictured an elderly man creeping around someone's yard with rifle in hand. What if the neighbors were home and happened to surprise him? It could startle him and poof, there go the bullets. It seemed crazy.

"Luckily no one was home and he ended up leaving and locking the shed," Brady sounded relieved. "The people probably left when he went to get his gun, but sheesh, I don't know what the hell he was thinking. Being on the ranch, he thought he could probably handle it, but he's not young anymore."

"Well that's good news. Maybe have a talk with him about toting a gun around, would ya?" She started laughing uncontrollably and couldn't stop.

"What's so funny?"

She pictured a cartoon in her head then managed to say out loud in the characters voice, "Come out, come out wherevew you aw, you waskilly wabbit." She imitated it precisely.

Brady howled with laughter. With the turn in the conversation, they ended up joking about how well they were going to get along. By the end of their fun, he said he'd look into flights.

Wednesday's call picked up on the plan. Brady had spoken to Steve about attending and looked forward to meeting the group for drinks on Friday. Jade teased she'd get him drunk just to see what happens. Brady said he'd check every one of his drinks before he swallowed. The battle of wills was all in joking until she changed the subject.

"Did you see Sonja at your game yesterday?"

"Yep, and we went out for something to eat afterwards."

"And?" she asked, hoping he'd fill in the blanks.

"And what," he responded.

"And are you interested? You know, like going out again kinda thing?"
Her voice showed no emotion, but she sat on the edge of her seat as a jealous
feeling crept through her.

"We talked about going out again."

"That's good." He's handsome, single and I can't stop him. Please don't
let him find someone until we have a chance to meet, she silently prayed.

"Are you keeping track?" He started chuckling.

"No, I was just asking. Have you booked a flight?" She refused to book an
airline ticket until she knew his was safe in hand.

"Not yet. What about you?"

"The only reason I'd go, is if you go. I wouldn't spend that kind of money
if you're not." With the meet in the fall it would be senseless, but Brady was
worth the extra cost.

"I guess it would be a lot for us both, wouldn't it?"

"It'll be almost fifteen hundred for me."

"Wow, how come so much? I can get a flight for two fifty then split the
hotel costs, it wouldn't be near that kind of money."

At least he priced it out, that's a good sign. "It's an international flight, so
just let me know when you book your ticket and I'll book mine right after."

"I'll let you know Friday night. I still need to figure it out. Well Hon, I'm
going to take a shower and get some sleep, I won't be calling tomorrow
because I'm working, but Friday for sure. Sleep well."

"Night, Cutie," she said.

Thursday she headed to the country. Her mom was updating the décor of
the rest of the house to match the modern feel of the addition. Wanting to
paint the bedroom she asked her daughters' opinions. Staying longer than
normal that evening, they figured out the palette. It'd been a month since her
last visit, taking the week before her surgery selfishly to deal and three
weeks afterwards to get back to normal. Jade left at ten to head home to bed.

And When

Friday passed quickly with an excitement brewing. She couldn't wait to hear Brady's answer and could barely contain the giddy feeling when her phone rang.

"Hello you," she said with a smile, seeing his number on the display.

"Hey you," he said with a dull tone.

"'Tis Friday, woo hoo and the end of the week!" He sounds tired, she thought. "How was work last night?"

"It was okay. Sonja was there and we're supposed to go out tomorrow."

"Isn't that good?"

"I suppose." Brady sounded distracted.

"Have you booked your ticket?"

"I won't be going, but I want you to go and have fun," he said in a quiet voice.

The weeks of talking, laughing and planning, even the past two conversations were positive. "Huh, what happened?"

"Tuesday when I talked to my Dad, he told me the doctor called and they could fit me into their schedule so I'll be heading to Casper."

Tuesday, he knew Tuesday and didn't say a word? Why didn't he say anything?

"Are you there?" Brady asked after several seconds.

"I don't get it." I leaned on him the whole time I was sick and he couldn't even tell me this back on Tuesday? "How long have you known?" she asked quietly.

"I've known for a while they were working on the dates."

"Why didn't you say anything? Why didn't you say…'Look, there is no way I can go because I may need to go for surgery'?" None of this makes sense. With him dating Sonja, perhaps he isn't telling me what's really going on. Maybe he's moving on, she thought. "Fine then, decision made," she said quickly, finding it hard to speak.

"I want you to go. You deserve to have some fun after all you've gone through. I know I should have told you when I first got the call, but I figured maybe something would work out. As you can see, it won't," he sounded remorseful.

"When do you leave?" She struggled to keep her tone even.

"Next Thursday and I'll be gone for a while to recuperate."

Again in a soft voice filled with "I'm sorry," but if he already booked his flight, he'd been playing with the Chicago thing, at least since Tuesday that I can prove. "I have to go," she said. Don't say anything you'll regret, her head spun and the result was a dangerous mix if she didn't hang up.

"Are you upset?" he asked softly.

She raced to put the words together, trying to find a way to hide her anger.

"Well, say something," he prodded.

"You knew you wouldn't be going for some time. You didn't bother to say a word and kept acting like you were going." She paused, trying to figure this out. Why wouldn't I be mad? If he'd given me any consideration he'd have told me from the onset. Instead, he built up my hopes and pulled the rug out, she thought. "We'll talk later."

"Okay Sunshine, I'll call you later."

"Bye," she said in a barely audible voice.

She needed to step out of her thinking and look at it from all angles before proceeding any further. Why would he tell her about his dad and not the surgery? Something doesn't make sense. He'd been through difficulties in the past and he'd pulled away into his own li'l cave to deal with them. He'd say he needed time, but always told the basics of what was going on, her brain began to analyze every possible reason.

Her being upset stopped his calls. As the days passed, she began to feel selfish for voicing her anger. Rarely did she dial his number, but did on Sunday, asking him to call. With no response, she went to work with her head filled with reasons for his behavior. Maybe he was trying to work something out or maybe he needed time to deal with the news. The not telling her sooner was unforgivable, but he was there for her and it was her turn to return the favor. He was a stranger, miles away, who'd taken the time by simple phone calls to give her support. It was time to put her head in perspective and give back what she received. Without hearing from him, she decided to write to clear things up Monday just before bed.

--Jade wrote:

Brady,

The only reason I wanted to go was to meet you and I figured you were blowing me off. Sonja and you went out, so putting two and two together, well, ya know. I didn't once think about what you needed and I'd look stupid no matter what I said. I don't know what else to say and I tried to call to apologize.

I've had time to think and realize I will lose my best friend if I continue to follow inside, instead of outside reality. All I want is you to be healthy and happy. I do mean that. You have much ahead and it's really not my place to pry about anything. It's time I'm there for you as you've been for me. Life is mistakes sometimes and I just made a series of them.

xoxoxo
Jade

Her phone rang Tuesday night as she was sitting down to a late supper.

"Hey," Brady's voice still somber.

"Before you say anything, I'm sorry."

"Ah, Sunshine, it's me who should be apologizing. You have nothing to be sorry for."

"Look, I am two thousand miles away and Chicago would've been fun, but what you have to go through puts things in perspective."

"I should have told ya on Tuesday or even Wednesday, but I just couldn't. I knew when the surgery was and knew we wouldn't be able to talk much while I go through it. I wanted to keep laughing and having fun with the idea of meeting. It was wrong and I should've told ya."

"We would've found other things to laugh and talk about like we always do," she said, not understanding his reasoning.

"We talked of meeting and being together, I just didn't want that to stop."

She tried to convert that into the Canadian woman language she needed. "You're saying it was important to have a plan to meet in your head so we could talk about personal stuff?" Was that the translation?

"Kinda. I wasn't blowing you off because of Sonja. She's nice enough, but not what I want and I decided not to see her."

"Look, Hon, we live far apart and I'm here for you. Right now your main worry is getting through this. No saying we won't meet someday, just our timing sucks." She giggled, hoping to hear his laughter.

"Yes it does."

She could hear him smile as he said it, but it sounded forced. "So you leave Thursday, huh?" She sent the package with her book and magazines airmail last Saturday. The post office said it would arrive within four to five days and she crossed her fingers it would make it there in time to surprise him as a show of support.

"Right after work I'm on a plane to Casper. I Figured I'd go a few days beforehand to rest up and get comfortable, visit with family and friends before I go under."

"Good idea. Take some time to enjoy. What's the surgeon going to do?"

"There gonna fix the muscles in my legs and put them back where they need to be."

"Are ya gonna be bionic, Hon?" She said with a playful snicker then continued to try and ease his fear, "the six million dollar Virginian?"

"Yep, that's me." He started chuckling. "Maybe I'll get them to work on a few things while there at it."

She tried to use the voice recalling the series. "We have the technology to rebuild him." She laughed outright and he finally joined.

It was hard to know he would pull away and be gone. What a pipe dream thinking they'd ever meet. He'd become a force in her life, the one who made her laugh, think and try harder at becoming the best she could be. Maybe the weeks away would end their friendship or maybe he'd miss her. It was rolling the dice at this point and there was nothing she could do but wait.

And When

Atlantic Dreams

Chapter Sixteen

Brady said he had hired a girl down the street to look after his dog, taken sick leave from work for the month and asked a friend to check on his house. By Wednesday night he said he was packed and ready, his tone robotic and emotionless as he spoke with Jade. He hadn't mentioned the envelope, so she tracked the package to find no update. Having just gone through her own challenge, she knew that nerves changed a person and didn't say a word about the gift, not wanting him to worry. Instead, she was a positive and supportive friend. They said goodbye and her phone stopped ringing.

The day after his surgery she finally received the delivery notification and sent him a quick email, not expecting a response.

--Jade wrote:

Brady,

Just checking in and hope you're not hurting too bad. Do hope you're being a good patient, resting and enjoying all the attention. I sent a package to your home the Saturday before you left and it was only delivered today. So whoever is looking after your house got it. I guess I should've told you, but I gave you my word I'd be there for you and I was hoping it would arrive sooner. I took time to create a book to keep you occupied while you go through this, a new project for me, writing. I thought to remain that sunshine you may need. You called every day to check up on how I was feeling during my surgery, so I decided to do the same.

If'n' you need me I am here. Get well, Cutie. Miss you,
J

To cope with the silence, she expanded her writing project and while revamping the first book, discovered her inner voice. As the days passed, she branched out to write different versions. Instead of moping around, she used the time to venture into a new idea since there was no guarantee he'd ever call again. Spending three weeks busy writing, one evening she received a surprise.

2 Dance: hey Sunshine!
Jadey: hey you...how are ya?
2 Dance: oh...I'm hurtin

Jadey: is it bad, Hon?
2 Dance: umm-Yep and darn near don't get no time alone. Next they'll be wanting to spoon feed me...grrrr!
Jadey: LOL, yikes!
2 Dance: and...I'm having puter issues being on dial up...Argh!
Jadey: you're the computer expert, aren't ya?
2 Dance: some say...but, oh ya know! LOL
Jadey: you still owe me that house call to fix mine!
2 Dance: always good with my word, Hon
Jadey: have dinner with me too? (official invite)
2 Dance: just dinner? What about the handshake?
Jadey: formal handshake?
2 Dance: uh huh...
Jadey: sure...and I think I'm going to another meet
2 Dance: really?

With his last sentence he was offline. At least he was alive and well. Jade smiled for the first time in a long while. The official meet in Atlantic City was planned, but she'd wait to break the news when he called.

It was another two weeks before he surprised her again. A message box popped up the first week of May as she sat working on the second book.

2 Dance: hey you!
Jadey: hey cutie, how are you?
2 Dance: doing much better
Jadey: are you home yet?
2 Dance: next week, almost done physical therapy
Jadey: are you moving around on your own?
2 Dance: might lose you...we've been having thunderstorms all day
Jadey: might misplace me...but I's pretty big, easy to find-LOL
2 Dance: LOL, ya know what I mean
Jadey: call me collect
2 Dance: that's expensive!
Jadey: you're worth it, aren't ya?
*2 Dance: *checks pockets for change* LOL*
Jadey: see you're in fine spirits as always
2 Dance: some things never change (smiles)
Jadey: call me and don't worry about money stubborn man...time to even up them phone costs
2 Dance: I's not the only one that's stubborn LOL
Jadey: oh ya know! I do miss you
2 Dance: no one else gives ya grief?
Jadey: boys only bug the girls they like LOL
2 Dance: hmmm.....ya think

He disappeared off the screen, the signal lost. His keeping in contact here and there was better than nothing. She emailed him a week later on his special day.

--Jade wrote:

Happy Birthday, Handsome!

Hope you're doing well and getting better all the time. It's been weeks since the surgery so thought I'd see how recovery is going. Work has been busy and at home I write every night. With spring, it's gonna get even busier with yard work, flowers etc...

It's been over month since I heard your voice, so I'm sending this little message to let you know I think of you and wonder how you are. Don't know if you're getting them and don't know if you get to see them before you get booted. I'm still waiting for the answer to me officially asking you out on a date. Being you're a man of your word, getting booted might keep ya safe from eating my cooking....LOL. I would love to catch up soon. Well, off to work!

Have a great day,
J

Over two months passed without a word and Jade invested all her time writing to not think about him. Her chat family assumed he was long gone and she joked to hide the hurt, saying he was magic, having disappeared without a trace. With a new pain-free start, she hoped he had the same burst of energy she experienced. The flip side was that maybe something went wrong.

"Hey, Sunshine, how are ya?" his voice was bright and chipper when he called out of the blue one evening.

"I thought you fell off the face of the earth."

"Nope, didn't fall off. I just needed some time to get back into the swing of things."

"The surgery was good?" He had talked about canes or a wheelchair when they first discussed his hesitation for surgery, she wondered if he was using either and that's why he disappeared.

"I'm doing just fine, Hon. I'm back to good as new." His voice was full of energy. "I'm sorry I didn't call you sooner, I just needed time to go through some stuff."

"I sent emails, but when I didn't hear back I figured you were gone or something happened."

"I got your emails and I should've called."

His apology sounded heartfelt, but he gave no reason for the lapse and she wasn't comfortable with not hearing an explanation.

"So what have you been up to all this time?" he asked.

"I've written three books and I'm saving for a trip."

"Wow, three books already?" he sounded impressed.

"You know the hamster, once it takes off there's no stopping it." Did I cross your mind at all this past two months, she wondered. A friend doesn't leave the other hanging.

"So you said you're planning to go to a meet, is that the trip you're saving for?" His curious enthusiasm was clear.

"I owe some people a big hug and I gave them my word. I just need to figure out the money side of it all." Little does he know I purchased the plane ticket a month ago, but should I tell him?

"Do you need my help? I could send you some cash if that would help," he offered. "How much does it cost you to go to this thing?"

"Where did that come from? I don't want your money. I'll buy the airfare, then pay off the credit card and charge the hotel." She had been watching her spending, planning to kick off her new life with her friends.

"I could pay for your hotel and that way you wouldn't have to go too far in debt."

"I should be fine." Why is he offering? Is he trying to make up for his time away? I can't be bought, doesn't he know that? "How was Wyoming?" If I ask details about his trip, maybe I can find out why he didn't call.

"It wasn't a fun trip, that's for sure. Don't get me wrong, it was nice to see everyone, but by about the end of the first week I'd had enough of being waited on." Brady described how his mom and dad were at his side far too often.

"So I guess you weren't a very good patient?" She chuckled as he told stories of how snappy he got. "So when you got home did you get a package?"

"I got it, but I had already read the magazines. I picked them up, thinking it was something to do while in Wyoming. Thank you for sending me something, that was thoughtful. I didn't get to the book you sent, but I'll work on it."

"There's no point now! That was to keep you busy while you were getting better." Her tone was indignant. He obviously didn't understand the time and care she put into it.

"Who says?"

"I finished that book and there's another hundred pages. Some things I even deleted and wrote differently so there's no point." She didn't want him looking at it after the fact, it sounded like an "I have to" somehow.

"Well you sent it to me, so it's mine and if I want to do them, I'm gonna." She heard him smile as he challenged her.

"Okay, go ahead. Just know the book is totally different."

"So who's all going to the meet?"

"A few, no one is saying for sure. The people putting it together are predicting a bunch, but you know how these things are. Only a handful showed for Chicago even though it seemed more said they'd attend. Many backed out."

"True and it always seems like there are ten women for every man who goes."

"Well, Brady, I should go. I'm expecting company tomorrow so I need to turn in early."

"Aha, out playing around! Who are you expecting?"

"Dan, the guy who lives five hours away," she said. He knew about the whole connection, she'd told him during one of their first calls.

"I see you have a line-up again," he teased.

"Nope, he was coming out this way, so we're going to sit and talk." Why am I explaining, you left weeks ago with barely a word, she thought.

"Uh-huh, chica-bow-wow," he laughed as he sang the tune.

"Dan's a very nice man and we're just friends. He needs to come to the city for supplies so he's taking extra time. Besides, he's got a girlfriend." Again she defended the situation.

"We shall see, Sunshine. I'll let you go, sleep well."

"You too, Buttercup," she said, then hung up the phone.

Unsure how to feel about the sudden reappearance, she immediately dialed Sarah, her close friend from New Jersey, to get an opinion. Sarah had dated from the net a few times, so she'd have the inside scoop on American male thinking.

"Hey lady, how are ya?" Jade's voice changed from unsure to comfortable the instant she heard her friend pick up.

"Hey baby, I'm fine, and how are you?"

"Well, I'm confused, Brady just called." She could've heard a pin drop with the pause.

"You're shittin' me! So where has his sorry mother-fucking ass been?"

"He said he needed time to get back to normal."

"It's about damn time! Did you ask why he didn't bother to call you?"

"I asked, but all he said was he needed time. I don't get it, if you've talked to someone for six months, wouldn't you be anxious to pick up the second you got home?"

"You gotta remember you're dealing with men, they just don't think like we do. Common courtesy would have told us to pick up the phone. Hell, I'd be missing that person I would've never stopped talking and dialed from my bed."

Man thinking, the one subject Jade sucked at. She thought about the many times in life when a man didn't bother to call saying he was going to be late, never mind keeping her posted on the big things.

"Did you tell him you're coming to Atlantic City?" They'd talked so often this past year they felt they'd known each other a lifetime.

"I told him about a trip, but I didn't tell him where or ask him to go. I said I'd have to see if I can save enough and then he offers to send me money to help."

"What? He hasn't called you in damn near two months and he's offering you money? That's a first for me, I never heard of a man doing that. Maybe he's trying to make up for losing time with you."

"That's exactly what I thought, but I don't have a price tag. I told him I didn't want his money. I'm not sure if I should tell him I'm going, even."

"Well you're coming right? Don't tell me you're not because I'd be disappointed."

"Nope, I'm coming. I just don't know how I feel about Brady since we haven't spoken in months. Sure he was going through something major, but communication shouldn't stop. No matter what I went through, we kept that line open. When I tried to pull away, he phoned even more…tit for tat, I'm thinking. What he did was inconsiderate."

With neither understanding Brady's offer, the ladies' conversation turned to the upcoming event and the people attending. They looked forward to spending time together. By the time she hung up the phone, Jade set her mind into the neutral category, not moving forward or backward when it came to Brady.

Signing into chat, in private she told Donna and Kara about the call. Kara was her twin in a way, born the same day a couple years apart and she was skeptical and analytical, like Jade. Donna's advice was to not take any shit from anyone. She'd seen a lot of crap through life and got the short end of the stick far too many times. Between her three confidantes, Jade felt justified not to blurt out any information about her travel plans.

Over the next three weeks, Brady's phone calls increased to every day, but it took a while to warm to the conversations. He kept in regular contact, even during the third week of July when he was away at a tournament he managed to call twice on Saturday just so they could laugh together. Jade kept the conversations on life's events. Cautious, she took her time and didn't simply jump back in. As he earned her trust, the conversations slowly lead back to how they used to be and it became easier and easier to open up.

"Hey beautiful, how are you?" his voice was all smiles and warmth that Monday evening.

"I'm well, young man, so tell me all about your trip."

"There isn't much to tell. Pretty much all weekend was work. By the time I finished, I'd sleep and get ready for the next day."

"Didn't you go to Civil War Battlefields or see some of the sights?" Jade would've made it a point to see it all.

"Nah, I'm not into that kinda stuff. To me, you see one museum, you seen 'em all." He sounded bored with the idea.

"It would be like walking through a moment in time. Just knowing something of that magnitude happened years ago in that very spot would be amazing." She sounded like a child with thoughts of an amusement park.

"You should've come with me. I could've gone to work and you could take my car and go venturing to all the places you want to see."

"I would've loved that. I could see all the historic places then meet you back at the cabin to sit around a campfire for a couple hours before turning in. It would be a perfect weekend with the smell of smoke in your hair as you get all cozy snug at the end of the evening."

"You like that kinda thing?"

"It would be great! I'd get some of the outdoors and roast marshmallows on a stick and curl up in a warm, comfy bed in a cabin. Tents just aren't my thing." She enjoyed fishing, being on a lake watching the star-filled sky on a dark summer night and curling up by a fire to watch the flames dance and the embers sizzle.

"Well next time I have to go away for a weekend, maybe you could fly up and join me?"

"Careful what you wish for, I just might." That would blow his socks off if I showed up in his hometown to take off for a weekend.

"Have you given any more thought to your upcoming trip?"

She hesitated only briefly. "My ticket is bought and my room is reserved in Atlantic City." He had asked several times, but she waited until she felt right about telling him.

"You're all booked?" His tone changed to excitement. "Atlantic City? What hotel are you staying in?"

"The Regent," she said. Having booked her holidays for a full ten days, she'd have time to spend with her friends. She'd stay with Sarah until the meet and then move to the hotel. After the meet she'd go back to Sarah's until the plane left. There was time to visit friends, shop, relax and spend time.

"That's great news! I'm sure you'll have fun." He sounded happy, yet she heard a questioning in his statement.

"It's that celebration finally and it'll give me a chance to relax from life."

"I know the feeling. I haven't done that in a long time."

He worked far too much in her thinking and she would really like to hug him for all his help. "Did you want to meet me still?" She asked in a serious tone.

"I'd love to meet you!" His response came in a rush of excitement. "I just don't know if that gives me enough time." She could almost hear the wheel in his mind spinning. "I'd have to take off after work Friday and drive five hours so I would get there around nine or so. We'd have Saturday and I'd have to leave Sunday to drive five hours back home." He was doing the math. "Let me think about it. What day are you arriving there?"

"I arrive in Atlantic City on September 20th and leave ten days later."

"What, why so long, isn't the meet only a couple days?" He sounded stunned.

"Well if'n' I'm going to pay that much in airfare, I figure I haven't been on a real holiday in ten years. I'm celebrating!"

"That changes things. I'll work on it and let you know."

"It's up to you. If you don't want to, that's fine. It's a long drive and you have your work and all." She gave him an excuse by putting the invite out and reasons not to show. I want him to be sure of his decision this time, she thought.

"Of course I'd love to meet you. I'm gonna see what I can do. It's been a long time since I took some time off."

She'd wait for his final decision, ever mindful him backing out of Chicago.

After the conversation that day, he called almost seven days a week and the conversations changed. It'd taken a long time to venture into the "what if" thinking again, but with regular contact they danced into possibilities. When Brady said he'd definitely make the trip, their talks turned personal, both thinking ahead as they began to discuss details.

Mary would be flying in from England and announced she'd stay for an extended holiday and a closer bond formed, knowing they'd be tourists together. Life was taking on new meaning, from years of struggle to going on an adventure for the first time. Looking at her drab wardrobe, Jade decided to treat herself to a new outfit. It'd been a year since she went anywhere that required nice clothes and she wanted something to mark the occasion.

Lisa excitedly offered to be her shopping partner and they spent Saturday wandering the stores and malls.

"It's about darn time you do something wonderful for yourself. You've had a tough couple years, it's time to enjoy. And, you're finally going to meet Brady! It's been years since I saw you take interest in any man." Lisa smiled at her. "Just think…you could be starting a whole bright new future!"

"I don't know about this. I'm nervous and not sure who I am anymore." Having fully healed from the surgery, life was different. Every morning she woke with a simple happiness, realizing she didn't have to worry about how the day would play out. Regaining normal capacity, she was able to maintain her home and a heavy blanket was lifted from her world. Of course with Brady back, life was falling even more into place.

"Oh you'll do just fine. I can't imagine what it'll be like for you. Standing face to face for the first time," Lisa said. "The great thing is you get to meet everyone else you've been talking to. This is something that they all waited until you were better and planned to go and meet you."

"Well most of them. Donna and Kara can't make it. Donna can't afford it and Kara has a wedding, but everyone else should be there."

"Okay, I'm going to the change room to try this on. Don't go too far," Jade said and walked away with a sundress in hand.

And When

After buying the cream and brown dress, Jade headed home and was trying on the dress and searching her shoe collection for the right look. Taking in her image in the full length mirror, she couldn't help but smile at the woman. Never one to wear frilly girly things she felt sexy for the first time in years. The phone rang and she smiled when she saw the number.

"How are you today?" Brady's cheerful tone came through the end of the phone.

"I'm great and you?" With every conversation or cam she felt closer to him. It'd been weeks since he'd announced he was coming and thoughts dabbled into a new arena, the attraction between them was so strong.

"So what's the news on Atlantic City, have they decided what they're doing?"

"Friday is a casual dinner evening just to meet or mingle. They're talking about Saturday being a formal dinner and dance."

"Really, how formal? Do I have to rent a tux?" He laughed and sounded worried in the same breath.

"Umm, don't think so. I think formal means no sweats, no sweat-shirts. It's not like we're going to a ball."

"Good, 'cause I don't do formal. I'd much rather wear jeans, dress shirt and of course my boots."

"I Guess I'm gonna see you all snazzed up like when you go dancing, huh?" She often asked what he wore when he was driving home after dancing. He described some of the most wonderfully colored shirts and it reminded her of Houston with cowboys decked out in purples, reds and stripes. A real cowboy wasn't worth anything without the shiny belt buckle and a great pair of boots, they'd said when leading her out on the dance floor. Some walked her back when she stepped on their toes or missed a step.

"Nah, I'm not gonna get all snazzed up. I'll wear my jeans and a sweat-shirt so I fit in with the rest." He snickered.

"Now wait just a minute, Buttercup," she started to reply when he burst out laughing.

"What are you gonna wear, Sugarplum, a ball gown?"

"I am so gonna poke ya in the eye for that, ya know." She hated that Sugarplum nickname. "And I should buy an evening gown all glittery and sparkles," she suggested, waiting for his response. When the line remained silent she asked. "Hon, are you there," then tried again. "Hon?"

"I'm having a visual, give me a moment," he said in a sexy tone. "I'm picturing you all sparkly and shiny. Wow, okay, I'm done…whew," he sighed and a huskier tone came through. "Wouldn't really matter, it's what's inside that's beautiful anyways," he said ever so smoothly in his southern accent.

"I don't know about that, you haven't seen me in person. What if you open the door and want to run the other way? Who knows what face to face could mean?"

"Do you think it's all about how you look?"

"For men it's all about visual and it could be I'm not what you picture. You could be disappointed." He was the one to say in-person is different, so how could he know it wouldn't be?

"Tell me this then, what if when you open the door you want to run the other way?"

He turned it on me, damn it! "I'd never do that. I'm a woman and we women see beyond into the real person way better than men do. Men, it's all about the looks."

"So you're saying I'm shallow?"

"No…I'm not saying that," she paused. "Well yes, I guess I am to an extent. Men have preferences."

"Oh come now, do ya think we men can't be connected deeper than visual? Then why have I been calling you for a year?"

Damn! He did it again, just turned it on me. "Umm…I guess we'll have to wait and see who goes running from whom." She wanted to drop the subject before she dug a bigger hole.

"Sunshine?" he started.

"Yes, Hon?" she hesitantly asked, knowing he'd corner her.

"What happens if we open the door and neither of us is disappointed?"

She knew it was coming. "Well…" she paused, trying to picture the scenario. "Umm…" she could hear him snickering at her, thinking he had stumped the hamster. "I don't know for sure…I'd do the proper formal handshake…." Still trying to picture what was supposed to happen, she knew her brain would probably stop, she'd get tongue-tied and with her luck trip or something.

"Then what, Sunshine," he said and chuckled continuously.

"I guess…maybe…umm…I give you that hug I owe ya for being there for me when I was sick." That was on the list for sure, she could never thank him enough for being her rock.

"And then?"

Oh, he's just having too much fun with my hamster. Jade reached for anything that sounded composed. "And…maybe we go out dancing and enjoy the evening, like a first date, ya know?" It sounded good and she hoped he'd stay on track.

"What if when I reach to shake ya hand…I take my other hand…and wrap my fingers in ya hair and kiss ya?" he said slowly.

"Umm…well…"

He burst out laughing.

"Oh ya know!"

"Hamster stall?" he managed to ask in between his chuckles.

"Yep," Jade said shyly. She couldn't imagine what it would be like if he kissed her. She'd thought of it many times, but now that it may happen she was at a total loss.

"Dancing, huh? Would you like that to be our first date? How about we go for dinner first?"

"Well you are from the South and I know how you follow the proper southern etiquette book and all. I figured this would be something you'd normally do being a southerner." She said in an exaggerated drawl.

"You have got to stop reading that book, I threw mine out." He laughed. "Besides, we've known each other so long I don't think there is any book that knows how things go between a Canadian and an American."

And When

"We could write our own book, north meets south!"

"If that's what you'd like, Sunshine, then that's the plan. I'll take ya out to dinner and country dancing for an evening. Go on the computer and look up country bars in Atlantic City."

She moved to the computer to research. There were no genuine country bars so he told her to search the state. "There is one, but it's far almost an hour away. Hon, our first date will be a flop, it seems. Just forget about it, we can do something else."

"Are you sure that's what you would like to do on our date?"

"I've always wanted to watch you dance, even if it's with someone else. We could figure out something else though. Men are supposed to plan the first date anyhow so you should make the plan." She put the ball back in his court.

"Who says men have to make the plan? And I'd want to dance with you, not just anyone."

"Well on page 137 of the Southern Gentleman handbook it says...'a true gentleman will always take initiative to ensure the first date is planned without flaw'," she pretended to quote from the imaginary book.

"That darn book again! I think you should bring that along when we meet so I can use my Sharpie to change a few things. I gotta warn I keep a Sharpie ready for any use I deem necessary."

"And on page 140, it says, 'the gentleman walks the lady to her doorstep, gives a formal handshake then bows at the end of the date along with a brief hug in appreciation.' So you see, Buttercup, I'm following what the southern etiquette calls for." She enjoyed using her playful southern voice to goad him.

"Uh-huh. Does it say what happens after the handshake, because I think there's a whole chapter edited out of that book," he teased, laughing the whole time thinking to stump her.

"Why, yes it does...it says and I quote...'she thanks him then curtsies and he kisses her hand like in *Gone with the Wind*.'" She could barely contain her laughter hearing his response.

"OH...MY...GOD..." He said then howled with laughter. She could almost visualize the tears he'd be wiping from his eyes from her smart mouth.

By the end of the conversation he said he'd plan the perfect date since that was what the book said.

Only mere weeks away until her plane ride, the buzz on the site was constant. Thirty-five members were already booked in at the hotel. Even Nicki, a spicy spit-fire of a woman from Philadelphia, would be there. Their friendship had grown since they found much in common, right down to their smart-ass sense of humor. Neither had been in a long-term relationship for years and both were building a connection with a man in another city. Tony from Ohio pursued her, but hadn't set a date to meet. The women became each other's sounding board, discussing their thoughts, hopes and men in their lives.

"Think about it Jade, when you meet normally in person, you don't take the time to really get to know the person. Meeting this way forces you both to invest time and see beyond that initial spark thing," Nicki said.

"I'm just nervous about what he'll think. I mean, what if we meet and he says no thanks."

"After all the time he's spent talking to you, are you crazy? Men don't take a year to get to know somebody. I've never heard of any guy doing that. It's not like you haven't seen each other on cam so he already knows what you look like. He's obviously really interested."

"We do have fun and laugh so much. It's weird, no one knows me like him. He can even tell when something's bothering me. It's like he's set up cameras in my house to know me this well. Part of me hopes that we...ya know what I mean?"

"I'm the same with Tony, he texts me all day with little notes saying, 'Love you babe' or 'Thinking of you' and I smile every time. I think it's only natural to start caring for someone who tells you things like that. Even when we argue about stuff he calls and we end up laughing about our differences. I think I'm really starting to fall for him," Nicki admitted.

"You don't have to tell me I'm the same fricken way. He hasn't said he loves me or nothing, but I don't think he's the type to say mushy stuff. He's like my dad was, always saying or doing things that tell you they care."

"Of course he cares! Sheesh, you are man-stupid," Nicki chuckled at her. "I believe everything happens for a reason so maybe your dad is looking down on you and sent you someone just like him."

"I'm surprised you said that! After I lost my dad I was so lost and I couldn't seem to get myself out of that alone feeling. My whole world changed and I didn't care about much of anything then Brady shows out of nowhere. I mean how many women are on that site, he could've picked anyone he wanted."

"Obviously he wanted you and he came in the nick of time, so quit analyzing it all. You were in a rough spot. I was the same way after my mom died. It was a long time ago, but I know that nothing seems right afterwards. I still struggle some days, but there are no coincidences in life. I think you meet the people you're meant to."

"I guess I'll just have to wait and see how this all plays out. I'm counting on you and Sarah to tell me what you think once you meet him since I'm such a dork with men," she said with a laugh.

"We got your back, don't worry. But you have to give the guy a chance, don't hold back."

Nicki was right, she'd have to let her guard down and allow whatever fate planned for them. Jade wrote Brady a letter the next morning to see his mind-set.

--Jade wrote:

Mornin' Hon,

Thought I'd help you smile today. 'Tis only eleven more sleeps until I get to meet you. The nerves are building, but you know that already. I am apologizing now for my stuttering when I open that hotel door. I'm sure I'll be in awe, which will then make me more nervous and jittery (hopefully not darn right clumsy) LOL.

Seems you are calm, cool and collected, whilst I'm sitting here kerflufelled. The nerves are so wound up and you are as cool as a cucumber. Maybe in the next while it will settle into your head and you'll start losing that firm control. Everyone gets nervous about meeting someone...'tis only natural, so rest assured if you are as kerflufelled as I am standing at that door I

will go easy on you. Being that I'm ever so understanding.
Enjoy Monday! Keep smiling!

11 sleeps and counting
Jade
Xoxoxo

"Hey Sunshine," Brady said when she picked up her phone the next evening.

She kept his words in the back of her mind at all times, his letter from months ago remained about feeling sparks in person. There's no telling what could happen until you meet face to face and she wouldn't believe he was coming until he stood before her.

"How are you today, my crazy Virginian?"

"I'm well, while you are kerflufelled, aren't ya?" He snickered at her.

"Yep, and I'm thinking that you have a few more sleeps and you'll be the same." She hoped he'd be nervous or she'd be the only dork at the meeting.

"Ain't gonna happen, Sunshine, you knows it and I knows it!"

"You never know, maybe you'll lose that cool as a cucumber thing on ya drive to Atlantic City, thinking wow…I's finally meeting the Canadian."

"Nah, I got it all figured out already. I figure I'll just open the door and stand one foot away to stop that hamster of yours then you won't be kerflufelled no more." He made the sound of a computer signing off as if to demonstrate how quickly he'd shut it down.

"That won't be good. I won't be able to form a thought. I kinda need that hamster, ya know?" she said with a smile.

"I'll reprogram that thing and you'll be just fine once I uncross a few wires."

"What time are you getting to Atlantic City do ya figure?"

"How do you feel about me coming up Thursday around noon?"

"Really, you want to come early?"

"I thought since you are coming all this way a couple days just wouldn't be enough since we've been talking so long. I thought we should spend more time with each other to see how things go."

"I can't believe you're taking time off. That's wonderful!" She couldn't contain herself. He's making this trip more exciting. First these people planned a party after her surgery to help her celebrate, then Brady came back, and now he was making extra time for her.

"Hon, I know you booked a room with two double beds and instead of you having someone you don't know bunk in, how do you feel if we share the costs of the room?" Brady asked.

"Umm...Oh...I's..." She paused while she wrapped her head around the idea. She'd dreamt about what may occur, but this was sharing the room. "I haven't shared a hotel room with a man in seventeen years," she admitted.

"Well there are two beds, so it'd be sharing a room with a best friend."

There was no one closer to her from the site. He'd seen her on cam when she looked tired with black circles under her eyes and he didn't even comment. No matter if they didn't click, he'd always be her best friend, she thought.

"Let's say one of us feels attraction and the other doesn't. Like let's say I feel a spark, but you don't. Wouldn't it make you uncomfortable knowing I'm sleeping in the next bed? And what if I snore?" She thought out loud and broke out in laughter.

"Do ya?" He chuckled.

"I don't know...I sleep alone. What if I do?" That crazy thought never entered her head before. "I'd be so embarrassed."

"I guess I'd have to use pillows to cover my ears or just go without sleep for the weekend." He started laughing.

"That's some holiday for you. You'll get back to work looking even more tired and ragged," she said, picturing a cartoon version of this all.

"Folks at work would ask "What happened to you this weekend, you look like crap" and I'd tell them it's da Canadian." They couldn't stop laughing.

"Okay, back to serious," Jade tried again. "Would you be okay sharing the same room with me if I don't feel that spark in person and you do?" she tentatively started. "Like let's say you like the Canadian, could you lie there all night and sleep knowing I'm four feet away?"

"I think I'd be the same as you. What we share is far more. It would be hard, but I respect our friendship."

"I guess we could share a room and that way I can find out if I snore." She giggled as she tried to figure out how to find out beforehand. "I have to remind you that I take a pill as soon as I open my eyes and then gotta wait for an hour before I can focus." She wasn't normal in the morning, that's why she booked her own room.

"Yep, I remember. I expect it, so please don't worry about it."

He'd been the one to help her get past her hatred of having to medicate. She had lived drug-free and when she'd started taking the thyroid replacements he'd talked her anger away.

"I figure I'll drive and pick you up from your friends place Thursday around noon or so, that way we can get to the hotel earlier and check the place out, kinda. I know you said you wanted some food and drinks in the room, so we could go shopping."

He had it already planned. "Really, you'll pick me up?"

"Once we get all the suitcases in the room and settle in, I figure we'll get ready and we'll go have dinner and country dance to the place you found for our first date," his voice was one of pride and warmth.

He would've just finished driving hours to meet and was willing to drive an hour to make her first date wish come true? She smiled ear-to-ear. "Really, you don't have to go through all the trouble, remember I said we could just find...."

"Now wait just a second there, Sugarplum. Wasn't it according to the Southern book that the man plans the first date completely?" He interrupted with a playful tone in his voice.

"I was just kidding!"

"We have something to celebrate and the plan's already made. Don't argue...don't say nothing, I'm in charge!" The smile in his voice was priceless.

"You're too much, Brady! I could almost cry, ya know."

"Don't get all mushy on me now. Hey, are you taking your cell phone with you?"

"I'm going to buy a cheap pay-as-you-go down there. The roaming charges would kill me if I use my phone."

"That's a good idea. That way I can call you when I leave Virginia and then call when I'm ten minutes away." He reassured her. "You'll have to email me her address so I know where I'm picking you up. I already programmed the hotel's address in my GPS so we'll know how to get around." Brady was way ahead of her it seemed, he thought of everything.

"I'm so excited! The next ten days are going to fly by. Promise me if I'm all nervous that you give me a good half hour to get my bearings, okay?"

Brady chuckled. "A whole half hour and then you'll be fine? I think it may take a bit more for that hamster of yours."

And When

Nervous in New Jersey

Chapter Seventeen

Her plane touched down in New Jersey just after noon on a Tuesday. It'd been an eight-hour day of travel, having boarded the plane at six o'clock with one stop in Minneapolis. Jade packed and repacked three times the night before, and now two suitcases stood beside her filled with clothes and gifts for the friends she was about to meet.

As car after car drove by she watched for her friend. They would have the day alone until Mary arrived later that night. A grey car stopped and out popped Sarah and her daughter, Tina, both with a big smile which mirrored Jade's.

"Hey, pretty lady," Jade said as she bent to hug Sarah, who was a good ten inches shorter. Seeing each other in person, the bond they had developed mimicked sisters.

"Oh my god, you are so beautiful in person." Sarah stood back to take a good look.

"Me? What about you? You're so pretty." Seeing her friend up close, Sarah looked young for her fifty years with a stylish blonde hairstyle, jeans and colorful shirt.

"And look at how beautiful you are," Jade said, hugging Tina, a vibrant young woman with a figure of a knock-out and a smile that radiated her mother's warmth. "I hate you already, you're skinny." The three laughed.

"I'm so excited to be here and you're exactly as I pictured," Jade said as they left the loading zone.

"I saw you standing there, but I wasn't sure at first. Then I saw your smile and knew it was you."

"I still can't believe I'm here. It's really nice of you to let me stay at your place."

"It's going to be fun, so don't worry about anything. This is a celebration, remember."

"So this is New Jersey," Jade said, looking out her passenger side window.

"Look at the bridge to your left." Tina pointed to a large metal bridge with letters placed on each of the girders. "Welcome to New Jersey" spanned the bridge. As they drove through neighborhoods, they talked and laughed at how alike they were. Showing her points of interest, Jade asked about the areas, wanting to fully understand where her friend lived. From mansions to ghettos, some houses were crammed tightly together in rows.

"Here crime is pretty high. This neighborhood isn't the safest," Sarah explained as they drove down a residential street. "There is such a mix of people who live here, so it always seems to attract some kind of trouble. Seems no one can get along," she said with distaste. "It shouldn't matter what color your skin is, people are people."

The cultural diversity was evident with Hispanics, Latinos, African Americans, Mexicans, whites, East Indians, all in large populations. "I don't think we have the same prejudice, but then again we don't have this many people. Our population is far less. Here you have this huge metropolis and states all linked close together. Where I come from is small town compared to the cities here."

When they stopped at a diner for lunch, one of Sarah's friends joined their table. It was a pleasant surprise getting to meet someone they had discussed over the year. Next, they picked up a cell phone and she texted Brady and Nicki the new number. After buying a bottle of vodka and mix to start her holiday, they arrived at Sarah's house, a modest three bedroom and as warm as her friend, a true reflection of her personality. They were joined by her daughter's children; even Sarah's son stopped by to meet Jade. All in all it solidified what they'd known all along, that they were now lifelong friends. Discussing the meet and her plan to share the hotel room with Brady, her new second family asked many questions, as if watching over her.

Sarah, a hopeful romantic, explained how she hoped Jade finally found the perfect man. "He took time to build things so that's a sign he's emotionally attached. No man calls for a whole friggin year if he ain't feeling it," Sarah explained her thoughts to her son. "I mean come on…you can barely find a guy who wants to talk for a week, let alone a whole damn year."

"I know what you're saying, but just be smart. I can see why a man would be calling you for so long. You are very attractive and a real nice person. My mom doesn't talk with anyone, so you have to be pretty special for her to keep up with you." Sarah's son said to Jade with a smile.

"Thanks, but she's pretty special herself," Jade replied.

They spent the day enjoying each other's company. At seven, Sarah headed back to the airport to pick up Mary while Jade prepared a late dinner for them all. When they returned, a woman with dark rich black hair, big brown eyes and thick English accent introduced herself as Mary. They sat around the dinner table and got to know one another. Mary's flight was far longer and the time change, wretched. Although it was eight in New Jersey, it was two in the morning in Mary's time.

"I'm so sorry I'm such a mess, I must look a fright. I'm exhausted from the travel," she explained in her charming English accent.

They talked over a couple drinks then headed to settle in for the night with Mary needing to catch up on lost time. The next morning they congregated in the kitchen and when Sarah left for work, the two spent time. Jade was a nervous wreck since today she'd meet Brady face to face. Only seven in the morning and she carried her cell everywhere, expecting his call.

"So besides Brady, who do you look forward to meeting the most this weekend?" Mary asked.

"I'm really excited to meet Nicki. We've spent so much time talking and she's very much like we are, relaxed and laid back. I also can't wait to meet Jill, Sandra and Steve. They've been so much fun in the room. What about you, who are you most anxious to meet?"

"Well I've become really good friends with Malcolm so he's definitely someone I look forward to. Candy and Sandra as well, but I'll be nervous to meet the bunch, I'm not one for crowds," Mary revealed nerves of her own. "I simply cannot imagine how you feel. I'm going on about meeting friends. I would be beside myself if meeting a man I'm interested in." Mary's smile showed her understanding.

Jade's phone rang at seven fifteen. "Morning, Handsome," she smiled ear to ear as Mary listened.

"Are you ready to meet? I'm just leaving work and should be there around noon," Brady said.

"I'm nervous, but excited."

"I'll call when I'm about ten minutes away, that way you can have your luggage ready and we can take off. Since this is our first meeting, I'd like it to just be us. I'm not one to meet everyone just yet."

"I got two suitcases and a carry-on, is that okay?"

"No worries, I got ya covered. Just be ready, okay?"

He definitely wanted a quick in and out away from prying eyes. "I will. See you soon," she said as he told her he just turned onto the highway heading to her.

She put down the phone and looked at Mary, who saw her jittery behavior. They sat talking until it was time to go upstairs to shower and get ready. Jade finished drying her hair, dressed then applied her make up with shaking hands. Once done, she turned to Mary. "How do I look?"

"You look fine, very beautiful even. My, you don't seem nervous. I don't know if I'd be as calm. Tomorrow I get to meet my friend and I'm sick with nerves."

Looking her best, it was nearing the noon hour when they went downstairs to await Brady's arrival.

"I guess we shall see you at the hotel tomorrow then." Mary smiled warmly.

"I guess so." Jade paced the living room. "Man, my stomach is churning. I can't believe I'm doing this. I must be crazy! What if we're not comfortable together in the room?"

"Just your luck, isn't it dear. There is nothing you can do about it, is there?"

Her phone rang. "Well, Sunshine, I should be there in about ten minutes. How's the hamster doing?" Brady joked.

"The hamster is on fast-forward and about to spin out of the wheel." She laughed. "How about you, are you nervous yet?" Please let him lose that cool demeanor, she begged internally.

"Nope, not one bit, we shall see you in ten minutes," he said excitedly.

They said goodbye and Jade increased her pace and Mary sat watching her walk back and forth, wearing a hole in the carpet. Jade couldn't even look out the window. I'll wait until he comes to the door. The teasing about how they'd be at the first sight played through her mind. Mary sat on a chair watching out the window. "Oh my, he's here!" she announced. "Brady pulled in and he's quite the handsome man." Mary smiled at Jade.

Jade stood arrow straight at the door with her knees ready to buckle. She held her breath when she heard the knock. Mary gave her a final look before turning the handle.

Her breath caught. Tall, dark and oh so good looking, far better than any of the pictures he'd sent. Brady stepped into the house with his dark sunglasses in place. Something else he teased he'd do, block her attempts to read his thoughts. Jeans, cowboy boots and a muscle shirt, hamster stall! Hamster stall! Hamster stall! His hair styled to perfection, a slight smile on his face. Even the black leather watch and silver necklace stood out.

Jade slowly stepped towards the man who'd been her strength and courage for a year. Forgetting the proper handshake, her nerves sent her forward to hug him briefly as she promised.

"Nice to meet you finally," she said, stepping back. "This is Mary from England."

"Ma'am," he said and shook Mary's hand.

"You are a good-looking man, I'd say." Mary smiled. "I do hope you two have fun. Be sure to meet up with us at the hotel tomorrow and make sure to take care of my friend."

Brady's southern accent came through with "Yes ma'am" and Jade could tell her friend was impressed. Brady was obviously anxious to go, barely five minutes in the door, they turned to leave as he said "Nice to meet you" to Mary.

"Have a great time!" she replied.

Spotting her suitcases, in one motion, Brady picked up the largest and was about to grab the second when she reached for it.

"Ready?" he asked looking at her with a boyish grin.

"As ready as I'm gonna be."

He made swift work of putting the cases in the back seat, then held the door open for her as she lowered herself into the seat. At 5'10" with shaking knees, it wasn't graceful. Getting into the driver seat, Brady backed the car out of the driveway to head to the hotel, following the GPS signals.

Come on hamster function, damn it! "Was your drive okay?" she stammered.

"It was just fine, Sunshine." Brady looked at her with a brilliant smile on his face.

"You're not nervous at all?" Please let him be, come on, I'm such a dork right now.

He held his hand over the console to show nerves of steel, then playfully shook it back and forth with a teasing grin. "Nope, I'm good."

"You're such a brat!" She said with a smile. Dang it, I'm like a school girl for crying out loud. Come on Jade, be charming.

"I think you're nervous enough for the both of us."

With his dark glasses covering his eyes, she couldn't tell what thoughts he was hiding behind them. She tried to look confident, but it seemed the ease of their conversations on the phone was lost. When Brady pulled into a shopping mall parking lot, she wondered about his plan.

"I figured we'll stop and get the stuff we need for the room," he said. She stepped out of the car and followed beside him into the store. When he grabbed a cart, she fell in step beside him. What is he planning to buy that we need a cart for? She questioned. His first stop was the camping section where he began looking at portable coolers and Brady caught her looking confused.

"This way we could put ice in the cooler and keep drinks, water and any fridge stuff cold in the room."

"That's a smart idea."

"Not just a pretty face, ya know." He smiled while using one of her sayings.

Making her laugh got rid of some of the nerves. They walked down an aisle where he stopped for a case of water. He's so sweet. He remembered I said I drank lots of water.

"What else do you like to drink, Sunshine?"

"How about some Pepsi so I can mix it with the vodka I bought yesterday?" She was on vacation and lord knows she could use a drink to relax her, or ten.

"Now we got a problem."

Jade raised an eyebrow. "What's the problem, Hon?"

"Coke is the real thing." He smiled brilliantly. "It's an American thang!" He used his cute southern accent and she couldn't help but smile.

"Coke, Pepsi, same thing to me." She could never tell the difference and mixed with Vodka, who cared.

"It is not the same, just so ya know." He hoisted two dozen packs of coke into the cart.

"Tis too," she said and stuck out her tongue then smiled.

"What else do you like?" he asked as he walked up the next aisle. "What do you like to snack on?"

"I like simple stuff like cheese, crackers, anything quick and easy really."

He turned and headed to the dairy cooler at the end wall of the store. As he stood looking at the options, she noticed two elderly ladies at the end of an aisle a few steps away, looking upward at the top shelf. Since Brady was preoccupied, she moved to ask if they needed her to reach something. They thanked her and asked her to bring down a box of cereal from the top shelf. Jade turned, good deed done, and caught Brady leaning against the cooler watching her with a big smile.

"What? I's tall so I helped!"

"You're so nice. What type of cheese do you like?"

After collecting sharp cheddar, multi-grain crackers and her favorite goldfish crackers, which she snatched up as quickly as a child seeing candy, they headed towards the cashier, talking with a little more ease.

Brady unloaded the goods onto the belt and Jade immediately took out her wallet to pay for her portion. She had wanted the cheese, crackers, mix and water and she'd pay half of the cooler.

"Put that away," his quiet request came when he saw her wallet.

"Nope, we agreed on half of everything, remember?" She smiled in a smart-ass way. I can't tell if he's happy he came, so I'm keeping things absolutely fair, her mind worked overtime.

"Uh-uh, that smile ain't gonna work with me, Sunshine." He paid the price the cash register showed. "Besides, I'm keeping the cooler and it was the most expensive thing. Unless of course you'd like to take it on the plane with you?" he said as he raised his shades and slid them to the top of his head. She saw a glint of playful stubbornness in his eyes, the "I win" look.

Look at his glimmering hazel eyes! They're not like mine which are much more copper than green, his are almost green/teal. Brady pushed the cart to the stand he'd taken it from then loaded the loose groceries into the cooler which Jade carried while he lifted the drinks and water. Opening his trunk, they carefully placed the contents in amongst his gear. Back in the car they drove the short twenty minutes to the hotel.

It was Jade's first time seeing a GPS. Brady joked that it was "his lady" that took care of him daily. Lucky machine, she thought. I'd take care of you too. She asked questions of how it worked. At least it's a safe topic. Soon I'll be alone with him in the hotel room with no distractions.

He pulled up to the front of their hotel before parking the car. Jade grabbed her suitcases and put them upright on the sidewalk while Brady opened the trunk for the cooler and cases.

"Be right back," he said and drove to find a parking stall.

Grabbing the luggage trolley sitting a few feet away, she proceeded inside to check-in with everything in tow. Once signed in, the clerk handed her two room keys just as Brady walked in with a small satchel and garment bag slung over his shoulder. Man, he's a vision. The nerves in the pit of her stomach increased. In the elevator, he asked which floor they were on and she handed him a key.

They found the room and opened the door to find two double beds, a TV, desk and the bathroom with a little mirrored dressing area at its entrance. Brady hung his clothing, dropped his satchel, then grabbed the cooler, heading for the door. "I'll be right back." The hotel room looked like the average and decorated in the late nineties with red and white coverlets. Painted a hue of gray, it hosted a small table in the corner with two chairs.

Jade neatly piled her suitcases one on top of the other out of the way then went onto the balcony to have a cigarette to calm her. Brady didn't smoke, so she stepped out while he was out of the room.

She finished her cigarette then leaned against the rail until Brady walked onto the balcony. As he leaned down on the rail he gently touched her arm, giving her a signal to back away. He shook the rail, only to find loose bolts.

"I don't think we should lean on it, the last thing we need is to explain how a Canadian ends up on the ground from this height," he said with a smile.

"That wouldn't be good, I suppose." She returned his smile. "So...am I what you expected?" Doh, that sounds really stupid! She cursed herself silently.

"No," he said with a serious look then stood back as his eyes moved from her head to her toes. "You're way prettier in person."

"You too, you're way prettier than I am." She felt herself blush. Oh man, try to relax or he'll think you're an idiot.

"Do you want to get some lunch?" he asked.

"I could eat." Jade had eaten only a small breakfast since her stomach was a bundle of nerves.

Once back in the car, Brady searched the GPS for a particular restaurant. They drove for twenty minutes to find it closed and he decided on another well known chain. "You have these up in Canada?"

"Never heard of it," Jade said as they went inside and took a booth.

Their small talk was interrupted when the waitress appeared. Jade ordered the mini burger along with a salad, Brady a steak and salad. At the salad bar, he guided her dish by dish, telling her his favorites. She tried every one of the many different offerings. At the table they spent the next while talking about the meet itself and the days with her friends.

At a pause in the conversation, Jade changed the subject. "Brady, I still can't thank you enough for being there for me all those months. I know you say it's no big deal, but for me it was a lifeline of sorts. It gave me something to look forward to. The ringing phone made things more bearable."

"Hon, I was glad to be there. It's no big thing, really," he said.

"Well, it was to me. I just wanted to say it to your face. Thank you for putting up with the hamster and all." Jade smiled just as her entrée arrived, three mini burgers with side dishes. "This is way too much food."

"Really, it doesn't look like much."

By the end of the meal, two burgers and half of her rice remained, she was too full for anymore.

Brady smiled. "You don't eat much, do you?"

"I'm stuffed," she replied.

"Do you mind?" Brady asked, pointing to her plate.

"Please do," she said and passed him her plate to watch him finish.

"I can see I best cut back on what I put on my own plate since I'll have to eat half of your food at every meal," he said with a wink.

"I can only eat so much, Hon."

"Works for me, it'll save us on groceries down the line." He winked then quickly grabbed the bill the waitress brought.

"Hey, let me buy lunch since you bought the stuff for the room," Jade insisted.

"Nope," he said and got up to walk towards the cash register.

And When

That First Kiss

Chapter Eighteen

Once back in the room, Jade stretched on the bed and yawned. "Sorry, I didn't sleep much last night or the night before. I had to be at the airport at four in the morning."

"That's okay, Hon," he said and grabbed the remote for the television then eased down beside her, propping pillows behind his head, seeming totally at ease.

He half sat, while she was fully outstretched on her stomach with one pillow curled to support her head. Jade looked at him, trying to figure out the man as he surfed the channels. His eyes concentrated on the screen and she took the time to take him in. He was striking in his looks with skin a golden brown from the summer sun and his hair looked soft, like fine strands of silk. Wide shoulders and muscled arms were revealed by the loose muscle shirt. How did I get so lucky?

"What are ya thinking?" He glanced at her.

Her eyes never left his, hoping she'd see into his inner workings. "I was just trying to figure out what you think about this all. I mean you drove a long ways, are you glad you came?" Jade didn't want to come right out and ask, am I attractive? That would prove my dork status.

Brady reached his right hand to her and his fingers touched the hair at her temple. Never losing eye contact, he moved down to the side of her neck and his thumb stroked her jaw line. "I am very happy I came. Come here," he said and motioned her to curl on his chest. He rubbed her back as she rested her head. His fingers, a soothing, calming touch, spoke volumes of his feelings for her. After all this time of holding her hand, he was lulling her nerves to a peaceful state.

Jade opened her eyes to feel his hand curled protectively around her shoulder holding her close. The television was playing a different show than she'd been watching.

"I'm so sorry," she quietly said. "I didn't mean to fall asleep." Oh man, how did that happen? I should be excited at our first meet and here I fell asleep on the poor man.

"It's alright, I'm glad you did. You haven't slept much, besides it was kinda nice," Brady said as his hand began slow movements through her hair. Picking up several strands, he followed them down to the ends, pulling them away from her head, weaving them through his fingers.

"Well...do I snore?" She giggled then held her breath for his answer.

"Sawing wood like a log!" he said with a grin ear to ear.

"Oh no," she said. Completely embarrassed, she felt her face turn red.

"Nope, I'm kidding. You breathe heavy though, that's how I knew you went to sleep." He smiled as she turned to hide her face. Well I guess I've totally broken the ice with falling asleep on him. She looked up to find his gaze watched her every expression as it danced on her face.

"Hon," she whispered then looked away from him.

"Here it comes," Brady said with a wide smile.

"Umm…" He'd always said he knew everything she thought by her eyes so kept them averted to get the courage she needed.

"Yes?" he prodded by poking her lightly in the back.

It's now or never, she thought. Meeting his gaze she watched his reaction. "Would it be okay if I kiss you once?" His eyes showed a surprise, then warmth.

"You sure you want to?" He smiled at her.

I need to overcome this shyness, she thought and half sat up with her left hand supporting her and moved closer. When they were inches apart she whispered, "I've been waiting a long time for this." Her lips were almost touching his, "I'm pretty sure." She watched his eyes darken, then closed her own and moved forward.

Brady remained perfectly still as her lips hesitantly grazed his lower, then upper lip. She felt the gentleness as he kissed her, his lips a silky softness. Asleep a moment ago, the tingling sensation brought her fully awake. She pulled away slightly to look in his eyes. Man, he's gorgeous.

His right hand at her lower back pulled her closer, while his left laced through her long hair and she started again, this time deepening the kiss. Her tongue entered his mouth as her fingers reached to his hair then slid to his chest. Lost in what she'd dreamt about many times, he was like a drug. Kiss him once…kiss him once…Jade thought as her tongue became aggressive and the warnings went off in her brain. Danger! Danger! Danger! Pull away! Her hamster that tried to keep up with the racing electricity, short circuited.

Her passion was matched by Brady with every stroke of his tongue. His hand felt like fire as he touched her bare skin at the base of her spine, sparking every nerve ending. Her loose shirt twisted from their embrace, he pulled her even closer and she heard him moan. With ease, he shifted and rolled, placing her on her back with his face above hers. He deepened the kiss and slowly entwined her legs, wrapping them together as if he couldn't get close enough. Fingers traveled down to squeeze her thigh then up to her side. Feeling frantically out of control, her hands traveled his back, not wanting him to stop. Their breathing heavy, the energy building, he pulled away to look into her eyes. His hazel eyes almost black in their appearance searched her own as her fingers stroked through his hair. Feeling his warm breath on her skin, the heat of him wrapped her so completely. He kissed her again, this time with a deliberate tenderness, a kiss so slow and intimate it sent shivers through her.

He pulled away and their eyes met. There were no words needed. Everything they shared, every moment they'd spent had brought them here and his eyes said he wanted her. Lost and found in him, this was the man she'd waited for. Her pulse raced in anticipation as his lips barely touched hers. His mouth lingered then changed within seconds as his tongue sought hers in a kiss filled with need. Neither able to stop what passed between them, his tongue moved with hers until her body trembled from the intensity. He pulled away breathing heavily then met her gaze once more.

"Brady," she whispered. "I'm not…I haven't…"

"It's okay," he whispered then kissed her neck gently.

His hand slowly slid upward from her thigh to stop at her side, his thumb stroked her ribcage, sending ripples through her. Every fiber of her being wanted him. "It's been a long time…umm, I haven't…" she said as her body began to tremble at his touch.

"It doesn't matter, Hon," he whispered. He branded her with heat wherever their bodies met. His hand leaving her tingling, burning a trail as it moved. He moved to cup her breast, his mouth covered hers. The soft moans escaping were beyond her control when his hand slid down the front of her jeans. Feeling the heat, she arched her hips upwards, grabbed the tail of his shirt and began to pull it off and out of the way.

And When

Their clothes were heaped on the floor, but neither of them had any recollection of how they got there. All hesitation gone, they were finally where they were meant to be. Her fingers slid down his body, feeling every muscle tighten as their tongues danced. She felt the hardness of his penis against her thigh and reached down to feel his length in her palm while Brady's mouth trailed down her chest to savor each hardened peak. When his hand slid down her abdomen between her legs, her body quivered at his touch. Taking a sharp intake of breath as his fingers explored causing jolts to run through her body.

His hand slid down the back of her thigh as he entered her in one slow movement. Her eyes fluttered closed, welcoming the feel of him as their mouths matched the rhythm. When he raised himself above her, she watched his eyes close in pleasure, his deliberate pace, slow and torturous. She wrapped her legs around him and his eyes locked with hers until the thrusting inside caused her body to quake. Her muscles clenched to hold him in. Closing her eyes, a moan of pleasure escaped as her body shook uncontrollably. He closed the distance and kissed her deeply as he exploded within.

His body limp on top of her, they stay wrapped tightly together as their breathing slowed. Jade's hands ran the length of him, enjoying the feel of his muscles as they twitched from the intensity of moments ago. Raising his head from her shoulder, he hovered above as he stared into her eyes and moved his fingers through her hair. He rolled to his back to bring her onto his chest. "Wow," he whispered. Curled together, the electricity soon reignited.

Every movement or touch was magical. They had spent the afternoon in bed, learning and laughing; their connection-undeniable. Showered, getting ready for their first official date, Jade blow dried her hair reflecting on the afternoon. I've never done anything this crazy, she thought. There was no regret, only wonderment. I feel more alive than ever. If Mom could see me now, she laughed at the thought. The shower stopped and Brady appeared wrapped in a towel. Water glistened off his body as he walked behind to hug her as she arranged her hair. Burying his nose at the side of her head he inhaled her scent.

"You're so beautiful," he whispered then kissed her neck. Squeezing her bottom, he released her.

She put on jeans, a colorful dress shirt and black heels then sat on the bed to watch him dress for their date. Jeans, black cowboy boots, a wonderfully colored angular striped cowboy shirt and the shiny belt buckle fulfilled every vision she'd ever had of him.

"You getting hungry?" he asked with a smile.

"Kinda. What about you?"

"Oh…I could definitely eat." He growled out with a smile.

As they walked towards the car they entwined fingers. Once in the car he plugged in his lady voice to guide them as the radio played. Jade sang along softly as he explained he always listened to this particular radio program.

"It's her voice and not the stories of love that I like, so don't get me wrong. She's the other lady in my life." He smiled at her.

"Uh-huh, you're just a softy, aren't ya?" She knew the tenderness this big, strong, tough guy could show.

"Me? Nah," he said with a smirk.

The ride would be an hour long and Jade wasn't sure what to talk about. Her private thoughts danced into the afternoon they'd just shared, replaying everything.

"Sunshine, why are ya looking out the side window all the time?" He poked his finger into her side so she'd look at him.

"Umm… no reason," she said.

"Fib-ber-fox," he grinned as he slowly said it, pronouncing every syllable. Another term she had introduced him to during their year of conversation.

She smiled bashfully, dang it! How does he know my thoughts? I want to hold his hand or touch him. I want him again, she thought with a blush. Okay make conversation on safe topics.

"I was looking at the scenery."

"What are you really thinking?" He grinned.

Why couldn't she say the words? We just shared something spectacular and I'm a fricken school girl. For crying out loud, just say it. "I was thinking about this afternoon."

"What about it?" He said with a playful grin in place.

"Well…it was amazing…and…umm…and I'm wondering if it will always be like that?"

"Yes it was." He reached to squeeze her hand resting on the console. "It will always be amazing with you."

Jade smiled. It'd been so long since she'd been with anyone and being man stupid, this afternoon was destiny for her, but she wasn't sure what he thought. "I just wonder about it all, ya know?"

"What do you wonder?" he asked with a quizzical look.

"Ya know how when you first meet someone everything is magnified and it's different at first. Is it possible to feel that for the next twenty years?" She silently wished she could have every afternoon with him for the rest of her life.

"Twenty years, is that all? I was thinking longer," he said with a wink. "Well, Hon, I think the start is always different and as time goes by you get used to one another more."

"Do you think when you've found the right one it always has that electric feel?" That's what his touch is like. They'd taken so much time to know each other beforehand.

"I don't know if it would always be electric. I think it changes with different moods. With time you get more comfortable with each other with electric moments."

"I don't think it would ever be just comfortable with you," she said with a smile. Her pulse quickened every time she heard his voice and sitting next to him, her heart raced faster.

They arrived at the place she'd seen on the website to find the restaurant deserted. They were led to a booth big enough to accommodate six people. The dimly lit room had a very country décor of wood, dark green walls and country music playing in the background. The waitress took their drink orders, leaving them to browse the menu after reciting the specials.

"Hmm, all-you-can-eat crab legs," Brady repeated, licking his lips at the thought. "What about you, what are you hungry for?"

"Oh, you don't wanna know," she said then blushed. I want you, she thought.

"Look at you." He laughed and slid closer to her.

After they placed their order, she noticed crayons in a small decanter on the table-top and immediately grabbed one to begin doodling on the paper top table. Brady watched as she quickly produced a likeness of a dog. Impressed with her ability, he grabbed a crayon of his own and together they created various pictures of horses, deer and cartoon characters, each having a talent for drawing, trying to best the other. By the time their food came, a quarter of the table showed the proof of their fun.

During dinner they talked about what they both dreamed of in life. Both wanted a horse ranch and playfully they drew one on the table, creating the picture as they envisioned one day. Jade drew a large sign at the top of the front gate while Brady drew the barn. He paused when she printed a name across the top.

"Huh? And When?" Brady asked looking at the picture.

"We seem to say that a lot. And when we get horses...and when we build the barn...I think it's perfect," she smiled. "What do ya say, Buttercup, to the AndWhen Ranch?"

"I like it." Brady picked up two crayons and drew a flag at the top of her cartoon sign, an American one.

"Umm Hon, shouldn't that be a maple leaf?"

"What do you think the other fence post is for? Of course mine will be bigger, though." He squeezed her ribs playfully.

"Oh ya know!"

After Brady helped with her meal, they headed to the bar at the other end of the building. Jade was excited she'd finally see him dance. The loud country music and the massive dance floor greeted them. Even though there were only thirty people or so out on the dance floor, line dancers showed their expertise in a multi-step, quick-paced song. Jade's jaw dropped at the intricacy of it all. "Can you do that?"

"I know just about every line dance."

With the next song, couples walked onto the dance floor and Jade watched them glide perfectly together to the lively tune. She looked at Brady, only to find he was watching her with a grin.

"You're so darn cute. You have this light sparkling in your eyes, taking this all in."

"It's amazing to watch older couples dance. It's like they've done this for so many years, each knows the other's moves. You can almost feel love pass between them. That's how I want to be twenty years from now."

"You think it will take twenty years for us to learn to be that close?"

"For me to glide effortlessly as she is, I'm thinking it would take a few years," she joked. They discussed many times the differences between the Canadian two-step and the real one. Back home she was a great dancer, but here a two-step was gliding in both directions, much the same as it was in Houston. She was watching the twirling, the special twists and turns; the couples made it look effortless.

"I think you should ask one of those ladies to dance so I can just sit back and see you in action." She pointed out several women who seemed to be excellent dancers. "I'll even ask them for you. I will explain my lack of skill and that I came all the way from Canada to watch you dance." He wouldn't go for it.

After a few songs, a slower paced two-step began to play and Brady led her onto the dance floor. Taking her hand, his arm went over her shoulder telling her to relax and follow his lead.

Holy crap, she thought as he began, she'd do okay for a bit then miss a step. "Sorry," she'd offer.

"It's okay you just need to learn it."

Finally the song finished. "I told you I need lessons." Jade blushed.

"All in time Hon, all in time," he said with a warm smile.

Well at least he didn't walk off the floor, so that was a good sign. They enjoyed their evening talking and laughing as she watched the couples in amazement. She tried another two-step to find she made fewer errors. Brady was a good teacher and kept her mind focused on him, not her feet.

As a slow dance began, Brady led her out on the floor, this time pulling her closer than before. It was far easier to match his slower footwork. As the song played, his hand at the middle of her back caressed her, his thumb moving back and forth. When she began to tremble he pulled her in even closer until her chest and his were melded together. Sure he felt her heart pound through the thin material, at the end of the song he leaned down to gently kiss her.

"You ready to get going?" he whispered, bringing her near. Jade nodded her head in agreement. Brady paid the tab, reminding her jokingly it was the man's duty according to the handbook.

The ride back to the hotel seemed faster and soon they walked through the lobby. Recognized by a couple of the people who arrived for the meet, they said a brief hello and made their way upstairs to the room. Once inside, they couldn't get close fast enough.

Jade lay utterly relaxed and content having been on the perfect date. Wearing her silk leopard chemise, she snuggled in the covers at the edge of the bed watching television as Brady brushed his teeth. She drifted off until his arm came around to spoon her. Bringing his stack of pillows close to hers, he sank his nose into her hair, taking deep breaths. His right hand lightly grazed the softness of the material as his hand wandered up and down the length of her side as they both watched the movie. The night would bring little sleep.

Opening her eyes the next morning she reached for her pill on the night stand. Taking her first gulp of water at nine thirty, Jade felt the bed move. Brady headed towards the bathroom, only to stop at the counter. She heard the filling of the coffee jug and the rustle of the packages left by room service. Knowing he didn't drink coffee, she smiled; he was doing this for her. She had told him her morning routine, about needing coffee to help focus. How sweet, she thought and sat up to watch his reflection in the mirror.

Peaking around the corner he said, "Mornin' Sunshine, I was going to make you coffee, but I can't seem to find the filters." His hair was tousled from sleep. Damn he's cute in the morning.

"That's okay, I'll do it." She showed him the filter and coffee all in one like a giant tea bag to place in the basket then snuggled into his side as his arms wrapped around her.

"Did I wake you?"

"Nope, I was up already, just waiting for you." Once the coffee was underway he led her back to the bed to snuggle until it was ready.

Hearing the final gurgle of the coffee perk, she put on her satin cover up, then sat sipping coffee at the small table trying to kick start her hamster as she watched Brady in bed with his back to her.

"What are you doing?" he asked as if he could see through the back of his head.

"Watching you, that's all."

"Why?"

"Just taking in the sight of you," she said and smiled at how wonderful it would be to wake to him every morning.

"Silly Canadian," he chuckled at her.

She took a quick shower, and then Brady stepped in giving her time to put on her make-up and dress. She made the bed and cleaned the room to start the day. On the table she saw his neatly folded sweatshirt, ready for when he came out of the shower. Curious about the front wording, she lifted the garment to reveal a NAVY SEALS logo clearly printed on its front. Lifting the shirt to smell his scent, she noticed the label. Government issued. Hearing the shower stop, she neatly put it back the way she'd found it. He had told her he was a Seal a long time ago.

Jade checked her image in the mirror as he got dressed.

"I see your O.C.D. is kicking in, the room is spotless!" He teased.

"I'm not obsessive. I just like to be neat and tidy."

"Uh-huh, O.C.D., I tell ya. They change the beds anyhow, so you don't need to make them."

She walked over to where he sat at the small table and kneeled between his thighs to kiss him. "Can we get something to eat? I'm starving."

"You too huh, I was thinking I could use with a big breakfast myself," he said smiling down at her. "What would you like?" The gleam in his eyes said he knew full well what answer he'd get. It'd been the topic of discussion for months.

"Biscuits and gravy," she replied immediately.

"Are you sure?" He grabbed her ribs to make her jump.

Before leaving, she used his laptop to send a message home that all was well. She had promised to keep her family informed and Brady had thoughtfully brought the computer along. He didn't wear the shirt he put on the table, she noticed as they walked out of the room.

Sitting in the restaurant, Brady ordered for her when the waitress came. There were others from the site in neighboring booths and they overheard conversations. Tonight was the first evening of the meet, but they kept to themselves, not wanting to bring in the rest of the world just yet. Within ten minutes a plate of heaven appeared before her and Brady smirked, watching her eat what she'd craved for so long. The last time she had eaten this was on a visit to Houston ten years ago. Eating until she was stuffed, she let Brady help with the last egg and biscuit.

After breakfast they ventured to a local pool hall for a couple hours. Jade showed her skill, much to Brady's dismay. They'd goad and tease each other relentlessly about the positions each maneuvered into by stretching their lengths over the table. Neither into gambling, it was a fun way to pass the time with laughter. I feel I've known him for years, she thought as she looked over at him before her next shot.

"How the heck did you manage to make that?" Brady asked, exasperated.

"That one was a fluke. I've never been able to do that before. Maybe you're good luck for me," she said, then missed her next shot.

She watched as he walked around the table. He leaned down in a stance with his legs spread. One leg stretched back, his body bent in half, eyeing down the length of his cue. Man he's sexy, I could watch him all day.

He sunk his shot. "Ha Sunshine, I've played a few games in my time. I think we should put a few stakes on the game. What do ya think?" He smiled wickedly.

"Umm…you mean money, ya wanna play for cash?"

"Cash is good too." He winked and she blushed.

At the end of five games Brady paid again. Jade tried to persuade him to take at least some money from her, getting a firm "No" in response. She even tried to hand him a twenty, telling him payment for the bet, but he wouldn't take it. She didn't like him footing the bill, the relationship had started to feel too one-sided for her liking.

And When

Back at the hotel, having a couple hours to kill, they lay together in front of the TV, talking and horsing around. He started it when he smacked her with a pillow, which turned into play fighting and then wrestling.

He tested her months of bragging that she was tough and pinned her down a few times. She managed to hold her own and during a heated tousle, she used all her strength to roll him off the bed and they both landed with a thud on the floor, laughing in hilarity. Once back on the bed he pinned her face down and sat on her legs with both hands held captive behind her back.

"What now, Sunshine?" He tickled her ribs.

"Oh ya know," was all she could get out in between laughing and trying to buck him off.

"Say it, come on say it. Who is stronger, huh?" he goaded. "Who wins?" He laughed at her predicament, enjoying every second.

"Okay, okay…you win."

Instantly he removed himself and curled her in his arms from behind. "Uh-huh, just like I thought, you ain't so tough, I can take ya."

"I think I did pretty darn good and you cheated with tickling. When we have the ranch, I'll show you how tough I am, you'll be hog-tied in no time."

"Uh-huh, I hear ya talking. Just remember who's got experience with ropes, Hon." He moved to twist their legs together so every part of their bodies touched and they fell asleep wrapped together.

When they finally woke up, he sat watching her get ready for the evening sitting comfortably in the chair. "Why are you so nervous, there's nothing to worry about?"

"I don't know, I guess because they all knew what I went through and this is the first time I meet them face to face. They've knew me at my worst, I guess."

After being upfront and honest about her life, she thought many would be looking to see the scar at the base of her neck. Dressed and ready, she put on a necklace and kneeled in front of him.

"Can you see the scar at all on my neck or will this hide it?"

And When

His finger traced the chain. "Nope, can't see it at all. Besides, why even worry about it, it's a part of who you are."

"I guess I'm ready."

In the elevator, he took her hand and squeezed it. "Every guy in the room is going to come after you, ya know?"

"Don't think so, I think every woman will be after you." She sneaked a kiss before the doors opened.

They entered the dimly lit room and took their seats at a table with other guests. Nicki sat a few tables away with Mary and Jade popped by to chat. Sarah would only attend tomorrow evening, having to babysit her grandchildren.

The evening went well and sharing laughs with people at their table, at times they disturbed others in the room. Brady's charm and her wit were unstoppable when added to the mix of the fun personalities they sat with. Once the jukebox kicked in, people circulated. Jade met Nicki a few times at the bar when they went to get a drink and they vowed to sit together the next night to spend more time. When the formal meet was over, some of the group went to the lounge to carry on, but Jade preferred to return to the room and keep Brady to herself. Once behind closed doors, they discussed the people they'd just met and how they differed from their personalities online.

Changed into a satin chemise, she curled up in bed. Brady wrapped them together so tightly she didn't know where her body started and his ended. His arm around her waist, she heard his breathing change and the inhale of her hair as the desire started. A switch he could turn on in her when the security and warmth of him suddenly became a fire. Lord, I could get used to this every day.

Jade woke the next morning with Brady sound asleep next to her, facing the opposite way. She tried not to disturb him as she took her pill then lay there, wondering what would become of this. They had spent a year getting to know one another and now in person, physically it was a magnetic draw, everything was in sync. Things did go faster that first day by her instigation and last night whenever she left his side his eyes followed. When they separated to talk to different people, she could feel his gaze. Sure enough when she checked, she caught his glance. As if by radar, they instinctively knew where the other was, a connection that defied explanation. He made her feel beautiful and desirable. The lingerie is in my suitcase, not worn, she thought. Turning on her side, she reached to weave the silky strands of his hair through her fingers then rubbed his back slowly as she heard him moan.

"What are you doing?" he sleepily said into his pillow.

"Umm..." she whispered and tried to find the words.

"Umm...what," Brady mumbled.

"Umm...Jade wants."

"Jade wants what?" Already his teasing starts. It's only his third sentence of the morning, but I can clearly hear him chuckle.

"Umm..." She let her hand wander up his back then down his left shoulder to the front of his chest and she scooted closer.

"I...can't...hear...you," his voice a playful melody.

"I wants you," she said softly, almost blushing at the thoughts in her head.

He turned onto his back. His left arm came around to hold her to him and ran up and down her back. "Ya think?" With a sparkle in his eyes, he became even sexier to her with his crooked morning smile.

"Uh-huh, I think."

After a leisurely morning, Jade got ready after her shower. Brady put a shirt on the table and remembering yesterday's, she held the garment up to look at the writing to find F.B.I. on its front. Bending closer to read the label inside the neck to find it also was government issued. The hamster started to race. What did he do exactly? He'd said several times he worked for a company contracted to the government, but why would this sweatshirt be here and why did he put it in full view on the table? Was this a hint?

After straightening the bed, she stepped to the balcony to have a cigarette and think. I'll wait to see what he wears, but what if he's some type of secret service? It would explain why he couldn't talk about his job. He told me right from the get go that even if we were married there were things I would never know about what he did, she mused.

His head poked out the door. "Is it nice out today?"

"Yep, it'll be warm again," she replied. Finishing her cigarette, she went inside to find him dressing, the sweat shirt gone and a muscle shirt in its place.

"Hon?" she started.

"Yes, Sunshine?" he said, bent tying his lace sitting on the edge of the bed.

"Umm…what do you do for work, I mean what is your title?"

"Just what I told you, I work for the government." He looked up. "Why?" He paused in what he was doing.

"Well yesterday there was a Navy Seal sweatshirt on the table and today there was an F.B.I. one. I know you said you were in the Seals, so are you in the F.B.I.?" She watched his eyes as his face became serious.

"I used to be." He bent to tie his other shoelace.

"Okay, so what could be better than an F.B.I. job that would make you not be one no more?"

"Well the C.I.A. is higher than the F.B.I," he remarked and went to the mirror to brush his hair.

"Okay, so are you in the C.I.A. then?" She held her breath.

"Nope, I used to be, but I got a promotion," said as casually as when he asked the temperature outside.

"Okay." She paused to let her hamster wrap around the information. "So you were Navy Seals, then F.B.I., then C.I.A. and you got a promotion to…" She waited for him to fill in the blank.

"Homeland Security," he said as he picked up his phone and wallet.

He's no ordinary computer guy. She went back on the balcony to digest what he'd said. It made sense why she couldn't read him, at times he'd catch her trying then suddenly he'd have no expression and block her attempt.

"You okay, Sunshine?" he asked, stepping onto the balcony.

"I didn't mean to pry, but I wondered why the shirts were out on the table. It kinda made my hamster go, ya know?"

"Actually, I brought those shirts in case you wanted to wear one. I noticed in your suitcase you didn't bring one, so I thought maybe you didn't realize it got chilly here."

I don't believe that for a second, he saw my suede coat. Did he go through my suitcases? If his job is that important, maybe he checked me out, she silently questioned. "You've seen inside my suitcases?" she gasped.

"You had them lying open, it's not like I went through them. And yes I saw the lingerie," he said with a sheepish smile.

"Aha, you were snooping!" She put her hands on her hips.

"It's not snooping if you leave them open, is it?" He brought her close, his arm circled her waist.

"I haven't even worn those outfits for ya." I should have, it just seems everything happens so fast between us all the time, she added to herself.

"You're so cute." He chuckled. "None of those things could possibly make you any more beautiful or sexier."

They left the room wound together and took a drive around the area to find a pancake place to stop at for breakfast. He wanted to venture out a bit and she left him in charge of all decisions. She was a passenger enjoying the sights.

Tonight would be the formal evening for the meet. Jade was anxious about Sarah and Nicki meeting Brady and spending more time watching them together. She had discussed him for months with the ladies and it was hard to describe how well they got along. She looked forward to their opinions once they got to know Brady. Last night was an icebreaker, but tonight was the big shin-dig with cocktails then dinner and dancing to follow.

Ending back at the hotel in the afternoon, they lounged together, curled up.

"I wish I wasn't going tonight. I'd rather make an appearance with you then come upstairs." Brady revealed as they were lying together.

"You don't have to go if you don't want to." She looked forward to thanking all her friends face to face. But last night few males attended, it must be uncomfortable being one of the few men.

"Okay, then I'll wait for you here," he said with a smile.

"That's totally fine, Hon, no worries."

He looked relieved. "I'm going to grab a shower," he said and got out of bed.

It's not exactly what she hoped, but at least he would meet Sarah. She was coming up to the room. Jade had promised to help her with her make-up.

She went to her suitcase and debated what to wear to the formal evening. Although she had bought the sundress for the occasion, it didn't suit her mood. She grabbed her alternate outfit and placed it by the bathroom under the sink, then waited for Brady to finish. She would get ready in the bathroom, wanting him to only see the end result.

She chose a fitted black skirt, lace crinkled material shirt that showed her curves and underneath, a shimmering camisole with a very low neckline. Matching necklace and earrings, her shiny black paten heels finished the look. With her make-up perfection, hair in place, she stepped from the bathroom to hear Brady's intake of breath.

"Wow, look at you!" He whistled.

She smiled, not from his compliment, but seeing him decked out in his black pants, white and black formal shirt, complete with his shiny boots.

"You're coming with me?" She was shocked. Earlier he had seemed elated he didn't have to go.

"Of course, do you think I would let you go down there looking like that without me there to keep the men off?" His playful smile and glint in his eyes showed he fully appreciated her attire as he came to hold her.

"Thank you so much for doing this!" She hugged him for still being her support.

"My pleasure beautiful, I's here for you." He kissed her passionately and she could feel his desire stir.

Their breathing heavy, he backed her towards the bed when the phone interrupted. Sarah had arrived in the lobby and asked their room number. A few moments later, Jade opened the door to see her friend in rose shirt, black dress pants and dress shoes.

"You look so pretty," Jade commented while giving her a hug.

"Me? You're flipping gorgeous, I feel under-dressed. What do you think about this?" Sarah nodded to Brady.

"Brady, this is Sarah, one of my best friends."

Brady stood, towering over her friend as he shook her hand. "Pleased to meet you, ma'am and I think she's pretty damn hot." He smiled mischievously.

"Wow, you are one good-looking man and so darn tall."

Sarah sat at the table with Brady while Jade lounged across one of the beds as they talked, meshing completely. Brady's comfort and ease with Sarah was a good sign.

"You gotta make me pretty for tonight. Sorry Brady, but she promised to do my make-up."

"Don't worry about me, go for it." Brady watched the first few minutes as Jade worked her magic, transforming her friend from daytime look to night-time sexy. He excused himself and said he'd be back shortly.

"Well?" Jade asked, anxious to hear Sarah's opinion.

"Oh...my...God, he is absolutely gorgeous, no wonder you fell for the man!"

"I know! I can't believe I'm so lucky and we get along so well. Do you see how we are?" Jade wanted to know Sarah's instinctual feelings with watching them interact the past hour.

"The man is just into you. His eyes follow you every move you make. He's so at ease and playful around you, it's like you've been together for years. But tell me the good stuff, what about the sex?" Sarah knew it'd been years for Jade and she had listened to all her nervous insecurities before she met him.

"It's incredible, Sarah. I didn't know it could be that way. Honestly it isn't just sex, sometimes he just wants to lie together and hold me. I've never been a cuddly kind of person until now. He's so tender and caring, we even play fought the other day and it was so much fun."

"You see, fairy tales do come true. That man loves you. He's called you for a year, came here to meet you and by watching you both together, I tell ya he loves you." Sarah's opinion mattered. "There is no way two people could be as close and not have deeper emotion behind it."

"Sarah," Jade paused uncertain. "I think I'm in love with Brady," she admitted openly. "Not just from this weekend, but from really getting to know him throughout the year."

"Shit, you don't have to tell me. I see it in your eyes when you look at him and he adores you, it's plain as day on his face."

Jade was afraid to let the cat out of the bag and asked Sarah to not say anything. For now, it would be their secret.

Brady returned a few minutes later to find Sarah and Jade polished and whistled in appreciation. "Are we ready, ladies?"

They entered the banquet room to find some participants already assembled. Everyone dressed for the occasion. After stopping to get a drink, the three continued to the table where Nicki sat with another woman and across from Jade sat Kendra. Nicki immediately started up the laughter and fun with them all and later, Mary joined their table.

After dinner, the hotel staff removed the dishes and the music started. The dance floor at the front of the room didn't stay empty long. Throughout the evening, Jade and Brady comfortably circulated the room together or separately. Jade would head outside with friends for a cigarette and on occasion he'd join the little group.

Watching him interact with others, Jade saw that he was always a gentleman no matter how much flirting was done. Being the best looking man in the room, many tried for his attention and no matter which table he sat at, eyelashes batted.

Kendra, Nicki and Jade, stood outside when another woman from the site asked, "Aren't you afraid of leaving him unattended with all those women?"

She hadn't given it much thought. "He's handling it all I'm sure," she responded and after the woman departed she second-guessed that response. "Should I be worried?"

Kendra was the first to speak up, "Are you crazy? I see it in his eyes every time he looks at you. There is no one else in that room as far as he's concerned, you are his only focus."

"Are ya kidding me? Look at you! You're absolutely fucking gorgeous. He'd be crazy to even look at anyone else. He came all this way for you and only you," Nicki said.

"What can I do if his eye did wander? I don't own him and monitoring or smothering wouldn't change a thing. That's not my style," she said. Jade didn't want him to stay with her out of obligation she wanted him to feel there was no one more perfect for him. The three walked back in to find him right where she'd left him, talking with a group of older ladies. Sarah left at midnight and the evening went well for the next hour.

As the event wound down, suddenly they were thrust into turmoil as accusations flew around the room, fingers pointing at Brady from one group. The anger was evident and having had enough, they headed to their room. Changed into her satin robe, Jade sat on the balcony overlooking the city lights, letting the anger dance in her head. After a few moments, Brady brought a chair out and joined her. Sitting six feet away, she watched him, then turned her head when he settled. After a long silence, he spoke in a gentle tone.

"That sure was a mixed up mess, huh?"

A couple who'd met through the site had had a public fight. While Jade tried to talk to one partner, the other turned to Brady and it had propelled them into a triangle.

"I don't know what happened. I spoke to her earlier when she was crying in the washroom. She told me she didn't feel attractive because her partner hadn't tried to be intimate with her in all their years of knowing each other. I told her she was crazy. She's beautiful, smart and funny. I don't understand how she can't see that. Then when all hell broke loose, I talked to him outside. I told him it's important to let her know things."

There were accusations that Brady had touched the woman and got caught red handed by the boyfriend. The story started with his holding her hand then changed to being in her lap. How could this happen? The boyfriend said he saw it with his own two eyes and warned her not to trust Brady. Looking out at the silent city, Jade took a sip of the drink she'd mixed. Sitting on the concrete with her back against the brick wall, her knees were drawn up protectively.

"Sunshine, you okay?" His soft voice brought her focus back to him.

"I'm fine." She turned her head to look at him.

"Fibber Fox," he replied softly.

"I just don't get it." She resumed looking at the city. "They're perfect for each other, like they're married already and yet...." Jade paused. "And now you're accused of God knows what and I just don't understand." The wind was taken from her sail. The time with him had been perfect and she never once doubted his sincerity. Now because of someone else, she questioned it.

The boyfriend had stared her square in the face and told her Brady was a player. He said he knew all along because of things he heard on the site. Don't trust him, he warned.

"I've been through a lot and life's too short. People gotta be honest with each other. When I see fighting, especially after drinking, everything gets all confused. Life could be over tomorrow for either one of them and they don't get it. They're perfect for each other and it hurts my heart to think they may never realize that."

Just like we're perfect, she thought. Does Brady realize that? She turned her eyes away from him, unsure what to think. Looking through the balcony rail she knew he was waiting to hear about his being accused. What do I think? They'd all been on a public site and it could very well be he had interests elsewhere. I live far away and these women are all close to him. Does he see the value in me? Looking around the room tonight, there were many available women and he could have anyone of them, so who am I to him? The thoughts turned in her head.

"You know I didn't do what they're saying, don't ya?"

Turning her head to face him, she took the time to really see the man before her. She played out the evening's event and the insecurities people tried to make her feel. I love you, ya crazy Virginian. You listen to my fears and are my voice of reason when I don't feel okay with the world. You've heard me cry when I talk about my dad and the frustration I feel in handling things. Jade knew exactly who he was to her and at the moment, he looked at her with such care, more concerned for her than anything else. His eyes said her opinion mattered. This big, strong, independent, Homeland Security man looked to her for validation and trust.

"I have no doubt you were holding her hand as accused. When she came to you she was insecure and upset, so I have no doubt you tried to comfort her. She'd been drinking and in her state of mind she turned to the best looking guy in the place, maybe to see if she was desirable." She saw his "oh whatever" look, at the comment about his looks. "Brady, we only met face to face three days ago and tonight I was asked why I didn't watch your every move in a room full of women. The answer was simple, what would be the point?"

"People asked me why I wasn't glued to your side too," he interjected. "I told them I know where you are at all times and I didn't feel a need to shadow you constantly. I said I can see you wherever you are and I you didn't feel insecure that I had to reassure you by being stuck to you." He paused reflecting on the evening. "I hope you weren't upset we didn't dance. I didn't want to have to prove to anyone how I feel about you. What we have is between you and me, not for that whole room."

She stood to go inside. "Brady," she said right from her heart. "I know who I am and what I want. I always hoped one day someone would see all I am and cherish that for the rest of my days. Only you know what you want in life. Either you want me or you don't and there's nothing I can do or say to change what you choose. My best friend made me understand a long time ago that I can't control life when he told me that all I could do is choose happiness. Well, I've made my choice." She touched his cheek then leaned down to brush his lips, putting the ball in his court. He's leaving tomorrow and tonight is all we have. I'll be damned if I'm gonna let the drama of earlier wreck it. Walking into the room, she removed her robe and settled into the warmth of the covers, leaving him to absorb her words.

He watched her for a long while, then brought the chair inside and closed the door. Within moments he slid behind her and gently nudged her to turn around. He looked at her with such caring then kissed her gently, as if to say he'd made his choice. They fell asleep hours later, wrapped together.

The sounds of the couple next door continuing the fight from earlier woke them at four in the morning. As raised voices invaded their world, Brady curled her protectively on his chest, both grateful they couldn't decipher the words, both upset that hours later the problem still escalated. The yelling didn't stop.

"Wow, promise me we'll never fight like that," she whispered.

"I don't think there's anything you and I won't be able to sit and resolve," he whispered against her forehead as his fingers brushed through her hair.

"I hate fighting. There's no point in getting that angry, ever." She never understood and had seen enough of it in her childhood. Suddenly there was silence for a few minutes. Looking at each other they thought they'd finally get some rest, until the sound of someone throwing up started. It was clear, wretched and loud.

"Eww…gross," Jade moved her hand from his chest to cover her ear.

Brady brought the covers up to help block the sound. "Good grief," he said. "That's a woman making that sound."

If he was attracted before, Brady would have a visual of what was going on next door. When it didn't stop, Jade turned on her side to get comfortable and he curled behind holding her, pulling the blanket up far enough to muffle the noise.

Waking the next morning, they drifted in and out of sleep from their disturbed night then slowly dressed for breakfast in a daze.

"It continued for a good while after you fell asleep," Brady said as he zipped up his jeans. "I think they had sex finally since the sounds were way different." He chuckled.

"Are you serious? She just hoarked her guts out and they had sex? That is so gross, barf then romance?"

"I was like, what the fuck? There is no way in hell I could look at someone after that and say yep, I'm turned on." Brady's face twisted and he wrinkled his nose.

"Why didn't you wake me if you couldn't sleep, I could have kept you company?"

"You were so comfortable. I just kept trying to cover your ears so you could get some rest."

At breakfast, the time ticked far too fast since Brady would leave at noon. Jade didn't want him to leave, but knew his obligations wouldn't let him stay. After paying the waitress they went upstairs to gather his things, Jade sat quietly on the bed watching as he packed.

"You okay?" he asked while moving about the room.

"I can't believe this is it." Please don't leave me, her heart begged. "I can't believe you have to go."

"I hate we live far apart, but when I get back from my business trip, I'll start planning to come see you in the next couple months."

"You want to see me again?" she asked softly, trying to hide her hope.

"Of course I want to see you again!" He gave her an "are you serious" look. "Monday I leave for Alabama, but when I get back I'll start the paperwork to travel to Canada."

"Don't you just need a passport?"

"With what I do, they have to approve me to cross any border."

Walking out of the hotel they found Nicki waiting for her taxi. Brady took his bags to the car then returned to chat until Nicki left.

"It's time for me to head out," Brady said and they walked to his car in silence. He unlocked the door and turned to face her.

"You look so sad." He moved the hair the wind blew across her lower jaw. "Sunshine, you have such a great big heart and you did all you could to help that couple. Don't worry about them, it will work itself out."

He doesn't understand, she thought as she circled her arms around his waist. "I think I'm falling for you Brady. I just want you to know that before you drive off."

"I know, Hon, me too...me too." He held her close.

Take me with you, her mind pleaded. Damn his work!

"It won't be too long before I see you again. It only gets better from here. The journey and overcoming the obstacles is the best part." He said as his hands rubbed her back. Taking a step back, his hand cradled her chin.

"A couple months," she said softly. She looked at him one last time. Please don't make me wait too long, her eyes begged. His mouth came down ever so gently and she kissed him goodbye.

Going back up to the room, the emptiness greeted her. All trace of him was gone, his clothes, his laughter, his scent, everything. Looking around the room, it suddenly didn't feel like a vacation anymore. "I should've kept one of his shirts," she said, thinking she would have something to hug. Her heart heavy, she dialed Sarah.

"So how was it after I left?" Sarah asked then remained quiet as Jade told her of the drama-filled night. "So how did you and Brady leave things? I'm worried at what damage this might have done to you two."

"He says he's going to make plans to come see me in the next couple months, so we'll see."

"That's great news! I just knew it by looking at the two of you. You make such a good looking couple and your kids would be gorgeous!"

"Yes they would, but let's see if he makes it to Canada first to meet the family." After the call, Jade curled up, missing the arm around her.

And When

To Build A Bridge Over Miles

Chapter Nineteen

Temperatures were dipping below freezing, but the snow still hadn't come by November, yet nothing wiped the smile from Jade's face. Coming home, she got into daily life, and with knowing Brady started the paperwork to come north, life was easier. Within the week of her return, he'd said he wanted to build what they'd started.

"So you're saying you want to commit to making this work?" She asked to be sure, not wanting to misread anything.

"That's what I'm saying. We just get along perfectly and to be honest, I really miss having you next to me. I forgot how it felt to have someone. I ain't giving that up." He chuckled.

"I miss you too. When do you think you'll be able to come here? I can't wait for everyone to meet you."

"I've filed the preliminary stuff and handed it in to the director. There'll be more, but I discussed it with him already so it'll just take time. I think I'll aim for February. With Christmas a month away, I gotta go to Wyoming. Then there's getting into the year, work gets a bit crazy then so I just can't see doing it until February."

Hearing that, she excitedly told the family about her relationship with Brady. Telling them all about his upcoming visit, he was instantly given an invite to every family holiday from then on.

"It sound's like Jade fell in love," Lisa teased at a family dinner.

"I guess I did." She was proud her life held a wonderful future.

Happy to get through the days, work and home seemed far less of a struggle. She constantly wondered what he'd think of her modest home with none of the bells and whistles. Will he feel at home here? This would be the true test, seeing where and how I live and then I'll fly to see his life. Her mind constantly planning ahead, she began to put money aside.

"Hey Sunshine, how is my beautiful Canadian?"

"Hey sexy man, how are you?"

"So what's new up in Canada?"

"Well, it hasn't snowed so I'm not totally freezing, but everything else is okay. It'd be far better if you were here. I have that snow shovel waiting for you," she teased.

"Oh, I have no problem shoveling, but I think I'd prefer making snow angels with you," he said with a chuckle.

"Snow angels? Are ya sure that's what you were thinking? I'm not sure if you know what a snow angel means in Canada, it might be something totally different in Virginia."

"Oh, I got a snow angel for ya." He laughed.

"It's been three weeks and I still miss not waking up to you."

"You're telling me! I was stuck on a base for a couple of those weeks. It's not good to have those thoughts running through my mind. The barracks were pretty darn lonely."

She pictured rows of cots on either side of the room with Brady clenching his pillow at night.

"I know you're waiting for permission to come up, but did you hear anymore?"

"I talked to my superiors about the red tape and that's why I called. They already have all your info since I had to put it in to come to Atlantic City to meet you, but now I'm working through more of it. They want more details, like where I'll be staying, your family, and stuff."

She answered the questions as he filled in the document. "What else are they gonna need to investigate, will they need my family's background info or just their names and addresses for now?"

"They have your address and phone number, so I'll submit this form and I think that'll be it."

"Hon, do they do this with everyone you're in contact with or is it just because I'm a Canadian?" His phone was constantly monitored. He said she was checked out a long time ago.

"Nope, it's just any foreigner, locals don't count."

"We have the biggest unguarded border in the world. We Canadians are on your back door so you'd think they'd realize we're safe." She could see if they were getting married then she'd expect to go through this. "What if you said you wanted to head to Canada hunting or fishing, what do they care?"

"Well since 9-11 things have changed, it's just how it is. I know ya not a patient one, but you're gonna have to learn to be."

"How do ya spell that?" She heard him chuckle at the jest.

"If it takes too long for the approval, maybe we'll meet up in that city just south of the border from you. You said it was a three-hour drive, so we could always do that the first while until I get permission."

"That way we'd get to see each other sooner. Oh, I'm excited! Don't make me wait too long because I'll go nuts."

"Well Sunshine, I have to get going, I just pulled in at the lanes, but we'll figure something out. I'm about as anxious as you are to get together."

"Okay Hon, go have fun, we'll figure out later."

"I'll call you on the way home."

Hanging up the phone, she loved how he made her feel important, even more so than before. He called more often and tonight, he said he missed her.

Nicki frequently called them both. She and Brady had been friends almost as long as Brady and Jade, the comfort level between them all, a good sign. Brady admitted it was nice to have other people in his life again, something he'd been missing for a long time. Nicki talked to Brady about Tony and he'd give her the male's perspective. Jade hoped that Nicki would find the same connection she did. Nicki had invested six months so far getting to know Tony.

At nine o'clock, Jade received a text asking her to come on the cam in five minutes.

Jadey: are ya here yet?
2 Dance: are we there yet? LOL
Jadey: hello cutie!
2 Dance: Sunshineeeeeeeeeeeee!
Jadey: so happy to see you...thanks for doing this
2 Dance: ya welcome....my pleasure since I get to see ya too

Jadey: should've dressed pretty for ya
2 Dance: ya are pretty
Jadey: awww
2 Dance: there's that smile I miss
Jadey: blushing
2 Dance: I remember stuff in the suitcase, picturing how red you'd be had ya worn it
Jadey: never got to see me girly...could've seen me in something different every night
2 Dance: or the same thing-winks
Jadey: ya not fussy?
2 Dance: nope.....ya wouldn't be either
Jadey: I kinda like being girly
2 Dance: yes you do...but after the fifth "oh my god" ....ya won't mind LOL
Jadey: that would start stuff over and over, we'd get no rest
2 Dance: and? Just so you know was on slow speed last time, I took it easy on ya
*Jadey: next time won't take it easy? *gulps**
2 Dance: nice visual ya just had LOL
Jadey: how'd ya know?
2 Dance: I could see it in your eyes
Jadey: well...I thinks you need to back that up smarty pants
2 Dance: look at you oh shy one...LOL
Jadey: as long as I get to fall asleep curled up with you
2 Dance: that's after I cuff ya
Jadey: cuff me?
2 Dance: lmao
Jadey: no cuffing
2 Dance: nice shade of red...lips even look red...whole face blush...LMAO
Jadey: just out of the shower that's why I'm all rosy
*2 Dance: hmmm......missed that in Atlantic City *snaps fingers**
Jadey: oh I thought about sneaking into shower...
2 Dance: I left the door open for ya every time so?
Jadey: I didn't know that
2 Dance: why didn't ya come in?
Jadey: on the list for next visit...what else did I miss?
2 Dance: now the hamster is thinking
Jadey: wondering if you left other hints
2 Dance: can see ya hamster is hitting the recall...LOL
Jadey: I remember every detail
2 Dance: no ya don't
Jadey: maybe you're adding stuff
2 Dance: nope, haven't added
Jadey: there is no way you could have been that attentive
2 Dance: uh huh

Jadey: ok smarty pants, do ya remember the mole on my leg?
2 Dance: details
Jadey: aha...ya don't remember everything!
2 Dance: if I remembered everything....you'd be worried
Jadey: ok then, next time I'll go over every inch with a fine tooth comb
2 Dance: promises, promises...we'll see in Feb
Jadey: ya talk a good game-but ya need the follow through, Buttercup
2 Dance: oh...think I followed up pretty dam good...how many wows did ya count...hmmm?
Jadey: ya got some proving to do buster brown
2 Dance: oh.....I hear ya
Jadey: have you gotten a flight yet?
2 Dance: been checking and getting an idea on how much it costs
Jadey: roh roh...neck sore, why ya rubbing it?
2 Dance: it's a bit stiff from work tonight
Jadey: if'n' you were here I could rub ya shoulders
2 Dance: hmmm...your touch
Jadey: liked to touch you
2 Dance: so soft
Jadey: like how you curled up behind me and your hands started at my hip
2 Dance: uh huh
Jadey: your breath was hot against my neck, against my hair
2 Dance: wow....she remembers
Jadey: remember it all, was so sensual...
2 Dance: yes you were
Jadey: your hands felt soft
2 Dance: legs entwined, couldn't get close enough to ya
Jadey: never felt like that before
2 Dance: wanted every part of you to touch me
Jadey: I wanted it never to end...feel like it was yesterday
2 Dance: uh huh me too
Jadey: wants that again, I'm selfish aren't I
2 Dance: not at all and wouldn't mind ya being selfish all the time
Jadey: think I would be...you'd never get any rest.
2 Dance: oh....but neither would you
Jadey: I could live with that
2 Dance: hmmm.....me too. Sounds like a challenge
Jadey: a challenge for February
2 Dance: uh huh
Jadey: there's lots don't remember clearly...kinda kerflufelled
2 Dance: we both were
Jadey: ya look tired handsome
2 Dance: I am, but needed to see ya. Its 2 am here so should sleep...can't wait to see you
Jadey: thanks for surprising me

2 Dance: my pleasure, as always
Jadey: xoxoxo...sleep well handsome
2 Dance: u do the same, rest well and we'll talk tomorrow
Jadey: night Hon
2 Dance: hugs-xoxoxo

The next evening she called Nicki to hear the progress with Tony, who hoped to visit her for Thanksgiving. Nicki admitted she was starting to fall for the guy and Jade understood completely.

"I can't wait! I hope it's like you and Brady who has nothing but great things to say about your relationship. I ask him questions about Tony and he gives advice based on you two. He said when you know you found the right one, it all falls into place, like you and him. You do realize if you move to Virginia we would live only hours apart. We could plan weekend getaways for the four of us once Tony gets here."

"He never tells me those kinda things." Jade was surprised to hear he bragged.

"Well you know how guys are they figure you're supposed to know it automatically."

"When he calls we discuss real life things, you know daily events and happenings, then we end up laughing or poking fun at each other. Well except last night, it was like he re-lived every moment and he remembered everything!" Jade detailed their conversation.

"He spent how long talking to you? Of course he remembers every detail! Now that it's real to him, he's thinking about it a lot and talking long-term, so he's going to look at all the details. That boy is not one to come out and say the words, he's more the type who does it other ways to let you know what he's saying. Like the other night, he said he can't wait to be with you all the time."

"He never says that kinda stuff to me. It would be so much easier if he'd tell me this is what I feel, think and want, instead of me trying to figure it all out."

"Why don't you just ask him things?" Nicki suggested.

"I guess I could, but what if he's not on the same page? That's kinda scary. I mean I really can see us living together and I don't want to just assume we will." Suck it up, Buttercup, ran through her head, the same advice she'd given many. I need to not be a 'fraidy-cat, she scolded herself. If we're going to stand a chance of making this work, it will take being totally open with each other, especially if he asks me to move. Her second lined beeped to find Brady on the other line. "It's now or never. I'll talk to you later." She said goodbye and returned to Brady.

"Hey you," she said with a smile.

"Hey girly, what are ya up today?"

"I just hung up from Nicki and discussing the usual girl stuff."

"Oh, oh, girl stuff." He laughed. "How is she doing with Tony?"

"Well, he's supposed to come down for Thanksgiving so we shall see. She's excited so I hope he comes through." Nicki's man promised to make the trek before, but something happened to change his plan.

"I hope for her sake he does. So what else did you talk about?"

"You, of course and ya know, stuff," she started.

"What about me?"

"Sometimes when I try to figure out stuff I end up in left field, so Nicki thinks I should just ask you things straight up."

"What kinda stuff? Fire away, I'm ready."

"Nothing bad, it's just after we talked yesterday, I thought about the time we spent together. You know how we are and I kinda wonder what you think." A generic way to bring it forward, a softer version so he wouldn't feel like he was under an interrogation lamp.

"Umm...I's lost, Hon. If there was a question in there, I'm not sure what you're asking," Brady sounded perplexed. Yikes, too generic.

"Okay," she said then took a deep breath. "You know when we joke about living together and how you say you'll re-arrange the furniture in the mornings just to keep me busy all day sorting it out. Do you really feel that's how we'll be? I mean, that it could work between us kinda...like living together one day?" Whew, I got it out.

"Would I be calling you all this time if I didn't?"

Shoot, he answered with a question. Darn it, I'll have to get more to the point. "I think we joke and play a lot with the idea, but for me, it feels like it could happen since we mesh so well. I didn't know if you felt that way or is it just something to poke fun at?" There, more clear.

"If you're asking if I can see us together at some point, yes I think about that all the time. There's still lot's we have to learn about each other first before I could really answer for sure."

"So you're saying, I just might not like tripping over your boots at the door and you may not like the way I cook kinda stuff, right?" Daily life is something that would be hard to learn from this distance.

"Something like that and how did you know I leave my boots at the door?" Brady chuckled guiltily.

"I figured you're a bachelor, so you probably throw off your sneakers and boots when you walk in. I've seen single guys' homes before. Shoe placement isn't a priority for many."

"I'll have you know I don't throw them, I place them." Brady defended with a smile. "I can just see Miss O.C.D. following behind me and straightening my stuff out."

"Uh-uh, I don't do that. I've learned not to move stuff that doesn't belong to me. Like in the hotel room, I straightened out just my stuff and didn't move anything you put anywhere."

"So you didn't go through my wallet or nothing while I was in the shower?" He teased.

"No, why, did you go through my purse? We sure know you went through the suitcases since you seen the outfits." Woo hoo! Score! She heard him break out in laughter at her one-upping him.

"Hey, now just a minute, Sugarplum. I did not go through your suitcases. You happened to be in the shower and it was lying right there on the floor with the top open. Do you honestly think I wouldn't notice?"

"Are ya sure I left it open? I was pretty sure I kept things neat, tidy and looking presentable at all times because of my O.C.D. and all." Woo hoo! Score two! I am enjoying this far too much, she thought.

"Nuh uh, I didn't open it, you left it open!"

Both were laughing hysterically, this is the first time she heard him tongue-tied. "I don't have nothin to hide, because you would've seen them eventually, so maybe I did leave them open, not expecting you'd be rifling through my lingerie."

"Oh ya know!" Brady tried to hold back as she zinged him with the comment.

"Anyways, back to what we were talking about. I know we both have stuff we have to learn about each other, I just need to know that we're on the same page. What is the outcome of spending the weekend together from your point of view? Remember your email from long ago? You couldn't tell how a person fit unless you met and could say they are a part of you, so I guess I'm asking if you can answer that now?" Brady was very much a part of her life and so far he didn't rely on her much. In fact, he'd only spoken to her once when really troubled. It seemed she relied on him far more than he did her.

"Well that's tough to answer a yes or no. I've never talked to any woman as long as I've talked to you. At first, it was like after a tough day I knew I could pick up that phone and you'd be there and it helped me relax. It just felt right. So yes, you became a part of me in a way. With planning time in Atlantic City, on the drive there I didn't know what to expect. We talked so long that I simply put in my head I was meeting my best friend until I opened the door and saw you standing there. I was like, oh my God, she's all that and a bag of chips and with all the time we spent together, everything just felt so natural," he paused taking a breath, putting his words together. "When I was standing at the car Sunday I hoped you'd ask me to stay. I didn't want to leave."

"I didn't know that, why didn't you stay? I was trying to not interrupt your life. I knew you had to fly out on Monday and figured you were anxious to go." I should've said what I was thinking, I knew it! Why am I always so careful? She mentally kicked herself. "I wasn't sure it was okay to ask. If ya didn't notice...I was kinda like a scared rabbit sometimes." She giggled at the analogy.

"Hon, you gotta learn to ask. I was like...why didn't she ask me to stay? I guess I kinda knew, but I wasn't sure."

"Are ya crazy? I never wanted you to leave. I wanted you to take me with you. You have to remember I haven't attempted a relationship in years so I don't know what a man thinks. I paced the darn bathroom door when you were in the shower and wanted to come in, but wasn't sure if that was okay with you." He thought I didn't want him, sheesh! "I wondered what you were thinking all the time, because I don't know how to read innuendos. The whole time I was like…does he want me?"

"Every time I looked at you, to be honest," his voice soft and warm as he revealed another hidden thought.

Doh! Why didn't I pick up on that, "Really?" She asked in shock.

"Yep," he paused, "I know I don't say things. That's just not my way to be all mushy and stuff, but when we were together it was like time stopped. We got along so well. Maybe I should've told ya when we were in person."

"We suck, don't we?" Jade started giggling. "You can't say the words and I can't do the actions unless I hear the words."

He started laughing. "What a mixed-up relationship we're going to have. How about I leave ya sticky notes and that way you know I've said the words and you'll know it's okay to say and do stuff."

"I can see it now I'll get up in the morning at your house and go downstairs to see your kitchen plastered with sticky notes of instructions." She reiterated her thoughts and he added to the scenario.

"Jade, it is okay to hug me when I come home. Have a good day."
"Jade if I'm looking at you, it means you can haul me upstairs."
"Sunshine, please don't move my boots, but it is okay to seduce me in kitchen."

"No wonder I can picture a future with you. I have no doubt you'd always do something crazy to keep me laughing. Picture it as we get older, our poor neighbors, I can see their faces as they constantly scratch their heads at us. 'Look at those two Ethyl, they're at it again.'"

They both created different scenarios of Brady chasing her around the front yard trying to trip her up. They dreamed up hilarious escapades of life and by the end of their conversation, his words left her with an excitement about the time ahead.

She needed to overcome her shy ways, he was right. She had to learn to ask for things, she'd never done that. It was time for her to be who she wanted and not so damn scared. After hanging up, she decided it was time to change her ways. First, she'd join the gym again. Having just pulled out of years of doing little because of the stupid tumors, it was time. She called Lisa and discussed working out and they decided to join together. Life was taking on a new bright shiny future and Jade was going to reach for it for all she was worth. Come hell or high water she was ready for change. The next morning she typed an email to Brady.

--Jadey wrote
Hon,

Thank you for last night. I guess I needed to know where your thoughts were. Being far away is tough and I'm a little out of practice...so I'm winging it. We're both not used to having someone, but we built a strong foundation even before meeting, so I don't think there's anything I couldn't work out with you. I know distance is the hurdle and I'll do my part by coming to you as often as I can, guess we just start planning.

We both work full time, have different national holidays and complications with you coming into Canada will take time, but once it's okay, my door will always be open. For now we can do as you suggested and you fly up to the nearest city to me and I'll drive down to the U.S. to meet you. Don't wait for an invitation (Mom's invited you for Christmas already...LOL).

Have a wonderful Friday, Happy Halloween.....BOO!
Jade
xoxoxo

Thursday night, Brady would be working, so Jade took the opportunity to visit her mom to catch up. Once home, she talked with Nicki to fill her in on how well the conversation went with Brady.

And When

Mysteries of Love Never Add Up

Chapter Twenty

The first snow marked the start of Jade's Christmas shopping on November nineteenth. She needed to send a gift south, something she'd never done before and she wanted to allow time. Last year Brady said he didn't get gifts at Christmas, that was just wrong and she was going to change that. Everyone should have a surprise waiting for them. Knowing him as well as she did, an idea sparked to get the perfect gift. In Atlantic City, he had really enjoyed the company of the older generation and explained that he respected the wisdom of the ages. What she had in mind was unusual and something he'd probably never seen. Too early for a romantic gift, she chose one with meaning.

Going to a local native art store, she asked to have a custom spirit chime made. They gave her a phone number of an artist to create one and she chose the materials to create one. Reading what each piece symbolized, she picked silver arrow heads, black leather, a raven's feather, and various beads. The lady she called asked her to bring pictures of Brady when she dropped off the makings tomorrow and said it would take two weeks to complete. Jade hoped the symbolism wouldn't be lost on her crazy Virginian. This gift would be created with heart and tied to him in spirit, a symbol to watch over him.

She spent time shopping for family, ignoring the wish lists from each member. Jade preferred to buy something they had mentioned during the year. It was far more fun when they unwrapped something totally unexpected.

Her daily regimen consisted of work, gym, writing, home, and Brady continued to be her outlet, offering laughter and fun to end her busy days. Lisa and Jade had faithfully attended the gym four times a week for almost a month already. They'd built up to a one-and-a-half-hour routine, proud of how far they'd come. That first week was a rude wake-up call. When she started, fifteen minutes on the elliptical darn near killed her and she'd had barely the energy to begin the weight-lifting routine the personal trainer set. One month later, a good half hour on the elliptical was merely a warm up for the weights then half hour on the treadmill or stationary bike. Jade left the gym with energy to burn instead of dragging her feet. Her calves were solid, her upper arms showed her biceps, yet she'd lost little weight. As with all things in life, she wanted results now, patience never a strong point.

She hoped by February, the month Brady planned to visit, her progress would be impressive. Jade wanted to get back to the woman before the tumors, someone he hadn't met. Recharged and alive, she never wanted to lose the feeling that kept her pushing towards her dreams. Life had finally turned in her favor.

Getting home Friday, at the end of November, she showered then sat comfortably in front of the TV, glad it was the weekend.

"Hey Sunshine, how are you?" Brady's voice was quiet.

"Hey handsome, you sound tired, long week, Buttercup?"

"You could say that," he responded in a monotone voice.

"Sounds like you need a vacation, you ready to head north and take a break?" She attempted to bring him around only to hear a deep sigh escape.

"I wish I could and that's what I need to talk to you about."

"What's wrong? This is something not good, isn't it?"

"I told you I gave your name at work, right?" he started, hearing her uh-huh response then continuing. "They told me today I could maybe lose my security level if we continue our relationship."

"What?"

"Because you're a foreigner, they mentioned my classifications could be taken away from me. I could maybe even lose my job," he said in a mere whisper.

"You said it would be okay and they'd simply run my name through their checks. I have a perfect background, so what reason could there possibly be for them saying that?" Jade tried to wrap her head around the news. How could Homeland Security say who someone can see and not see? That just doesn't compute. I'm a Canadian, for crying out loud, she thought.

"I know you're upset, but it's how it is. I have contact with a foreigner and for me to come up there I had to tell them all about us." He paused. "This is my career!" His helpless tone came through.

"Huh? We had contact for the past year and you said they monitored your phone all this time. You gave my name before we went to Atlantic City and there was no problem, so what are you saying exactly?" Her eyes welled with tears as she waited for his response.

"I'm not sure, I'm trying to figure it out and I'm confused about it all. I know what we have, but I also don't know if I'm ready to go further," he sounded tortured.

"Why would you say you'd just need to fill out papers? You said the challenge of making this work would be the best part and told me not to worry, that you were taking care of everything to make this happen because you wanted this. Did you know this might happen?"

"Yes, I knew it could, but I didn't think it would."

"Why didn't warn me? Why did you say it would be no problem?" Her anger stirred within. He should've prepared me, she thought.

"I don't know why I didn't tell you, I guess I should've. I just wanted to figure it all out first and wanted to spend more time to see what I feel. You know, wait and see where this might lead." She heard him exhale. "I'm so confused right now."

Did I really just hear him confess to not knowing what he felt? Was it his job or did he never care? She played his words repeatedly in her mind, 'wanted to spend more time to see what I feel.' I asked him several times. Did I imagine the past two months? Her hamster recalled every word he ever said. Am I crazy? Did he not say those things? The tears that slowly formed in her eyes spilled over. How could he not know? He talked for weeks about coming up, anxious to see me and meet the family. They had laughed and planned his trip, so how could he not know his feelings? Her mind reeled, trying to put the confusion into words. He had called for a year, talked of future, even joked of the horse ranch they'd own one day. And when we are together…and when we build the ranch…and when we buy new horses…it was something they dreamed of working on side by side.

Careful to watch her tone to not give away her tears started, she asked. "Brady," she paused. "Are you saying you don't know who I am to you and that you don't care?"

"Ah Sunshine, I don't know any more. I do care, but I'm just not sure what that means."

The sound of his words stabbed through her. People know their feelings! He told me outright he wanted this and couldn't wait, she recalled every memory.

"Jade?"

She sniffled, not able to hold back anymore.

"Ah, Hon," he said so quiet and soft.

"I don't understand." The words tumbled out between the tears. "You told Nicki you could see a future for us. Just this week we were planning for February. You said you looked forward to it. We could meet just south of the border the first while if work got in the way. I don't understand what happened that suddenly you don't know who I am to you." She hiccupped in between the tears. "You don't know what you feel?" She hiccupped again. "I'm sorry, I hate crying."

"Ah, Hon, I didn't mean for this to happen. I was excited about seeing you. It's only when they talked to me today that I started really thinking about things. I hate that I'm hurting you."

"I hate that you're hurting me, too. I can't believe you changed your mind." Her heart was breaking. This whole time he knew this could happen. The thoughts raced through her mind since none of this made sense. Did he find somebody else?

"I didn't change my mind about you I knew the odds of this working out. The distance would be hard and finding time and all. Now that it may mean my job, I'm just not sure. I'm afraid of losing you in my life, but also afraid of what it could mean." He sounded upset.

How could any government do this? What they shared had nothing to do with his job. I never asked details and he kept his mouth shut. Why wouldn't they simply investigate or ask me? Interrogate me? How can they just say he would lose his job without even calling to check? she wondered.

"You're so far away and I took a lie detector before I met you in Atlantic City and I'll need to take another one in February. I just don't know what to do. I don't want to lose my job. Maybe I need some time," Brady said.

"Time for what?" She was shocked that he'd simply drop a time bomb, then walk away, leaving her with this pain. "Either I am worth something to you or I'm not. I can't fathom how you invested this much time and not know what you feel. You said we were on the same page, two peas." Jade quieted. "What am I supposed to do, forget about the past year and all the time we spent?"

"I don't know," Brady whispered through the phone.

What am I supposed to say? That's okay go live your life I'm fine? I'm not fine, far from it, she thought angrily. "I don't want to talk, I'm about to start really crying and I don't want you to hear that." The sobs were coming and she didn't want to let him hear how badly he'd hurt her, feeling foolish enough for believing him earlier.

"Please don't cry," Brady's voice pleaded.

"I'll talk to you later." Jade hung up, not able to contain her tears any more. She sat on her couch and let the sobs come as her head raced. I was cautious after he first disappeared and we built up to meeting. I asked what he wanted. How could he suddenly not know, am I that man stupid? She dialed Nicki.

"What's wrong?" Nicki heard her crying.

Jade inhaled deeply. "He changed his mind. I can't...even talk and...I'm worried because I hung up. He sounded...upset. Can you call...to check to see...he's alright? He may...need a friend." Jade hiccupped.

"Sure I'll call him, what happened? You sound so upset, I'm worried about you."

Jade tried her best to explain what had transpired, but was sure she lost some of the words. Hanging up, she received the text from Nicki within minutes.

I tried calling him, but he won't answer. So I text him and asked if he was okay.
He responded: 'No'.
I said then why did you dump her? Why couldn't it work? I'm confused.
His response: 'DUMP HER? F-ing great
She called and said you changed your mind and she is devastated. Said how could she be so stupid after all this time?
No response

Nicki called after a few more attempts to reach Brady and calmed Jade down long enough to talk about his change of heart. By the end, Nicki said none of it made sense and promised she'd try reach out to him tomorrow once he'd stewed on it all. The next morning, Jade opened Nicki's email.

I definitely think you two have a communication block. You may have heard something different last night because you were upset. I am so confused, I have no idea what happened with you two, but he's not talking to me. I think you should call him to clear the air. I don't think he had the same conclusion about your call as you did.

She dialed Brady on Saturday, he never returned her call. Sending texts with the same result, on Sunday she wrote an email.

--Jade wrote:

Brady,

I couldn't let you see me that upset. I wanted to make sure you were okay so I called Nicki and asked her to check. I don't know if she got the full story since I was mixed emotions. Thought we'd talk once I could absorb things...and I don't want to talk to anyone until I understand, so waiting for you to call. This is our first fight and you won't talk?

You say you are afraid to lose what we have so we need to deal with this. I'm not angry, just confused. I tend to want to control my emotions before dealing with things as you saw last night. I'm sorry I cried...wish I could have held that in.

It's up to you...I can't make you talk to me or want to. If you want me out of your life, though it's not what I want, I'd thank you for all you've done for me and walk away, wishing you well. Please don't leave me with unknowns, that is just too hard and something I don't deserve.

Jade

With no word back, Jade robotically went to work Monday morning. It'd been three days since she'd heard a word from him. Coming home she checked her email and answering machine, disappointed. Finally she received an email Thursday morning.

--Brady wrote:

It's not really important who said what and what's said between you and Nicki. I know you talk and most likely there was a communication problem. It is very easy to take things wrong when listening to someone who is upset, hurt and not thinking too clearly. You needed someone to talk to and let all of the anger and stress out. Like you would do for a friend, Nicki was trying to figure out what was going on and how to help. Glad you could call her and glad she was there.

I am not mad at you, I am mad at myself. I also tend to control my emotions before I step back into things. I just need some time.

Brady

He'd stubbornly pulled away like she had. They really were two of a kind, even when dealing with problems. The week continued without a word and she carried on as best she could. At the gym Lisa noticed the change.

"Brady and I are having a disagreement." Jade told her, not wanting to explain further.

"Is everything okay between you two?" She asked cautiously.

"I don't know, I'm waiting for him to call me so we can sort it out." Jade cracked a smile, but it did little to improve her mood.

By the end of the second week she couldn't leave this unattended to. Two weeks was far too long and an uneasy feeling that something was amiss started. Whether instinct or the wealth of suggestions from her online family, it was time to get to the bottom of things. In one last-ditch effort she wrote a letter asking him to come to the table.

--Jade wrote:

Brady,

It's scary to think you could just disappear from my world without another word. You promised to never do that and said, "I'm always good with my word." I'm trying to believe that you are trying to figure out who I am to you and that's why you haven't called.

I'm sorry if knowing me has confused your life. What were your words-"that you've seen it's easier for people to text & email than to sit and have a conversation," well, over the year we talked about everything. We're both stubborn smart-asses and we've talk about the good, bad and hard turn's life takes. I thought maybe I had finally found someone who understood when you said you wanted to build on what we have. Now, I have to adjust to not hearing from you. It's been hard and it feels like you're punishing me.

I realize you voiced your thoughts and concerns. The way you worded things was very thoughtful. Perhaps that was your way of letting me down gently because you don't feel anything for me. Maybe you're scared to feel again after so long, wondering how it would turn out. Not sure, I need clear and concise or I don't get it.

I was ready to do whatever it took, even if it meant me coming to you more often. It would be hard, but with time we'd figure it out. "The challenge was the best part". You got the approval for Atlantic City so we know they'd give you it again if I came to you. I don't know what changed, that's where the confusion starts.

I've thought long and hard these past years about my life. We've both admitted to the void we feel. You said "you choose your own happiness," I really thought about that, but at times it requires two to choose. I stayed safe within my world in a routine life. Going through the tumors made me realize I want to miss someone, look forward to them, meet life's struggles and sit and laugh about it afterwards. Life was never meant to be safe. Anything worth having comes with risk.

When you said you wanted the relationship, I believed we'd found the beginnings. I looked forward to every moment and I thought you did as well. Must be a reason you kept building the connection for a year. I got to know the man inside long before setting eyes on you.

You say you need time and I don't know how long that means. It's been two weeks and it would be easier to just talk it out. I haven't said anything to anyone, but people see I'm not my usual self. The longer we go without talking only makes the hamster work more. This won't fade or go away...you know how I am, if something's in my head it tends to stay there. (Don't make me come down there and sit ya down. LOL)

Brady, you have been a gift to my life, I told you that long ago, but I have a feeling there is much I don't know that you need to tell me. I have thought of every possible thing from the best to the worst so I am prepared. My only request is don't make me wait too long for the conversation I deserve. I will continue on whatever level you decide as long as the lines of communication are open and honest. There is never a need to feel you can't talk to me, friends first.

I wait to hear from you.

Jade

She followed her routine without the voice she looked forward to. Nights she'd lie in bed, willing her phone to ring, only to fall asleep in the wee hours of the morning.

"Hey," his voice was barely audible three days after the email.

"Hey," she responded with little life as she sat having coffee before the start of her workday. Grateful to hear from him, she knew the call would be short since he started work in a half hour.

"How are you doing?"

"Not good."

"Me neither and I want to say I'm sorry. I know I should've told you sooner about the possibilities, but I just didn't think it would happen."

"I don't know what to think. What aren't you telling me? Have you met someone else?" The gnawing in the pit of her stomach told her something was rotten in Denmark.

"There's no one else, it's my work that's causing the problem."

"You've been the closest person to me for over a year. You're my best friend, so I thought you would have been open with me. Not telling me was wrong. There isn't anything I haven't told you, I didn't withhold anything, so I gotta wonder why you didn't warn me."

"I just pulled into work. I'll call you tonight and we can talk when we have more time. I just wanted to call this morning to see if you're okay."

"Well I'm not, but I'm back to familiar ground, I suppose." She didn't sugar-coat anything he should know that leaving for two weeks made it worse. "You go to work and we'll deal with this tonight."

"I promise I'll call. Try to smile today, okay?"

"I'll talk to you later."

She hung up and got through the day and had barely stepped in the door that evening when the phone rang.

"Hey you," Brady's voice reflected their mutual mood.

"Before you say anything, I want to apologize for cutting you short when I fell apart. I needed to get my head together."

"I don't blame you, so there's no need to apologize. I'm the one who should be saying sorry since this is my mess."

"Something isn't adding up. I want to let you know I've prepared myself to deal with anything, no matter how hard it is for me to hear. This is your one chance to say anything and I will handle it as long as it's the truth. So I'm going to ask you outright if there is anything you need to tell me?"

"Wow! Where did that come from?"

"I've come up with every possible scenario from you don't feel anything for me and never did. It's too much to risk. You want me to leave your life. I was just a notch and you were playing. Right down to maybe your sister really is your wife. Trust me, I've had time to think for two weeks." Jade gave him everything she and her friends discussed.

"Oh my God, you've really been all over the map, haven't ya?"

"You may not understand this, but I have a great big heart and I've forgiven things far worse as long as it's the truth. You helped me through so much and became my best friend. I will always be grateful, even if it ends here." She meant every word. There was never any point in holding onto people who didn't feel the same. It was a losing battle. If he doesn't care about me, what can I do? You have one chance Buster Brown, she thought.

"Hon, it's not that I don't care for you, because I do. I talked to work before we even met. They've known about us from my phone records, so I had to explain you from the start since you're from Canada. They gave me the go-ahead for Atlantic City, because I told them about how we met and that this was to celebrate you coming out of things." He paused. "When we met, things got closer and I told them what was happening with us and the plan. I did a full report and they told me three weeks ago what could happen. I didn't know what to think or feel." Brady sounded tired.

And When

"So what have you figured out?"

"I still don't know. I'm as confused as ever. I don't want to lose my job, but I also don't want to lose you."

"So the past two weeks of us not talking, hasn't helped?" He left me hanging only to give me the same answer? That thought aggravated her. "You must know what you feel inside. Who am I to you? Better yet, what do you feel when you think of me?" she asked since she knew exactly what she felt. No question. No doubt.

"I do care for you, you're my best friend. I just don't know what this is until we see more of each other. With you being so far away…oh, I just don't know."

"This is what I don't understand. We were planning to see each other in February and even discussed for the first while me driving to the U.S. to meet you. So how come all of a sudden it's a worry with work? You suggested that to avoid any problems."

"I know I said that, but with time and us seeing each other more, what do we do at that point if we decide this is what we want?"

He'd always have his job to contend with, but could Homeland Security really have the authority to tell people who they can care for and not? What if they want to get married one day, could they really fire someone because of who they loved? So much for the good old U.S.A., forever touting about freedom of choice being a right, the government who upheld those laws would break them?

"I don't know what you want me to say." She struggled for a moment. "Am I supposed to go away, is this where it ends?" Something gnawed inside, this just doesn't make sense at all, I'll research things, she decided.

"I'm not saying it's ending at all. I don't want to lose you and I enjoy what we have, I'm just not sure where it could go."

"I guess you have to figure out what happens. We haven't even seen each other again. We've only met once and I guess we'll never know if you don't want to try." It's pretty point-blank, she thought. This ends up nowhere. No more flirting, talking of future, plans or dreams. It would be "How's the weather" conversations when he called, if he called. He doesn't see this from my perspective. It's not fair that he built things just to tear them away.

"I'm not saying we'll never, I'm just saying I don't know right now. I'll figure something out, I promise." Brady offered.

The conversation left her uneasy after hanging up. Once you cross the line from friendship to lover, it's impossible to go back. How do you get back to friends once they ripped your heart out? I've never been in this position. I don't know what the hell to do.

On December seventh, Jade received a call that his Christmas gift was ready. Totally having forgotten she'd commissioned the work, she asked Brady what to do with it during his regular call.

"It's something I had made specifically for you and I'm not tempting fate to throw it away." Superstitious perhaps, but a spirit chime carried a spiritual tie and it would be bad luck in her thinking.

"I'm surprised you got me something after all this."

"I ordered it weeks ago, before this all…" She left the words dangling.

"You can sent it if you want to. I'm leaving for Wyoming for the holidays though, so I don't know if I'll get it in time."

She sent it airmail the next day. Brady called four times a week and his words were like nothing had changed. Flirting constantly, he danced into the thoughts of future, joking of their ranch and being together. She kept her guard up, unsure if he was calling out of habit or obligation.

Talking to her chat family, all were skeptical about his explanation. One went a step further and put Jade in touch with a private eye. She gave him the information and he said it would take a couple weeks. He told her to start using her computer and he guided her to many available sites. Nightly, she began taking a closer look at the facts, finding inconsistencies in Brady's information. His address showed as being listed to his parents and when she asked, he casually explained the property was titled to them and he had purchased it for a great price when they moved back to Wyoming years ago. Digging further, she turned to background searches where Brady's history of homes included several different addresses. His current one was in a totally different town than where she'd sent the letters and package. The searches linked several names to his-siblings, for the most part, but one name she couldn't tie to him clearly. Researching that name, she found another trail with no clear answer. For every question that spun through her mind, she checked. Even while she was contacting State Records Department for public documents published in his name, she maintained normal conversations with Brady and carefully slid in questions he'd answer without knowing. The more she asked, the more information he exposed to look into.

There were never any definite answers, just inconsistencies. She spoke to investigators in Washington who provided tidbits of information about Homeland Security. She turned to Paul, a friend who worked for the Canadian government who knew someone in the U.S. hierarchy. Jade never gave him direct information, but explained the story. He would look into the power and regulations of Homeland. Never wanting to breach any confidences or do anything to jeopardize Brady by poking around, she was careful to watch where she went for information and what she said. The long process enabled her to draw conclusions by putting bits and pieces together. Without direct evidence, she'd have to wait for the private investigator's final report before confronting Brady.

Within a week, Paul spoke to the expert in Homeland, a higher up from Brady's organization. His reasons about his job preventing him from being with her weren't true. Although she was a foreigner, there were protocols and procedures that were followed with great success. It was simply a matter of a thorough investigation. His level of security would be suspended temporarily to allow time to investigate, but he'd be reinstated with no worry. With her having a clear background he could have married her if he chose. Brady's excuse seemed to be all smoke and mirrors. Hearing this, she called Brady the next morning.

"Hey Sunshine, this is a surprise, you're up extra early." Brady's voice was warm and jovial.

"I just needed to hear your voice." She needed to feel the same comfort it always brought her, but didn't this time.

"Oh, oh…what's wrong?"

"Nothing, I guess I'll let you get back to work." He could have married me if he wanted, kept playing through her mind.

"I'm worried. This isn't like you at all."

"Did you get your Christmas present? It shows delivered in the system." She changed the subject. I'm not even sure you live at that address. You think he would have mentioned the delivery two days ago, her mind assessed everything.

"Yes I did, but I haven't opened it. I'm saving it for Christmas."

"Okay, I have to go to work. I'll talk to you later."

"Try to have a good day, Beautiful."

"Bye."

With his excuse a lie and time to think it through during the day, she dialed Brady's number that evening, ready to tell him. She left a message, but he never returned her call. Three days later when she didn't hear from him, she sent an email.

--Jade wrote:

Brady,

I tried calling you, but no response. I'm going through stuff right now that's troubling me and I'm afraid of relying on you because I wonder if one day you just may not be there. I have been thinking about things and I just don't see the whys behind stuff people do and say.

I want to be honest with you about everything, because I'm sure you'll wonder how I come up with some of the thoughts I have. I must get ready for work, but I just wanted to say I know I don't always say the right words. Things just don't come out properly when I'm troubled.

Jade

It would be three days before she got a response, one which would force her to wait.

--Brady wrote

Jade,

I am sorry I missed your call. I told you I'd be leaving for home, but I guess you must have forgotten. I didn't bring my phone with me so my sister called my mom to have her relay a message that she turned my phone off because it rang. Don't know if that was you calling, work, etc...

I know from our last conversation that something was bothering you, especially because you called in the morning and said you just wanted to hear my voice. 'Tis a tell-tale sign that something wasn't right. You made a choice to not tell me and I left it alone. I will not pry or force you to talk, but I knew you were not telling the truth. Rather you just say that you're dealing with some stuff and trying to work it out then to fib. Besides, you are not one to be able to hide anything, I knows ya! LOL

I do hope you have a great holiday. This is the first time I've had a chance to check my emails-been out doing stuff with the folks.

Take care and be safe,
Merry Christmas, Beautiful

Brady
xoxoxo

And When

When Dreams Shatter

Chapter Twenty-one

December 31st, with a new year about to begin, Jade sat on her couch looking at the envelope she'd received that morning by courier. It showed its U.S. origin and she'd been waiting for this. In front of her was the report from the investigator. She'd called a week ago and he informed her that he'd sent it. Now, she hesitated to open it. This would answer everything the past weeks of research couldn't and give her the truth about his job. Slowly she peeled the tab and pulled out the four pages.

Jade read through the first page and came to a dead stop near the bottom to read '*Brady Gibbs, married since 1994, resides at the attached address with his wife and two male children.*' Stunned, she turned to the next page to find more details. The report was thorough, giving his wife's maiden name, her family, their spouse's names, along with his siblings, their partners, addresses and every detail. It even had the date of purchase of his current home, including pictures.

The blood boiled as tears began to fall. "Oh my God, what have I done? I slept with a married man?" Her heart pounded at the thought, her stomach churned. I'd never stoop to something like that, she thought. "Why? Why did he do this to me?"

She picked up the phone and frantically dialed Nicki. "He's married! Good God, Nicki, he's married!"

"Are you serious? Oh my fucking God! What a fucking asshole! He lied to us all. And all his advice about relationships, what a jerk! He was supposed to be my fucking friend. Why would he pretend to be something he's not? That's ridiculous! You didn't do nothing wrong; there was no way for you to know." Nicki tried to exonerate Jade from any responsibility.

"Nicki, I had an affair with a married man, for fuck sakes! I would never have crossed that line, ever! Did I miss something? I thought I was so careful. Were there clues? What man lies for fourteen months?" Jade's fury raged.

"You didn't do anything! This is all on him. He fooled us all and don't you dare blame yourself in this or I'll come up and kick your ass. None of us could've known."

Jade's next call was to Sarah.

"You gotta be shitting me, what a lying mother-fucker! I'm so sorry Jade, I can hear how upset you are. Fucking men! He was too good to be true. I'm so sorry this happened to you, but you listen to me, don't you dare blame anyone but him," Sarah said, stunned by the news.

"I'm so fucking mad. He could have told me at anytime he was married and I would have cared for him as a friend. There was no reason to ever go there. He was my best friend! In Atlantic City he could have told me face to face and I would've hugged him to thank him and been his friend. I just don't understand." Her tears wouldn't stop. "I want to write his wife and tell her. How could he do this to his two boys? How dare he lie and use me in some sick twisted game!"

"Now hold on there," Sarah interrupted. "You don't want to do that. This woman has no clue what he's up to. Do you really want to be the one to tear up her life?"

Jade's hamster stopped in its tracks. "Wouldn't you want to know if you were his wife? I sure as hell would if I was Mrs. Gibbs. I'd rather be informed."

"No, I don't think I would. Maybe she does know and just doesn't care or has gotten used to his ways and gave up. You don't want to bring her misery. He's doing that all on his own."

"I need to think about this. I'm so pissed off. Happy fucking New Year to me I guess." Jade said. "It's four hours away and what a gift, he tore me apart."

She spent New Year's Eve replaying their history, looking for signs she might have missed along the way. Am I blind? He was caring and thoughtful, always. From the start of this until they met in person he was her support through so much. Why? They were physical once, so it wasn't sexual, he could get that locally. He didn't come to me with his difficulties, so I wasn't a shoulder he leaned on. What did he get? Why did he build this connection? He had sat in a room full of people that weekend and had shared, talked, laughed, while and not one person suspected. Why?

She cried until she was empty. Heavy-hearted at the stroke of midnight, she knew only one person knew why. Jade sat at her computer, a blank page on the screen. I'll write a letter to Brady, one that will tear his world apart and force him to realize I won't let him do this to me. He'll probably try to run, but I'll close off all exits and block him in. I want my so-called best friend to explain.

And When

--Jade wrote:

Brady,

I was honest with you about everything: My fears, my life how I lived and what I was going through. You know about my family, friends, work...everything! I was at the most vulnerable point in my life when we met, had pulled away from the world, trying to deal with what I was going through. Did you view that as an opportunity? I know the truth. All of it!

Your parents live at 2749 Dale Cove...nowhere near Wyoming, is it? You have not lived there in years. That's a fact. Phone: 555-1741.

You live at 508 Havern and it's not where you keep horses, but where you keep your FAMILY!

Your wife is Jenny Gibbs (Skeets). You said you were divorced years ago, remember? They bought the house located at 508 Havern in April 1998, taking title "WITH HIS WIFE." Your two boys are Dylan and Cody, born a year and a half apart.

Your wife's older sister is Michelle Diggs, married to Albert Diggs. They live at 17293 Arbor Field in Ashburn. Phone: 827-9017

Wife's younger sister is Karen Boson, married to Daniel Boson then divorced in 2002, she now lives at 37456 Young in Nashville, Tennessee. No avail phone number.

Her parents' are Gerald and Margaret, live at 28412 Clodend Drive in Sterling. Phone: 914-0494

Should I keep going? Yes I have a bunch more information. Your family-your neighbors-everything...I even have the number of your bishop...perhaps I go there. Do I keep digging? Maybe go to your boss Stacy Hardin, or do I just get the truth from your family and relatives? I'm sure they'd be quite interested in talking to me, don't you think?

Why didn't you just tell me the truth from the start? Why did you share that weekend with me? You're MARRIED! You could've told me when we met you were married and ya know, I would've been your friend anyways. Then you build lies for the next months, only to make up more lies saying you didn't want to lose me. What the fuck? I have no idea if this is a hobby for you...how many others are there? None of what you've told me is real. How do you do it? How can you affect someone's life and think nothing of it? Bet you're laughing now.

You may think you can just disappear, but that would force me to contact all the people in your life (EVERY FUCKING PERSON). I have nothing to hide and I've done nothing wrong to you, EVER. What I want is the truth! What did you get out of all this? Why did you pick me? I have so many questions.

I have spent tonight printing information; every email, message, conversation, picture communication, reports...every detail and it is on several thumb drives to be sent where I choose.

You know, I sit here and keep hearing your voice "I'm always good with my word," Boy you use that lightly, don't you? Did you really think I wouldn't start looking? None of it made sense. I am sitting here thinking how it took years for me to trust again.

I am caught in a moral dilemma right now and this won't go away. The only thing that will help me decide is to hear from you by telephone in a certain timeframe. No emails, Mr. Computer Expert, I will not even open one from you. Besides, the thumb drives eliminate that you could erase information by sending me a virus, so don't bother. You are on the clock and it's all on you to give me the answers I want. Without that, I simply continue, even if that means contacting your family, work, relatives, neighbors and bishop. You made me cross a line I never would have and betrayed every sense of the word "friend." Nothing you've told me is real. Guess that's your New Years gift to me. Hope it was worth it.

Jade sat re-reading the email for hours, tweaking it to ensure it reflected every bit of pain. Satisfied, she saved it, not ready to send it yet and printed out all the documents as proof. Saving it on two thumb drives, she crawled into bed at four thirty in the morning, drained.

Hearing her cell phone beep from the other room, she opened her eyes a little after eight in the morning. Taking her medication, she got up, feeling utterly alone and sick. Pouring a cup of coffee, she turned on the computer then sat quietly in her living room as tears rolled down her face as it booted up. Her cell phone on the coffee table blinked, telling her she received messages and she flipped it open to see '*Happy New Year Sunshine.*'

Her anger back in an instant, it was time to place the rage as she typed '*How's your wife?*' and hit send. She went to the computer and opened the draft of last night's letter and hit the send button. Within seconds she received Brady's text '*What?*' in response then replied. '*You have mail, best fucking read it.*' He'd be using his Blackberry to open her letter and she moved back to the couch and waited.

Within ten minutes her phone rang the familiar long distance ring. Picking it up, she braced, ready to deal.

"Hey you," Brady's voice shook.

"That was quick. I didn't expect you to call. I thought you'd turn tail and run."

"Of course I'd call. We need to talk," he said with desperation in his voice.

"Ya think? I don't know if there is any point in it myself. You'll just lie and I'll question everything you say," her voice cold and sharp as daggers.

"I know I lied to you and I'm sorry. I have nothing left to hide. It seems you've been pretty thorough so what would be the point of not telling you the truth?"

I'll have a hard time believing anything, but I hold the upper hand, her mind working two steps ahead of him. He has no idea just what I know and what I don't, she thought.

"Do you know what I'm feeling right this moment? I feel stupid to have ever believed in you. The one thing I can't seem to find out is, why? That is something the investigators couldn't give me. Sure, they offered theories and to tell the truth they felt horrible about having to tell me. Their letter they started with 'We are sorry to inform you,' at least they have a heart, not that you'd know about that would you, having a heart, know what I mean?"

"Ouch," he said softly.

"All this time I thought you were my best friend, only to find out I was a notch. Do you really want to talk about ouch?"

"You were not a notch. That is far from the truth!"

"Really," she almost laughed. "Then what the fuck was I to you? A game, someone to have fun with and twist into knots?" Her voice shook as it got louder. "Why don't you just tell me why the hell you lied to me, what did you get out of it?"

"Jade, this was not about having fun. It wasn't a game and it never was." Brady's voice quieted. "I really care about you and as stupid and wrong as that may sound, I care. You probably don't believe that and I can't say I blame you, but it's the truth."

"Is that what you call this, care? When you care for someone you're honest with them. You trust them. You tell the truth. You don't lie or tear them apart. No, that's not care. I think you need to check the dictionary, Buttercup." Her words came faster.

"It wasn't all lies. I didn't lie to you about everything! What we shared is real. Everything we talked about was real. The only thing I lied to you about was that I was married."

"Well that's kind of a big one, don't you think? Oh…and the children too, another biggie. Why would you sleep with me, is that what mattered to you? You were my best friend, damn it! What we shared was far more important. You've made me an adulterer without my even knowing. Do you have any idea how that feels?" Tears slid down her face with having to say the words.

Brady sighed heavily. "I am so sorry. I probably will never say that enough to you if we live a hundred years. I knew it was wrong and I should've told you. I just got lost in it all." Brady paused to take a deep breath then exhaled slowly. His tone filled with emotion. "It didn't start off that way. When we started talking, I never thought we'd ever meet and the more we talked, the closer I felt. You became my best friend."

He took a long breath. "Then Atlantic City came up and I started to think about my life and how I was feeling. We flirted about things, but on the drive to Atlantic City, I decided I was going to tell you, but I wanted to meet you after all the time we'd spent. I had lied by putting 'divorced' on that stupid profile and I wanted to make things right."

He paused as if recalling the memory. "Then you were standing in front of me and I was lost looking at you. I couldn't say the words. I realized I really cared for you. We got along so well, it was like I just…I…oh I don't know." Brady's voice trailed off as he exhaled deeply.

Jade sat quietly, not willing to interrupt his explanation, waiting for him to come clean.

"My marriage is not what you think. My wife and I stopped being a couple years ago. For the first few years things were good and then it began to change. She didn't want to do things together any more. It's like we lived separate lives; she did her thing and I did mine. She said maybe it was time to have kids since we settled into this existence, thinking it was the next step. She got pregnant and from then on life really changed. We focused on being parents and did all the right things, but it was never about us. When the first one came we got so busy. At times she treated me like a child, not a husband. Within a year of the first, she started warming up to me finally, but she only wanted to make a baby. She never touched me again after that and things just completely broke down. Pregnant again, she pulled the strings. We became strangers sharing a house. To support my kids I took extra jobs since she won't work. I've been like a robot, getting up and going through what needs to be done. The only time we talk is when it's about the kids or money. We never have physical contact. It's like that's why she married me, to quit working and have babies. I tried to fix what was going on, but she didn't want to talk. It's been like that ever since, so I stopped trying." Brady sounded ashamed he was telling her, speaking softly. "I don't get a say in anything."

Brady's confession sounded like every other married man who found himself in a mess as the couple grew apart. She heard his loneliness, but wouldn't let him off the hook. "Why wouldn't you simply divorce and do the right thing?"

"Ah Hon...I love my boys. I can't imagine not being there for them. I know that sounds stupid and you probably don't understand, but I would do anything for them."

"What you're doing, Brady, is teaching them that marriage is a cold home-front with mom and dad not talking, showing affection or loving each other. Did you think of that? Children are smart. They pick up on things that you don't think they can. You work so much you rarely see them. You're a paycheck that leaves before they're up in the morning and gets home long after they're in bed. What part of that do you think helps them? And what kind of life is that for you or your wife? Marriage is about building a life together mentally, physically and emotionally. You're holding each other back from ever being happy. Maybe you should talk to a therapist to hear what this does in the long run."

"I've thought about that. I do wonder if what we're doing is hurting them. Then I think about what divorce would mean. With the economy taking a nose dive, the house we paid for is worth not even half of what we paid for it. We couldn't sell the place if we tried. With the credit cards and debts, how would I support my kids and pay this huge debt?"

"Why didn't you end it long ago? Not saying you regret having children, but when a marriage starts to dissolve as you claim yours did, why bring kids into it? You were married a few years at that point and said it started to break down. Why wouldn't you realize it just wasn't working?" Jade tried to fathom how his life had unfolded to the mess he was in.

"I don't know, I guess I should have seen it. I thought it was just a phase, you know how you hit speed bumps and you figure you'll pull out of it. I figured it would work itself out somehow. Looking back, I should've known."

"Do you love your wife?"

"Kinda. Not like I'm supposed to though, not that way."

"What do you mean? There are no kindas in love. You said that, remember?" She used his words against him.

"She is a good mother, but it's not the kind of love you're supposed to have. I'll always worry about her like a friend, but I don't want to be with her. I'm not attracted, she's not attractive…" Brady paused. "I just don't know, no more."

"Brady, only you know what you feel and no one can tell you what that is. I think you know the difference between love of a partner and love of a friend. Love is when you can't wait to be near them, touch them, laugh with them and share everything. It's a very different feeling from friendship. You want to work at building a life and I don't think I could lie in a bed next to them for years not wanting them. That's just wrong!"

Jade tried to imagine his wife beside him every night like a cold log. What did she feel? How could any woman go years with no intimacy or conversation? Was it true or just his version?

"Look, I have to get going," Brady said. "I ran to the store in order to call you, but I have to get back. Can we continue this conversation tomorrow?"

"I don't know."

"What? You're saying you don't want me to talk to you anymore?"

"I needed to hear the truth and you've given me some of it. I need some time to decide what to do about this." She wondered what the right thing was. His words added to the appeal of Jade's idea of telling his wife.

Perhaps that's what their marriage needed, a good hard look at who they'd become and how they lived. Maybe this would shake his wife enough to start caring and scare him into never doing this again.

"I don't want to lose you!" His voice was desperate. "I can't imagine not talking to you. I understand you need to figure out things and I wouldn't blame you for anything you do. Tell my wife, tell my family, but please just tell me we'll still talk."

"We'll see," she said in a barely audible voice.

"Can I call?" He asked, sounding hurt.

"One condition," she said. 'I best set the ground rules and let him know I'm in charge, she thought.

"Anything"

"No more lies. I want the truth." He still doesn't know how much I know. I'll have to watch every word that comes out of his mouth. What's the point? Maybe I shouldn't talk to him.

"And nothing but the truth, I swear to God."

Having learned so much over the hour, she needed time to absorb. Who's to say he's not lying? His words, filled with pain, could be all part of a bigger picture. I'm far smarter than you ever imagined, so now what do I do? I thought he was scared to feel again and that was his hesitation. Before I go the report, he still talked like we'd be together. I'd definitely want to know if a husband ever cheated, that's a given. Trust and loyalty were everything and there is no way I'd want to remain blind. How degrading would that be? Sitting at home thinking everything is wonderful only to have him playing around? I'd end it, she thought.

But what's his wife's version? How did she view their marriage? There were always three sides to a story. If I lived in Virginia, I'd be able to find out things. I could befriend his wife. That would be the only way to hear her side, or live across the street and watch how they live. Do I phone her, write her?

She sat motionless, unable to think straight from lack of sleep. Her family phoned to wish her a Happy New Year and she managed to hide her troubles. No sense telling them, they'll be horrified. Her phone rang again to find Kara, her Louisiana friend on the other end.

"I just hung up from Mark and he said to call and check on you. He sent the report last week and said he'd leave it to you to tell me. So what's going on?"

"Brady's married with kids." She filled in her friend with little emotion to her voice, detailing all Brady told her.

"What an asshole! Just because his sorry life isn't working, doesn't give him the right to do this to anyone. Especially not you, he preyed on you."

"I don't know what to feel or think."

"I'd report him to his church and let them deal with him. They'd haul his wife and parents in for a meeting and force them into counseling to either repair or end the marriage. At least you would be putting it in their hands. I know how the Mormon faith works. Think about it Jade, he needs help and his wife has a right to know what he's been up to."

"I'm struggling with what's right. Do I affect many people or do I affect one person?"

"In his religion, this is equal to killing someone. It is that big a sin according to his faith. So ask yourself this, if he killed someone, would you report it?"

"Of course I would! I couldn't let him hide from that. This isn't taking a life, this is damaging one." Jade was a little shocked at the severity of his faith.

"To them it's equal, so he knows perfectly well how big this is. I used to be a member of the Latter Day, so I know all about this." Kara gave insight and by the end of their conversation, Jade was even more confused about "the right thing."

Her phone rang several times that day, her chat family concerned for her well being. She told them what Brady had said and received different advice. Her friends wanted to help her and the thoughts were split many ways. Some believed he was a man trapped in his circumstances, falling in love with her. Others felt he was a coward and would hurt someone else the same way if he got away with this. One said she should walk away without another word, but to Jade he was her best friend, the one who'd been there when she needed someone. All these people knew bits and pieces of him. So what's best for Brady? Actually, what's best for Jade? She needed to find a way to deal with the immense guilt.

Exhausted, she decided to turn in early, too tired to think anymore. Lying in bed she talked to her dad, the words drifted as she was feeling troubled and twisted inside. "Hey Pops. It's your bonehead daughter. God, if you're listening, please forgive the mess I'm in. I don't know how I got here. I'm in a big mess and I'm torn up. It seems Brady is married...why was I allowed to meet him? God, if you're listening, did you have a bigger plan? Why would you let me fall in love with someone and then throw in that he's married? That's just unfair... I thought you sent him to me...You would have liked him, Dad....funny...smart...everything I've ever wanted.....He's perfect... I thought I was careful Pops...he was my friend...do I tell his wife, what am I supposed to do?" Jade's voice raspy and half asleep. "Dad, I need your help...I don't understand...I thought life was changing....I thought Brady...I was ready to change my life...I have to do the right thing....God if you're listening.....forgive me... I didn't know..."

And When

Admissions of a Soul

Chapter Twenty-two

The ringing phone woke Jade, her voice a raspy croak when she answered. "Hello?"

"Hey you, were you asleep?" His voice came through the wire.

"I dozed off," she said, checking to see it was eleven-thirteen, then moved to her darkened living room to the love seat.

"I'm sorry, should I let you go?"

"What's up?" Her head ached, the thoughts jumbled.

"I just need to talk to you for a while." Brady sounded tired.

"I'm listening."

"I've been worried about you all day and I want to be sure you're okay."

"I'm not and I won't be," she said in a gruff tone. Is he worried about me or is he worried what I'll do with this all?

"I didn't expect you'd be and I know ya hamster, that's why I phoned. I figured you'd have more questions, so I'm here to answer."

"With every one you answer, two more come. It's like a big puzzle with many pieces. I don't know if it's worth it."

"I know it's a big mess, but just start asking and I'll tell you anything." He prodded like he always did when something troubled her.

He sounds heartfelt. Well, heartfelt according to what I used to believe was genuine. If he hurt others, I'm definitely writing his wife, she thought.

"How many women are there? If you've been having problems for years, how many affairs have you had?"

"One, you are the first and the last," he answered immediately.

"I don't believe that, you were on a dating site. Who's to say you don't have many women?" She tried to become more alert to not let him off with simple explanations.

"I have talked on websites and in chat rooms, that I admit, but it was just talk. I guess as a way to deal with my life."

"Brady, people have friends in life to go to. If that's the case, why didn't you just post as married on your profile, why did you hide the truth if you only wanted people to talk to? You were talking to my friend Pam at the beginning, even planned to meet and set it up three times, so don't tell me you didn't, because clearly you did."

"I don't have friends really. Sure I got buddies, but no one I can really talk to about things. I used to have people I could open up with, but once I got married, Jenny didn't want me to have female friends so I stopped talking with them." He inhaled, Jade's cue to let him finish. "As for the site, I posted divorced because I'd been on other sites and when I put married no one would talk to me. If I put looking for friends, no one would take the time. I knew it was wrong, I shouldn't have done it, but I just was looking for conversation, something I've been missing for years."

She was about to interrupt then thought better of it. Just listen, figure this out, she lectured herself.

"As for meeting your friend, I told you what happened with that when we first talked. I had just joined the room and she was the first to chat with me. We talked for a couple weeks and Pam suggested we meet. When I agreed, she started talking about physical stuff and I cancelled. She apologized and said she understood and I told her it was friendship and nothing more. We set it up again, but she ended up cancelling. Then we decided on a time and as it got closer to the date, she wanted to meet in a hotel room. I was like 'what the fuck?' There was no way and that's when I stopped talking to her completely. It was about her putting a notch for her and I wasn't about that."

As she listened, Jade tried to recall their conversation from a year ago. His words were the same, but Pam never elaborated, perhaps this was the reason.

"Why would you allow your wife to make you give up friends? That doesn't compute. If someone wanted to marry me, he'd best accept I have best friends, most of them single men, or we won't get married." Jade saw a side of Brady she never knew existed. Is he spineless in a way? She wondered.

"I don't know really. Jenny was fine with my friends the first couple years then she slowly started making it more difficult and every call became a fight. Suddenly she didn't like them and since we'd been married for two or three years at that point, I figured it was easier to just stop than fight about it all the time."

"I'm shocked you'd let someone control you. If that's your story, there is only one way for me to know the truth, I'll need to speak to your wife." She pushed the envelope by reminding him of her options. Her goal was to stop him from doing this to anyone else's life. "So why did you pick me, of all people? That's what I can't figure out. I was sick at the time and had been through so much, did you see me as easy pickings?"

"Oh My God, Hon, I am so sorry you feel that way." He exhaled as if hit by a blow. "You were far from easy pickings. When I first joined that site I got emails from women and some of them were nuts, so I went into the chat room to watch. It didn't take me long to figure out who was what. I avoided the crazies and just laughed and joked around. That's when your friend started talking to me. Then I was in there one day when you came in and I watched how you weren't like anyone else, you dodged the attention with your smart-mouth comments. I saw how everyone else respected you and you were different. I was curious, so I checked your profile and shot you a couple lines in the room." He chuckled warmly. "You came right back at me with smart-ass answers. I was like, 'What the hell?' This girl is something. She's pretty, smart and funny.' The rest you know because we started talking at that point."

"But Brady, when I sent you the letter about the tumors, why didn't you open up then? I was honest with you, so why didn't you just tell me you were married?"

"I don't know to tell the truth. I almost did right at the start, but I wasn't sure if you'd be okay with it. The longer it went with me not telling you, the harder it got to say. I did try to, many times. I just couldn't since I had lied to you already and I knew how you felt about honesty. I was scared and with the distance I thought we'd never meet. I didn't want to risk losing what we shared. With time, you became the person to help me through my days. We laughed so much and with what you were going through, I wanted to be there for you, to give you what you gave me."

She silently weighed his every word. I want to believe, but I can't see his expressions or his life. What if this is just more bullshit? "I sit here wondering about everything and I don't know how much is real and how much isn't. I don't know if anything we shared meant anything. I keep thinking about how close…how you'd look into my eyes and wrap me so tight…keeping me safe…the feelings…." Tears started, her heart shredding, as she replayed their time together. "We were…so intimate…and we laughed, I was sure…of…" Her voice drifted, and not able to speak any more, she rubbed angrily at her eyes.

"Ah Hon…" Brady sighed deeply, his tone gentle and loving. "I know you find it hard to understand this all or believe in me, but what we shared was real, all of it." He paused for a moment. "I couldn't hide what I felt for you in person, you have to know that. We spent so much time together before we met, everything that weekend was real."

His voice felt like a warm embrace. "I wish we could have this conversation face to face so I can see it in your eyes." She stumbled for a moment. "I fell in love with you that weekend." The hurt tearing at her wouldn't stop. "I thought it was the beginning of something…I thought we'd be starting…I was so stupid to think…..to know…." She couldn't finish.

"I feel so horrible." His voice choked with emotion. "It was all real. I think that's what made me question things. Meeting you and being with you made me look at where I was in life. I left there wanting to change things. I didn't want to live the way I had anymore and I was sure about it all, I felt so ready. Then when I got back home, I realized I'd hurt my kids and I didn't know what to do. I figured the best thing for you was to let you go. How could I ask you to stay?"

"So the work thing wasn't true, that wasn't real? You ended things, knowing you'd made this big mess?"

"I filled in paperwork to meet you. I had to tell them long before because of your Canadian phone number on my phone, that's all true. I started the paperwork after Atlantic City and planned on coming up, but honestly it could've meant my clearances if I did, that's what made me look at it all."

"If they would have said you're cleared and it was okay, you would've come here to see me?"

"I wanted to see you and I would've come."

"When were you planning to tell me about being married? You know I would have eventually flown down to your place and what would've happened? I'm sure that's the last thing you need is me on your doorstep." It wasn't computing. How long would he have kept this charade going?

"I sound like a jerk, don't I? To tell the truth, I think I would've told you when I was sure of what we had. I guess with only seeing you once I was thinking I needed to see you again to make sure. In November when we started planning, I thought if the feelings were the same when I saw you again, I'd tell you right then." His tone took on a playful note. "Of course you'd probably kick my butt some with finding out, but I felt there wasn't anything we couldn't get through together."

"Don't you think that would've been a huge risk to come here and then tell me? You know I'd be angry, did you think it would be that easy?"

"Oh, I know you would've torn up one side and down the other, but I figured I'd find a way to make it up to ya. When I got to thinking about it all, I was having a hard time with the idea of leaving my kids. Then the job problems added to it and I felt like there was never gonna be a way, that's when I told you I was confused."

Jade kept trying to see this from his standpoint. If he divorced, could they find a way?

"I did some checking on Homeland Security," she said cautiously. "It is possible to be with a foreigner, even marry one. There is a lengthy investigation, but there are those in Homeland who've married people from all over the world and Canada is one of the least threatening countries. Your clearances would be suspended pending the investigation, but they'd be reinstated."

"How the heck did you find that all out?" He sounded stunned.

"I know someone who knows high-ups in your government. My friend told your story to his friend and checking was done. You may be angry, but you've been checked out by one of your own, one of your company's top management." She waited for his wrath.

"Wow!" Brady exclaimed. "You're something, I'm rather impressed. You're one smart woman."

"Not just a pretty face, ya know."

"No you're not. Never were." He said then laughed. "The company I work for is contracted, so some of the rules may be different."

"It was the director of your company, but I did everything to protect you. My friend gave me what-for with getting involved with a married man. He was not too pleased at your deception and dragging me through this. He wanted to report what you did to your superior and said, 'Give me the word and I'll pull the trigger,' but I told him no."

"What does that mean, Sunshine?"

"It means one word from me and his friend would wreck your career." She wanted to be sure he knew just what she could do. Not that she'd go that far, but to let him know she had leverage in getting the facts.

"Holy cow, I wouldn't blame you if you did. Whatever you decide to do, I deserve. There is nothing you could ever do for me to be angry at you." His voice was steady, he believed what he said.

"I don't want to wreck your job, that's not what this is about. Your life is a big enough mess, so what good would that do? It would only trap you further into unhappiness. I'm not here to get even, I don't want retaliation. I need to do the right thing for everyone involved." God had brought her Brady when she really needed someone. A little misguided on his part, but maybe she had it wrong and he brought her to help Brady sort out his life? Her head swam with trying to understand the whys of it all.

"What is the right thing?"

"I don't know." A deep sigh escaped her. "I need time. I feel so guilty for what I've done. That's tearing me up and right now, the man I call my best friend I know nothing about. I don't know anything about your real life." Jade paused. "Send me pictures of your wife, kids, home, anything about how you live. If you want me to understand this, you have to show me the real Brady."

"If that'll help, I'll send them," he agreed readily. Something she was sure he'd refuse.

"Do you think you can sleep, Hon, it's almost one in the morning?" Brady asked.

"I'm worn out and could use about a week of sleep."

"Sleep well, Beautiful, and I'll talk to you tomorrow."

Over the next week, Brady called every day to ask what she wanted out of life. Jade felt pressured to answer what she couldn't. It frustrated her to no end as she waited for some cosmic sign to tell her how to handle this all.

--*Jade wrote:*

Brady,

We are both in a tough place and yet I remember how wonderful it used to be. I'm sure you lie awake like I do thinking, "What the hell happened?" And you ask what I want. What I want doesn't matter. A couple of months ago, I wanted to see if we had what it took to start to follow the feelings. I knew it meant eventually moving, starting a new life, new job...I figured we would work side by side. I'd learn how to country dance, we'd build the ranch, grow old, tease one another and I'd curl up in your arms every night for as long as time allowed. That was what I wanted, but that changed at the end of November.

What we had was worth watching the other's life grow, change and yep, I'd still be making fun of you when you called from the Old Folks home. You were my best friend. It wasn't what I wanted, but I thought to hold onto the friendship you said you didn't want to lose. Well, that changed in December.

Anyone would be struggling with this all if they were in my shoes. There is no answer to want. You say you're unhappy, lonely and miserable in your marriage, so you know that life is not what you want....never stopping to figure out exactly what you want for your next 50 years...so here we are, thinking about what will make any of this okay.

You say we choose our happiness in life, so what has Brady chosen? You are no longer happy where you are. I don't know what I feel anymore. Is that why we met? Am I supposed to do something with this all?

There is no black and white. This has been really difficult and I'm sure you never saw this coming. I know this affects your life, but there are no easy answers right now.

Jade

And When

Reasons to Believe

Chapter Twenty-three

Over the next weeks, Jade struggled with the feeling that she'd spend the rest of her life feeling empty and lost. To add to her misery, her phone displayed calls from several long distance numbers dialed from the U.S. during office hours. Different numbers appeared daily and not one left a single message. Computer research proved unsuccessful and Brady believed it was his work investigating as a result of her nosing around. Afraid to answer her phone, it seemed to Jade that everything was going from bad to worse, they argued regularly. Brady still hadn't sent the promised pictures after two weeks so Jade stopped answering his calls.

"What are you doing girly, what's going on with you and Brady?" Nicki asked.

"I'm waiting for him to show me his life like he promised," Jade said. "With getting all these unknown phone calls, I figure he should know what it feels like to have no clue what's going on, don't you think?"

"He sent me a text asking if I've talked to you. He said he's been trying for days," Nicki advised.

"It's only been a week. I guess his butt must be twitching." Jade smirked. "He calls and I let it ring and ring. Let's see how he likes to worry."

Nicki laughed. "I gotta hand it to you I'd be on the phone demanding he give me what I want. After tearing up your world and ripping your heart out, you sound rather calm about this all."

"If this was a fight between you and me and you needed me to do something to resolve things it would be done instantly. That's what you're supposed to do when you've pissed off a friend, make amends."

"I see your point. He deserves to have his butt twitch then, but how should I respond?"

"Heck, tell him every day, I don't care."

"I just texted him back that, 'Yes, every day.' Let's see what he comes back with. Aha, here we go. He asked, 'What's going on. Why won't she talk to me?' Probably because you're treating her like crap, you dumb shit! I don't know, maybe you should talk to him. I mean sure he's an ass for what he did, but he's obviously worried. He does care for you. I saw that with my own two eyes."

"Just tell him I'm upset and leave it at that. Maybe to him it's insignificant, but it sure isn't to me. He doesn't have to worry every time the phone rings, does he?"

"Okay, it's sent. I can't believe how strong you are, you sure got balls, girl. Remind me never to get on your bad side." Nicki giggled. "Have you figured out what you're going to do?"

She had weighed the pros and cons, even drafted the letter carefully to give his wife all the details in a kind way. All the proof, copies of emails and pictures, sat printed in a pile on her desk. Mulling it over with friends, she still received mixed ideas and with the mysterious phone calls adding to her stress, she hoped something would force a decision.

"He came back with 'What did I do?' Can you believe him? You ask a guy to do one thing that's real important and the dumb shit forgets." Both laughed.

"Shit, he's texting me!" Jade picked up her cell to see a strange code being sent. "What the heck is this? Nicki, I can't read this. It says to receive file go to something or other and type in a code. What is that?" She watched her cell as another two texts with different codes appeared.

"He's sending you your pictures, girlfriend. I guess the boy figured it out." Nicki giggled as she said it.

"I can't receive pictures on my phone! Great, now what," she said and went to her computer with cell phone in hand. Finding the website, she discovered that she didn't have access. "This is great I can't open them on the computer either."

"Text him back and tell him it's not good enough."

As she started typing, her phone line beeped with an incoming call. "Okay girly, I have another call. I'll get back to you later, but thanks for keeping me informed." Jade said goodbye and picked up the beeping line.

"Hello?"

"Hey you, did you get them?" Brady asked.

"Did I get what?" She barked at him. Dammit, why did I pick up? Shit!

"The pictures I just sent, the one's you wanted of my family." He sounded desperate, like a child who suddenly did as told after being asked a hundred times.

"My phone isn't capable of receiving pictures." Her response should have chilled him to the bone. "It's pretty clear you had no intention of sending them."

"I forgot. When you wouldn't answer my calls I got a hold of Nicki and she reminded me."

At least he was being honest, she thought. "You say you're afraid of losing me and with all that's going on you forget about the one thing I ask for?"

"Is that why you haven't been taking my calls? I was worried sick something happened to you and that's why I got a hold of Nicki. Why didn't you just remind me about the pictures?" He sounded frustrated.

"It ain't easy when you're left guessing and not knowing, is it, Buttercup?" Jade snapped at him.

"Wow, you're upset."

"Look at the mess I'm in...your mess! Then you say I need to remind you how to make things better?" She barked. "If I did something to you, I'd sure as shit make up for it right away. I wouldn't ask you to remind me. With all these phone calls, I don't even feel I can answer my phone anymore."

"I get your point. I'm sorry about this all. I promise I'll go home tonight and send you the pictures. I seem to always be hurting you, don't I?" He sounded rushed, talking rapidly.

"Where are you?" She could hear odd noises in the background.

"I'm at the out with the kids."

"This isn't good-you have your kids with you."

"It's okay. After I heard from Nicki I just wanted to send them right away and talk to you to apologize. How have you been?"

"Look, spend time with your boys. You shouldn't be talking to me when you're with them."

"Can I call you later? Will you pick up?" he continued in a playful voice. "Now that I got a hold of you, I want to be sure you'll talk to me again or I won't hang up the phone."

"Do as you promise and I'll pick up." Jade gave her word.

"Okay, I'll talk to you later tonight then."

Hanging up, her thoughts went crazy. What did I do to deserve this? Did this happen for a reason or is it just my shitty luck? Three months ago I was incredibly happy for the first time in years and now I'm miserable.

His text came at ten p.m., asking her to come to the webcam. She didn't race to the computer like she used to, today's conversation proved he had forgotten about her. When his face popped up on the screen, he smiled and waved. In that moment her heart softened, she longed for the time they were happy to share moments like these. Where were the feelings that everything would work out wonderfully? Where did our laughter go? She'd been so angry, but to see his face brought back memories, the good ones.

Jadey: Got two new numbers today from New Jersey and Washington DC
2 Dance: Oh boy
Jadey: Computer said-Mountain Pass, NJ and DC
2 Dance: Cell phones?
Jadey: Land lines-unpublished ones
2 Dance: Could be work, will try to find out
Jadey: What did you tell them, are you blaming me for all this?
2 Dance: Not gonna blame you for any of this
Jadey: That would be the easy out for you though
2 Dance: Just because it's easy-doesn't make it right...calls still in afternoon?
Jadey: 9:41 and at 3:36-I'm afraid to answer-don't want to say the wrong thing
2 Dance: I hear ya. I put you in a mess
Jadey: I don't blame you for it all
2 Dance: Well....I take at least 99%
Jadey: I had hopes, was like a snowball...couldn't stop...the more we talked
2 Dance: I's the one that kept it up without saying a word, so it's my fault
Jadey: If only I wouldn't have kissed you that first time...I attacked ya
2 Dance: Wasn't attacked...sheesh
Jadey: Made ya smile though
2 Dance: Just like you
Jadey: Thought we needed a laugh
2 Dance: Need more than one...

Jadey: It isn't gonna get any easier, is it?
2 Dance: Don't really think so, can't really tell. I'm more confused than ever
Jadey: I just think if I weren't here no more you'd have an easier time
2 Dance: How would it be easier? Think at this point...even without you here, ya still would be here
Jadey: Huh? If I go, I'm gone, no more worrying
2 Dance: I would worry! I care!
Jadey: In 6 months I'd be forgotten and a distant memory
2 Dance: Don't think I'll ever forget you
Jadey: I'll disappear, change my number
2 Dance: NO disappearing!
Jadey: This is so hard...I keep remembering...
2 Dance: I keep playing things over and over again of our time together
Jadey: I was thinking about our drive to dancing today...I wanted just to touch you
2 Dance: Not while driving...sheesh!
Jadey: Pull over...LOL
2 Dance: Lmao
Jadey: Thought I was crazy for thinking it
2 Dance: Wonder what would happen if we could be together
Jadey: I think about it all the time, is it wrong of me?
2 Dance: Hmmm no, was wonderful together
Jadey: Didn't the feelings scare you kinda, that we got along so well?
2 Dance: Not at all.....what's the word...excited, happy, crazy feeling....
Jadey: Lost?
2 Dance: Yep
Jadey: Can only imagine if we were together, I felt so happy
2 Dance: Scary, eh
Jadey: Never been like that...was wonderful weekend
2 Dance: It all was wonderful, every single second, even before we met I knew inside this was special
Jadey: I never felt anything like this before
2 Dance: Makes two of us
Jadey: Really?
2 Dance: Yes, really
Jadey: Thought I was a dork during the weekend...felt so nervous
2 Dance: Not at all Hon
Jadey: Its wrong...but at times I wish...
2 Dance: I wish, hope, dream and fantasize
Jadey: Me too
2 Dance: Play it constantly in my head
Jadey: To be honest, I do too....every moment replays
2 Dance: Do ya ever add to it, like if we saw each other again?
Jadey: I wonder about things

2 Dance: Dangerous, huh

Jadey: I dream and wake up feeling lonelier

2 Dance: Me, too...think the possibilities would be crazy if we could be together

Jadey: The first time you put your hand on my back...I imagine what it would be like always

2 Dance: Yeah...couldn't stop wanting, pure passion and connection

Jadey: Such a close feeling...it was like we were one

2 Dance: Yes it was

Jadey: I met my equal. Thank you

2 Dance: I am glad and fortunate to be able to say the same

Jadey: Do you think we will see each other again someday?

2 Dance: What do you think?

Jadey: Think you'll say no

2 Dance: Don't want to say no, but also don't want the hurt to be constant. Worried about you!

Jadey: You want to see me...but you are afraid of hurting me, huh?

2 Dance: I know sounds crazy, how could I hurt you more after what I have done

Jadey: You don't see yourself leaving your marriage, maybe down the road?

2 Dance: Don't know what to think or do. Can't tell you something when I'm all mixed up

Jadey: Maybe if you kept seeing me, one day you'd decide or maybe if you don't see me you'll miss me...darn, this is hard

2 Dance: Yeah it is, I do miss ya all the time

Jadey: You still don't know if I'm what you need and you may never know if I go away

2 Dance: Don't know what my life needs

Jadey: Would you meet me one last time?

2 Dance: What? To settle everything face to face, like to say goodbye?

Jadey: I'm sorry...don't think I could be around you...oh ya know!

2 Dance: Hon, I get lost too with things. Would be wonderful to see you, but don't know from there

Jadey: Sometimes I feel...I remember so much...everything and how close we are

2 Dance: Feel it too, Hon

Jadey: Why is it we can't let go?

2 Dance: Maybe cause we never felt like this and it feels so right inside

Jadey: Yet it's all wrong on the outside. I can't imagine not ever talking to you

2 Dance: Don't have to tell me...I feel that way too

Jadey: Even through all this...oh I don't know no more

2 Dance: Ya trying to walk away, aren't ya?

Jadey: No, yes, no...I'm trying to understand. Maybe in 6 months you'll miss me and decide things aren't the same without me

2 Dance: Don't think they will ever be the same. Please don't cry, Hon...
Jadey: I'm so confused
2 Dance: Ya saying want a six-month break?
Jadey: Don't know any more. Show me your life...
2 Dance: Will do that right now
Jadey: Do you want me to leave does that make it better for you?
2 Dance: Wouldn't make it better
Jadey: Would make it easier though wouldn't it?
2 Dance: At this point...
Jadey: I haven't done anything
2 Dance: It won't ever be over with you...not sure
Jadey: What do you mean not sure?
2 Dance: I's all mixed up and now these calls started. Would ya friends have said things?
Jadey: My friends wouldn't do anything and family doesn't know yet.
2 Dance: People you contacted or ya friend raised flags...If it's from my end it most likely be my job
Jadey: Well if it's your job....do you trust me to fib?
2 Dance: Has nothing to do with trust...I do trust ya, but ya got no poker face
Jadey: I think you wish I wouldn't have checked things...made a mess kinda
2 Dance: You had every right...the mess is mine. It's all my doing
Jadey: I'll make this better
2 Dance: How?
Jadey: Will talk to my friend ask if he did anything...retrace with the people who investigated and find out if anything has been said.
2 Dance: Stop...
Jadey: Will do whatever it takes to fix this
2 Dance: Take a breath...relax
Jadey: Will make sure your work is okay
2 Dance: STOP! There is nothing you could do or I could do. Even if you check and re-check ya might never know if there was a breach and maybe they just calling to see if you know me. They got your number off my phone
Jadey: I won't leave until I know you're okay
2 Dance: Umm?
Jadey: What?
2 Dance: Nothin'
Jadey: Fibber fox
2 Dance: I don't want you to go even if this all falls out
Jadey: I just need to feel okay again...so angry, then felt bad, then angry again
2 Dance: I'm so sorry
Jadey: Don't frown...this would be easier for me if you were living a happy life

2 Dance: Don't think it will ever be easy. I need to think this all out and need to fix my life
Jadey: The right thing to do is always the hardest. We were brought together for a reason
2 Dance: Guess ya right
Jadey: Maybe I's here to help you somehow
2 Dance: Think I's beyond help
Jadey: You are perfect (the fibbing is not good), but you're human. You just picked the wrong woman...gets feisty and fiery.
2 Dance: Yep...you sure are just like me, feisty and stubborn LOL
Jadey: That we are
2 Dance: Two peas in a pod...you best go to bed its late, thanks for chatting with me
Jadey: Sweet dreams
2 Dance: U2 Hon xoxoxo, I miss ya!

Had it been wrong to talk about seeing him? Am I supposed to ignore what I feel? There's no off switch to shut it down. He said he doesn't want me to leave, but...? I wonder if he's just as lost. He obviously thinks about me so this wasn't about meaningless sex, like a typical cheater. It's hard knowing, but would it have been worse not knowing? With everything out in the open would he make the choice to change his life and get a divorce down the line? He wasn't in love with his wife and hadn't been for years. Maybe once the economy straightened out he could sell his house and change his circumstance. If he stayed with Jenny, it meant life with no intimacy or joy. Many divorced and split the time between parents. It took having feelings to make him see what's missing, just like me. Is that why we met? She wondered.

Receiving the pictures, she opened them to see two miniatures of Brady staring back at her, but the third was harder to look at. For the first time, Jade saw the woman he'd given his life to and tried to picture Brady standing at the end of the aisle. Jenny was average and looked like a lady who lived for her children as most moms did. She didn't fuss with her appearance and having two sons with Brady's genes, she probably kept busy. Do they have his smart-mouth ways?

There were many differences when she compared herself to Jenny. Impossible to gauge what Brady saw in each, the contrasts were staggering. Jenny was an average build while Jade was bigger with curves. Dressed in her sweat-pants and t-shirt, while Jade was stylish. Her long flowing dark hair was opposite to Jenny's short red, tie-it-back look. But what did Jenny feel for Brady, is she unhappy? Her expression showed she'd rather not be in that moment, but is that all moments? If she's unhappy too, they're both wasting time in this short game of life. Why stay and never find real love?

And When

The mystery phone calls stopped within two months without explanation, but Brady still pushed at trying to regain her trust. They argued constantly as she asked the same questions in a different ways. Getting frustrated with forever weighing his words, there was no way she could prove anything. His patience was endless and said if it took a hundred years to repair the damage, he'd do it. She waited to hear that he loved her, but he couldn't tell her with a certainty why he wanted her to stay. Without seeing each other, she didn't have his actions to gauge.

Jade knew exactly what she felt. For every tear shed, every angry word, every twisted feeling, it showed he meant that much to her. Nightly, she lay in bed and asked for help with the mixed-up roller coaster of emotions. What am I supposed to feel? Is he looking up at his ceiling right now, wondering how life could be? He had numbed himself over the years with get up, go to work and come home. Maybe that's punishment enough.

And When

Moving Ahead, Recording the Lesson

Chapter Twenty-four

Jade watched the news of yet another celebrity caught cheating. The infidelity broadcasted to the world in a quick five-minute blurb. Over the months it seemed everyone knew someone who had cheated. Unfaithfulness was a common-place event these days and it was no longer shocking.

It had taken six months of debates, talks and wrestling with it all to come to her decision. It wasn't her responsibility to make things right, it was his. Brady would have to answer one day to someone much higher up. Having searched her soul, she didn't want to hurt his boys or Jenny. Believing that everything happened for a reason, she left karma in charge.

With his secret out, Brady talked freely and often ranted about the debt he faced alone. With Jenny refusing to work, he prayed fall would change that when his youngest attended school. It was a shock to learn tidbits of his life at home and the endless chores awaiting him every night. He did the yard work, cleaning, laundry, and he even made his own meals.

"That doesn't even make sense. You work two jobs, for crying out loud! If I were a stay-at-home mom, you bet meals would be made, the house cleaned and the wash done. I just don't get it, why don't you tell her to get off her ass?"

"I hear ya and I've talked to her many times, she just doesn't see it that way and it ends up in an argument. There's no point even talking," he replied after reiterating a fight they'd had.

"What does she do all day?"

"She takes the oldest to school, then goes back home. When I ask her why things aren't done she says she didn't feel well. Honestly, I don't think she pulled out of the depression after the pregnancy."

"What…she has it made! Come on, depressed for four years? There are medications to get past post-partum." It seemed Jenny was unhappy in life as well.

"Sometimes when she gets upset, she'll throw it all at me, like everything is my fault and she resents me."

"That's nuts! What's wrong with this picture?"

"I used to try to tell her all the time, but I give up." He exhaled in frustration.

"When are you gonna understand that you can't make her better? It takes two. My sister and husband both work to pay the bills and they share responsibilities. It's teamwork." Why didn't he see that? He's vibrant, fun-loving, and I can't imagine him going home to this. Jenny must feel the same way, she thought. Both don't realize they are absolutely miserable.

"I tried to make her understand for years, but I don't bother anymore. I do what needs to be done and keep my mouth shut."

"Have you thought to try to spark up the romance? Like if you came home with flowers and took her to dinner? You know, romance her." Jade hated saying the words, but it's what Brady needed, a friend to help him find a happier life.

"I don't know if I want to. So much has happened, ya know?" He sighed, his voice one of sadness. "I don't think of her that way. I just don't feel…well, I'm not even…I'm not attracted to her and I don't even want to go there."

"You gotta do what's right for you, but you have to start looking at the big picture. This just isn't healthy and it's ridiculous to live unhappy."

"What about you? You're one to talk. You don't look for anyone or date. What about your happiness, Sunshine?"

"I'm not meant to find someone." The hurt pulsed inside. I did find him, he's just an ass, she thought. "I have my writing to keep me busy. Speaking of which, did I tell you I met a man on Friday for coffee and he looked at my books? He loves them and made arrangements for me to meet someone," Jade excitedly revealed the news.

"Who's he setting up the meet with and how did you meet this guy?"

"I met him on that writer site. He's writing his memoir and was supposed to bring it to the coffee shop. I'll read yours, if you read mine kinda thing, but he didn't, which was kinda awkward. He took one look at my work and made a phone call to a lady named Linda, that's who I'm gonna meet. He didn't tell her much just that she needs to see this and I'm to call her Monday."

"I wonder what that means. Maybe she's someone who can help you get these things off the ground."

"Ya think? I have no idea how to go about things."

"I'm keeping my fingers crossed." His voice was filled with excitement.

They ended their conversation and Jade began the work of double checking the work for mistakes. When she wrote, the words raced to the pages, but with reviewing things she noticed the corrections needed. It took three days and many long hours to get the books polished for the stranger, but by the time her appointment came, she was ready.

Walking into the designated meeting place, Jade grabbed a coffee then sat waiting at a little table. It was the end of July, the coffee shop nearly empty. Constantly checking the time, her nerves kicked in. What am I doing here? She's gonna think I'm a nut job, her head kept saying. When she had called on Monday to set up the time, the woman answered with her full name, "Linda Fraser speaking." Jotting the information down, Jade used her computer to see a picture which was tied to many links. Clicking several, her jaw dropped. Linda was an executive at a national magazine.

Jade was still waiting at twenty-minutes past the arranged time and she bashfully dialed Linda's number, who apologized profusely for being late and promised to arrive within ten minutes. Good to her word, she walked in eight minutes later. Friendly, warm, they talked and got to know each other a little. At a pause in the conversation, Jade hesitantly passed Linda the folder containing the first volume. In silence, this stranger read through the first pages and skipped throughout browsing as a multitude of expressions played on her face. Humor, sorrow, frowns...Linda appeared totally engrossed as twenty-minutes ticked by before she spoke.

"How long have you been writing?" Linda asked.

"This is my first attempt."

"You've got to be kidding. This is brilliant! I don't think I've seen anything like it. You have such an easy conversational style that it makes the reader want to continue."

"Really, here I thought you'd tell me I was nuts." Jade snickered.

"I really like this. It's an amazing concept." Linda smiled from ear to ear.

"Well if you like that one, I've done a couple more." She handed the other two volumes over.

"Are you kidding me? When did you start this and how did you come up with the idea?"

Jade explained the motivation and how she tucked them away until the meeting last week. At the end of the two hours, Jade was ecstatic when she left with a list of tasks to accomplish for Linda before their next meeting scheduled in three weeks.

Walking out of the shop, she texted the news to Brady and immediately her phone rang.

"I was waiting for your call. What did she all say?"

Jade rattled on so fast, she thought that she had lost him in the details.

"Congratulations!" His voice took on a serious tone. "Hon, you are destined for great things in this life and I knew it from the moment I met you. You have an amazing personality-that just can't be denied. You're going to make a difference in this world."

Why did he have to say that? She wondered and felt a tug at her heart. "Really, you think that about me?"

"Really I do. You are a remarkable woman. I'm not one to say the mushy stuff and I wouldn't say it if I didn't really mean it."

Unsure about her future, her fan club had officially opened as Brady encouraged her to move forward, full steam ahead. For the next three weeks, Jade worked her full-time job during the day, then until two in the morning every night. Weekends started at eight and finished at three in the morning, nothing stopped her. On that Sunday afternoon, she stood nervously on Linda's stoop, her hands filled with the results of her efforts.

At the antique dining table in Linda's cozy cottage home, Jade went through every bit of homework. Linda reviewed every piece, ecstatic at Jade's ability. When Jade hoisted three more volumes onto the table, Linda's jaw dropped.

"You can't be serious?" Linda stared at the pile before her. "That's unheard of! Most authors take a year to complete one book. In three weeks you've managed to complete three more and all this?" She waved her hand over her now crowded dining room table.

"I want to keep building on the series." Jade felt on top of a mountain having climbed the peak. Maybe God put her in a mess to help her find this hidden talent?

"Do you mind if I take these with me? There is someone I'd like to show them to." Linda sifted through the pile and chose four volumes.

"If it'll help me get these out there then absolutely, but tell me what do I do now? How does this all work? All I know is how to write, kinda."

And When

You Can Call Me Ann

Chapter Twenty-five

Jade finally packed her bags for a vacation a year after the first meeting with Linda. She had talked about this trip many times, but something had always come up to foil the plan. Now, with her books safely in the hands of an agent, she could take a long overdue rest. She looked forward to seeing Nicki in Atlantic City, Sarah in New Jersey, with her first stop, Virginia. It'd been two years of sharing life's ups and downs with Brady. They'd had only short breaks once in a while when they disagreed, but her phone never stopped ringing for long. They'd laugh about their battles, both being stubborn and pig-headed. With the airline and hotel booked, she'd land in Virginia then take the train to New Jersey.

She'd also get to meet Brett, a new friend from Virginia. After meeting on a writer site, they'd spent the past year working together. "Mr. Gadget" she nicknamed him, being a self-proclaimed techno wizard who helped with her books. Without him, it would've taken forever to accomplish everything needed for the agent. Their meeting online was strictly friendship and they offered each other help and support. They'd talk about everything from soup to nuts. She even told him the story of Brady.

Still mired in his loveless marriage, Brady hadn't faltered in contacting Jade, their friendship was strong. It astonished her that a man would keep in touch three years running and even thought about writing Guinness to see if he'd broken any records. With her books on their way, he'd jest about her future fortune and volunteered to invest to set them up for a life of travel, leisure and the ranch. Jade envisioned a life of writing, horses and travel. Brady said he'd keep her on a strict allowance and their humor-filled battles were constant.

What if I did hit it big? The thought played in the back of her mind. Linda predicted her books would top the charts, but Jade wouldn't believe until it happened. Signing the contract with a New York agent, she asked Brady what he'd do if she suddenly would be able to afford the dream.

"Wouldn't that be something, I can see us together as plain as day. You'd be busy writing and I'd manage the horse ranch and at nights we'd curl up together, living the dream," he said.

In reality, they hadn't seen each other in two years and the question always lingered about the connection they shared. The hurt he caused two years ago was a memory. She honestly thought he'd leave her life when she finally decided not to expose things to Jenny. She had braced herself and stopped initiating contact, not wanting him to feel forced to continue in friendship. Leaving it his decision, she shut off the pain and logic won out. There were never going to be answers or guarantees, the turmoil of it all only kept her stuck in hurt. His circumstance and a border separated them. She set new boundaries and let go of romantic illusions. Looking back, she never would've pursued writing without meeting him. Now, the biggest unknown was how they'd feel standing face to face again after so long. Had it fizzled into their comfortable friendship?

There was always the internal voice of doubt, and every few months she'd run his information on the computer. For two years she didn't find a trace. Three months ago, his name appeared on a profile without a picture and that same gut feeling started. Feeling somewhat underhanded, Jade artfully created the phony profile of Just Ann, placing her near Brady's hometown then sent him an email. At first he hesitated, but with time the conversations flowed. When he sent Ann a picture, it confirmed he was on the net again. Taking on a new a lingo and atrocious spelling to hide behind, she mirrored Brady's life. Ann was with someone, but unhappy. Her boyfriend had cheated and they were rebuilding their relationship. Obtaining information about Brady on the sly, Jade needed to be careful not to reveal things during their phone calls.

2 Dance: Hey Sexy!
Just Ann: hi Brady
2 Dance: how ya doin tonight Ann
Just Ann: tired how r u
2 Dance: me too...been a long week
Just Ann: sorry to hear ur worried of ur job in the last mail
2 Dance: me too, it's not a good time since the company is moving
Just Ann: do u stil have a job? where they movin
2 Dance: still employed and in Washington to different building
Just Ann: when they movin
2 Dance: a couple months
Just Ann: so u be keeping ur job?
2 Dance: have other things lined up so I don't worry too much
Just Ann: realy?
2 Dance: got a couple other leads
Just Ann: jobs ain't easy to com by
2 Dance: if you look hard enough, bound to find something or someone
Just Ann: is it local?
2 Dance: one in South Carolina...other is in Texas
Just Ann: lots I no r goin out of town to work, u may move?
2 Dance: yep...see them go too. Not looking for that, but thought is there. I do like Texas
Just Ann: where in Texas

2 Dance: Dallas
Just Ann: that a long ways off
2 Dance: yep
Just Ann: would be easy u bein single n all
2 Dance: somewhat easy, the hard thing is stuff you leave behind
Just Ann: friends n family?
2 Dance: not easy to move to a new place, especially from family. If I get the job...wanna run away with me? LOL

I wonder why he never told me about some job in Texas. I knew he was having difficulties at work due to the economy, but he never mentioned a possible move. Would he disappear? Jade wondered as she placed her words carefully.

Just Ann: don't know
2 Dance: if only it was all that easy
Just Ann: we movd here 3 yrs ago
2 Dance: you will always miss where ya came from
Just Ann: u can start meet people on web- start plans 2 move their
2 Dance: haven't gotten that far...not pointed in that direction yet...besides, wouldn't be right to be looking that way when I'm not there, especially for the other person
Just Ann: i talk to a Colorado man. Is farthest away i talk to
2 Dance: true, can meet from anywhere in the world
Just Ann: u meet any from far?
2 Dance: yep...far as Michigan
Just Ann: tell me about the ladies in u life
2 Dance: not much to tell at this point really just been putting all my effort into work
Just Ann: in ur mail u say u met sum in past-must b storys
2 Dance: oh yes, but that is some time ago from today. Been at least 6 months since I actually met someone
Just Ann: what was last one like
2 Dance: well, she was great, at first
Just Ann: but
2 Dance: ya know the scene...ya catch eyes and she was a city girl. She was on a site playing cards so we talked ...then decided to meet for dinner

Well that was one he met local and the furthest away, Michigan? Jade pushed on to see if he'd admit to a Canadian he held onto.

Just Ann: how long b4 u said no future with her
2 Dance: oh...about two weeks
Just Ann: that quik? no one turned ur head 4 longer?

2 Dance: she didn't really like the country boy style. Tried the long distance thing, but that didn't work out as well.
Just Ann: what was that 1 like
2 Dance: at first really neat...was different, but became one sided in getting there
Just Ann: from where?
2 Dance: New York, got to be lonely going out when they were not around

New York, that's six hours away from him? That's three he'd mentioned in this short conversation. Is this real or make believe? Jade wanted to hear all his secrets.

Just Ann: would u do long distance agin
2 Dance: for the right woman...would do about anything
Just Ann: I am suprise u never met close to right 1. U r good lookin man
2 Dance: I's okay....not all that
Just Ann: I met 1 i realy conect with hes just far away. And some I met won't go away
2 Dance: I know the cling thing
Just Ann: tell me ur cling story
2 Dance: they don't know what they really want...just want attention though
Just Ann: who where when?
2 Dance: Norfolk, middle of last year. She was nice...
Just Ann: ?
2 Dance: went down for the weekend and didn't pick up on the cling thing until it was over
Just Ann: just 1 weekend- how long u date?
2 Dance: started there and went out for two weekends...was still around for the next two months
Just Ann: Is that the longest I have 1 for 3 yrs
2 Dance: really?
Just Ann: from where i use to live
2 Dance: what was wrong with him?
Just Ann: he don't know til I gone how he feel-never knew what i meant to him
2 Dance: ya never really know how you really could miss someone until they have left

That is four women now, one local, one in New York, one in Norfolk, and one in Michigan. He had admitted he talked on the computer many times, but insisted he never met anyone. Jade knew his schedules. He even called when he traveled for work, so how could he have found time to meet all these women hours away from him. How could his wife not know? She analyzed every word internally.

Just Ann: thinc u will fall again?
2 Dance: I always hope I will
Just Ann: I use to know what love is...it disapears tho-starts okay n changes
2 Dance: seems like it's all great, then someone pulls the rug out and the world ain't the same as it was
Just Ann: people change
2 Dance: lot of different ideas on what love is and how to treat people
Just Ann: how u treat the 1s u date in the past
2 Dance: I treat them the way I want to be treated, with respect
Just Ann: but cling ones u got 2 be direct or they stay
2 Dance: blunt works well with some...others just don't hear ya all to well

"Respect," Jade said out loud. "What is wrong with you, Brady?" Is he moving on and looking for someone closer? She'd understand that, but the not telling her definitely wasn't respect.

Just Ann: ever have to tell some 2 leave
2 Dance: shame to admit it but had to. Showed up at work then at the house waiting on the porch...kept wanting to talk and make things right, saying she would change. That's when I knew she was clingy
Just Ann: don't u ever meet one u feel something for?
2 Dance: I have. I wonder how life would be all the time
Just Ann: ur perfect woman, what she look like
2 Dance: don't have a set hair color, height or build
Just Ann: most men have wishs
2 Dance: most men do, but they miss out on a lot if they go by a wish list. Basic thing I don't like is someone who is dependent-I need her to be able to think for herself...Just cause you are with someone, doesn't mean your goals and ambitions have to go away
Just Ann: and?
2 Dance: want someone to share thoughts with. Even to slap me behind the head and wake up for thinking differently, play fight, love tap, wrestle
Just Ann: never done that- u?
2 Dance: yep all for fun...it's been awhile, but was great fun.

Jade instantly thought of their crazy wrestling match in the hotel room. Is he remembering time with me? There was no way someone ended up on his doorstep or his work. His work had guards, and his home, a wife and children. Could most of this be a lie?

Just Ann: what happen with ur marriage
2 Dance: grew apart
Just Ann: how long u married
2 Dance: 8 yrs...
Just Ann: any kids

2 Dance: nope she couldn't have any
Just Ann: how long divorced
2 Dance: almost 3 yrs now
Just Ann: was that a reason for break up
2 Dance: it wasn't the reason but yeah probably had a part in it, think its part of the big plan...u?
Just Ann: i cant have no more, have one but she on her own now
2 Dance: is that a no?
Just Ann: 2 many risks for my age
2 Dance: okay, so if the risks weren't there....would u?
Just Ann: yes with right person but dont mean I can
2 Dance: think health of the person does come first...ya might not be able to, but there's always adoption
Just Ann: most men want own bloodline 2 see themself in kids
2 Dance: well, most men think of themselves and not both parties
Just Ann: would u adopt
2 Dance: tis an option...wouldn't adopt unless both parties were in agreement

Kids, why would he ask if she wanted children? What would it matter? I'm utterly confused. Perhaps he is seriously looking for someone to take on his children if he left his marriage, Jade thought. This is making less and less sense.

Just Ann: u r different where is the man part of u?
2 Dance: pulls out his man card LOL
Just Ann: don't u just hook up?
2 Dance: nope, really don't believe in just sex it's more to me than that...what if it's good and you want more, do you just keep hooking up?
Just Ann: mayb 2 fill a void
2 Dance: so you shut off all feelings?
Just Ann: surprise u never have, mos men do
2 Dance: a long time ago...do have wants and desires
Just Ann: im surprise u never had one nights, if i were single i think id be lookin
2 Dance: just not how I am
Just Ann: i should get goin hell be home soon-great talkin to u
2 Dance: yes it has been...thanks for spending time with me
Just Ann: pleasure, goodnite Brady
2 Dance: sleep well Ann.....hope to see you again

Maybe he used whatever means to convince these women he was genuine, knowing he'd never follow through. His stumbling block was always the love of his children, so why didn't he say he was divorced with children? It would be more plausible if he really was searching for a new partner. Jade just wanted the truth. Over the next while the continued conversations were inconclusive, nothing was clear.

2 Dance : Hey you
Just Ann: u been hidin?
2 Dance: went out dancing on Saturday but didn't stay too long
Just Ann: how u been?
2 Dance: work has me busy lately, wish I could be on here more but need the work
Just Ann: all work no play?
2 Dance: yep, need to get out and play
Just Ann: r u closer to find some one?
2 Dance: nope
Just Ann: u have to get out and find a lady
2 Dance: yep...understand I need to get out there...just not sure
Just Ann: not sure of?
2 Dance: of what to do really...at a point that I am just stuck
Just Ann: u is as free as a bird
2 Dance: ya don't have to be taken to be stuck, Hon...even times when ya free the way is not always clear
Just Ann: go meet n decide, u have 100s to choose from, put u picture up-women will flock
2 Dance: well ya know how the flocking goes
Just Ann: sortin takes time
2 Dance: yeppers...lots of time
Just Ann: u just got 2 find a nice lady
2 Dance: I like talking to you and you are really nice
Just Ann: u 2 but I shuld go, he'll b home in 5 minuts
2 Dance: sleep well....thanks for staying up to talk
Just Ann: night Mr Brady
2 Dance: night Ms. Ann

"Don't you get why Ann is a nice woman? She's me, you dumb ass. Hello?" Jade said as she signed off the computer. It was like a knife through her at times when he never spoke of anyone special. It seemed no one meant anything to him.

She researched bars and clubs in Virginia so that Ann's emails would detail where she went on weekends. Brady's last email said he believed he'd seen her out with her boyfriend. Jade pictured Brady trying to run into her made-up persona. "Humph, serves him right to waste gas money chasing a ghost. If only you knew, you dumb ass!"

On Monday, while out of town on business in California, Brady called Jade at work to ask her to jump a plane and meet him. He'd be there from Tuesday to Friday and she promised to look at flights when she got home. Signing on to her computer, she saw him suddenly pop on her screen, talking to Ann.

2 Dance: HEY!
Just Ann: ur mail said u was gone
2 Dance: just got to California this afternoon now sitting wondering what to do. LOL
Just Ann: how long u there 4
2 Dance: until Sunday evening

He'd told me to make arrangements to come until Friday. With his telling Ann Sunday, Jade probed further.

Just Ann: go out dancin
2 Dance: went down to the bar, bartender was reading a book. There is no dancing place around here
Just Ann: u should'v asked som 1 to go with u
2 Dance: don't have a lady to take
Just Ann: any girl would take u up on free trip to California
2 Dance: I pick Ann
Just Ann: cant, things r gettin better at home 4 me and him
2 Dance: cool...but if ya could? Just getting ya thoughts on it
Just Ann: cant say realy

She knew he'd probably shit himself if Ann agreed. Jade had half a mind to tell him yes, then buy a ticket. What she wouldn't give to watch his jaw hit the floor, seeing her waltz off the plane. If she were rich she would, just to watch him squirm.

Just Ann: hows ur love life
2 Dance: what's a love life? LOL
Just Ann: u r not trying
2 Dance: nah, not really...went dancing the other night
Just Ann: and
2 Dance: was awesome to get on the dance floor
Just Ann: no lady turn ur head?
2 Dance: oh one did, but can only turn it so much
Just Ann: ?
2 Dance: she's married...why I said can only turn my head so much, but she is a great dancer

Just Ann: maybe u may have a chance
2 Dance: no chance if married, even if she said they were splitting....not until it is official. Seen it happen-they say getting separated and then things turn around
Just Ann: u been there?
2 Dance: nope I haven't, but seen a friend dragged around in it. Nope the leaving part has to be on her own
Just Ann: isn't it hard when u see someone and can picture urself with them
2 Dance: oh, it's hard...I always got a picture of that in my mind and how things would be
Just Ann: we got 2 get u settled
2 Dance: that is a big task
Just Ann: find u a nice lady-tall n smart n likes dancin
2 Dance: tall works...dancing is a plus
Just Ann: just dont know what wil hold ur attention
2 Dance: ya gonna be my reference-ya have a big heart and ya willing to work things out to go the distance...ya very caring, there is just something about you
Just Ann: all women r like that
2 Dance: nope not true
Just Ann: we nurture
2 Dance: ya more than a pretty face, Hon

Jade nearly fell of her chair. Does he know it's me? Is he starting to get a clue?

Just Ann: work thru much over the years-life not easy, things change
2 Dance: people let things change
Just Ann: don't let things change...sum people forget others
2 Dance: dunno how they forget
Just Ann: forget to work hard instead of givin up
2 Dance: some work just not to deal. Stay at work longer so they don't have to deal with things at home
Just Ann: i should get going, rick taking me out tonit
2 Dance: was wonderful to catch up with ya, don't want to get ya into trouble
Just Ann: by Brady
2 Dance: niters Ann, have fun

Jade signed off with a heavy sigh. He just admitted he worked long hours to avoid being home. It's funny that he said he wouldn't cross the line if a woman were married. You certainly jumped leaps and bounds over that line with me, she thought. It's like talking to two different men sometimes.

And When

When Brady called Jade on Saturday, she asked when he got home and he said Friday night. His stories didn't add up, was he lying to Ann or calling Jade from California? Sick of not knowing, she started looking at airfares and working out dates. Finding a seat sale, she booked time off then emailed Brady her plan. She'd fly into Dulles for a day in Virginia and they'd do lunch or dinner, then she'd hop a train to visit her friends. Monday's phone call didn't go the way she expected.

"One day? Why only one day? And seriously…'We can do lunch or dinner?'" Brady said angrily.

"You're busy and I don't want to interrupt things. This way we could at least catch up then you continue on with normal life." If you only knew I'm Ann, you'd be happy it's just one day, she thought.

"Why spend all that money to come here if you're only going to stay one day?"

"Nicki and Sarah want me to visit and you work all the time. How long would you expect me to stay?"

"At least a week, if not more," Brady replied instantly.

"A week, how would that work? There are things I'd like to see while I'm down there, but you have enough with juggling everything."

"Don't worry about my schedule, that is my life and I'll worry about it. I say at least one week, maybe two."

"One whole week," she whispered while tossing the idea around. With knowing he played on the net maybe it would be good. "I could go to your games and pretend I don't know you. Be a spectator kinda thing and I could ask Brett to take me to Washington to be a tourist. Are you sure, Brady?"

"I'm totally sure. Think of how fast the first meet went. We only had three days and that wasn't enough. I want way more time."

"That was different. I never wanted that weekend to end." The memory danced around in her head. "Are you serious about this, because I plan on going online tonight and booking? I'm not kidding." Is this right, is this wrong? She asked silently. Would he even be there or leave me high and dry?

"I say book it. That is, if you're not chicken?" He started making clucking sounds.

"Okay, Buttercup, I'm booking it. I ain't no chicken."

They ended their conversation talking about the plan. He probably assumed something might wreck the plan as it had every other year. Maybe he expects it to fall apart, but little did he know, nothing would stop her from stepping on a plane. It's time to stand face to face. Jade booked an airline ticket to arrive at Dulles Airport and depart from Atlantic City, then immediately called her friends to let them know the dates.

"Woo hoo, my best friend from Canada is coming," Nicki screeched.

"Are you sure it's okay, I don't want to put you out or anything?"

"Are you kidding me? It's not the Ritz, but my door is open." Nicki sounded excited. "So what's the plan, have you talked to Brady?"

"I told him I'd come for a day, ya know, just to see him face to face, but he wants me to stay a week, if not more." It sounded strange saying it out loud and she expected Nicki to yell at her.

"He hasn't seen you in two years, so of course he wants to spend time with you. You gonna tell him you're Ann and that you know he's playing again?"

"I don't know. I wonder how he's planning to make time to see me. He works two jobs so what is he gonna do, stop in between? When I asked him, he said it isn't up to me to worry about his schedules."

"Well he's right, if he's asking you to come for a week then leave it to him to figure it out."

"Nicki, what if he leaves me high and dry at the airport? Who's to say he'll even be there?"

"I don't think he'd do that. He's been talking to you for years so obviously the man cares for you or he wouldn't keep dialing your number. You'd get to see his life, but of course you never know. If you look at the whole thing all together, he said he'd come to Atlantic City and he even made extra time for you by coming early. I know he's an ass for being a lying schmuck, but do you honestly think he'd desert you? You guys are friends."

"I'll talk to him more. It's two months away and if I get a sense he's not going to meet me, I'll spend a night in Virginia then take the train to your house early, if that's okay?"

"Absolutely, you don't even have to ask," Nicki reassured.

"Okay, I'll let you know more once I get more info from him. I can't thank you enough."

Next, she dialed Sarah's number. "Hey Lady, I booked a flight tonight, so how do you feel about seeing me end of July?"

"Baby, that's great, that'll work out perfect because I leave for Georgia mid-August." Sarah's voice relayed her excitement. "Now I hope ya don't mind, but I don't live an exciting life or nothing, so you'll probably just be sitting around a lot."

"I could care less if we do nothing the entire time I'm there. I'm coming to see you. You know me, I have no life. Between work and the books, I haven't been out in how long?" Her social life would start again someday. With her books, there'd hopefully be travel, new people to meet and somewhere along the way she'd maybe find another Brady, one who was ready for her.

"So have you talked to Brady about this, does he know you're coming out?" Sarah listened while Jade explained it all.

"Baby, the man has been calling you for years. Do you think he's not going to show when he can actually see you? You're crazy if ya think that. Remember were talking about men, they're all about the visual."

"I know, but with seeing how he plays with Ann, I gotta wonder what's real. It darn near tears me apart thinking he's lying, but I don't know if he's lying to Ann or to me, I have no idea."

"There is no telling what the truth to that man is. He's married and alone still, his life is a mess. He is lonely, miserable and trying to find happiness. I feel for the guy, because he's in the same situation many people are when they find out they made a mistake. Lots of people get stuck in life and don't know how to get out of it. He's your friend and always will be."

"If he finds a hundred different women to talk to or be with, there's nothing I can do. I think I'm going there to say goodbye in a way. Not totally goodbye, just to end the future stuff he always talks about." She'd given this much thought. "Face it, Sarah, I live far away. I am connected to him, but he hasn't changed his life so he doesn't want anything more. There's no point in talking about things like that and I need to explain that to him."

"I know. You got put in a bad place and I have no doubt he loves you. Right now he's stuck in the wrong place, but you never know what the future holds. Look at you with your books. Things may change one day down the road and maybe you'll cross paths again. Hell, you could move closer and maybe then he'll be ready."

"Can you imagine?" Jade snickered at the thought. "I'll be rich and buy the house right across the street from him, just because I can. He'll drive by every day as I sit on the front porch sipping umbrella drinks." They burst out laughing.

"Oh, I can see it now, you'd be torturing the man," Sarah said chuckling.

"Yep, I'd make friends in the neighborhood and maybe ask him to tend to my house while I jet off to Hawaii for the winter. Living life, having the dream and he'd watch it all. Better yet, I'll build the ranch just outside of town where he'd see the horses every day. Maybe he could walk me down the aisle if I meet my dream man. He could give me away, wouldn't that be something? He'd regret not making the right choice then," Jade said with a laugh.

Sarah's chuckling stopped. "Honestly baby, I think he regrets not making it now. I could tell by watching you two, he really loves you. It's just sad he never did anything about it. What man spends all these years keeping in touch if not for love?"

"I have no doubt he felt something for me, but maybe it's changed. He hasn't seen me in two years and he's obviously talked with others. Maybe he's trying to replace me."

"You'll never be replaceable lady, you are one of a kind and he knows that. I don't know what will happen with you two. I just hope one day you find someone who will never let go." Sarah's hopeful voice still looked for a fairytale ending. "I know you're in a tough spot and I wouldn't have the courage to do what you're planning. I would have a hard time standing face to face and letting go of a dream."

Sarah had met that one man who altered her life years ago. They'd lost touch over time then bumped into each other again and maintained a close friendship ever since. Some people just aren't forgettable and always hold a place in your life, that's who Brady is.

"I'm hoping I have the courage. There's no telling what I'll feel looking at him. I may not feel anything, or I might slap him across the face and tell him the truth about Ann. I told him a long time ago I would always be there for him as long as it was the truth. When I found his name on the site I told him I understood and asked him outright if he was on the net. He flat out said "No," and I know it isn't the truth. So I'm going to focus on my books and hope one day my life takes off in a different direction." Maybe Brady would have to sit back and watch her dreams take hold before he figured out what she meant to him, but it would be too late. "Sorry for ranting, I just get lost with things."

"No need to say anything, I feel your pain. I'm looking forward to seeing you again and be sure when you're down there to keep me posted. If there's anything that makes you uncomfortable you come straight here, you've got a place to come to if you need." Sarah offered her home as an escape.

"Thank you Sarah, I just may need to jump a train sooner than I think."

And When

The Plans of Goodbye

Chapter Twenty Six

2 Dance: woo hoo!
Jadey: hiya Hon
2 Dance: hiya, *wolf whistles*
Jadey: your cam froze
2 Dance: ya made it!
Jadey: did not!
2 Dance: uh huh...brrrrrrr
Jadey: okay says your webcam is not available?
2 Dance: please deposit another 25 cents and the window will go up...LOL
Jadey: there he is
2 Dance: ya sooo blue though
Jadey: blue housecoat, Buttercup
2 Dance: hmmm...tis not the color...tis what's inside-dang, think I need to work for hallmark
Jadey: LOL
2 Dance: Ut oh...see leopard underneath Hon
Jadey: oh ya know- 'tis just jammies
2 Dance: nice!
Jadey: you seen 'em, I wore it the first night
2 Dance: hmmm, first night of what?
Jadey: been so long ya forgot, must be getting old...LOL
2 Dance: oops froze again
Jadey: some expert you are, try again...says not available
2 Dance: hmmm...I get an error message too
Jadey: wasup with that?
2 Dance: there we go. Get your money ready for our race-$20 bucks!
Jadey: I'm getting into shape...you just might lose that race
2 Dance: let's see ya progress
Jadey: don't know if you'll see with what I'm wearing
2 Dance: nope...can't really....think ya need to take it off...lmao
Jadey: don't think you remember me enough before to make comparisons
2 Dance: oh...I measured!
Jadey: I's getting muscles, see biceps
2 Dance: wow you look good, Hon! Legs are looking good too, but ya know....
Jadey: what I know?
2 Dance: ya still gonna owe me $20 LOL
Jadey: calves have big muscles, can outrun ya
2 Dance: don't think so
Jadey: oh ya know!
2 Dance: I got power and speed

Jadey: you may be fast, but you'll be watching the girls jump all over
2 Dance: nope.....watch that from the finish line...get the front view angle
while I hear the Bay watch theme in the background LOL
Jadey: are we racing in swimsuits?
2 Dance: u certainly can
Jadey: I gots a Speedo picked out for ya!
2 Dance: oh no!
Jadey: orange one, soooo cute
2 Dance: if that's the case...then I got a piece of floss ya can wear
Jadey: Canadian racing attire if'n we're gonna do this right
2 Dance: does it got a maple leaf on it?
Jadey: it's just a maple leaf
2 Dance: <only does stars and stripes
Jadey: I'm gluing it to ya!
2 Dance: a loin cloth?
Jadey: just one leaf LOL
2 Dance: uh huh, don't matter, not gonna be able to see it from behind
anyhow
Jadey: oh ya know
2 Dance: nothing but the tail lights. LOL
Jadey: bring ya cash smarty-pants
2 Dance: will hold a hankie for ya for when ya lose
Jadey: won't you be eating crow when I win
2 Dance: lmao....come to your senses yet?
Jadey: I'm gonna be timing myself at gym on the treadmill
2 Dance: how far we running 100-200?
Jadey: 100
2 Dance: meters or feet?
Jadey: meters of course-endurance a lil bit, oh yeah, you's old now...LOL
2 Dance: I'll be the star...
Jadey: don't count ya chickens, Buster Brown!
2 Dance: ya just gonna see a puff of smoke-oh, and bring American cash,
US$
Jadey: no Canadian money? It's good up here ya know
2 Dance: yep.....good in only one place-unless ya pasting it on ya
Jadey: Oh my God!
*2 Dance: dollar bill tassels *pokes**
Jadey: Not!
2 Dance: Is it just me or is it getting really hot in here?
Jadey: it's you...ya brat
2 Dance: I love it when you type real slow, getting kerflufelled? LOL
Jadey: do you wonder what it will be like to stand face to face?
2 Dance: oh, if I told ya...ya wouldn't sleep tonight
Jadey: so ya do miss me?
2 Dance: ya got that right! Oops time for bed Hon, it's late

Jadey: thanks for surprising me tonight was good to see ya
2 Dance: ya welcome...thnx for coming out to chat
Jadey: night Hon
2 Dance: xoxoxo.....sleep well

She marveled at how completely different his tone was compared to the conversations with Ann. Watching him on the cam, he looked like a child at a toy store, even his eyes smiled, he seemed anxious to see her. There's no way he's fibbing, she thought. Ann gets cautious Brady, I get the real one. In a week they'd be face to face again. Will he still be able to tell what I'm thinking? She wondered, hoping she'd have a poker face by then. He suggested a trip away to an amusement park or the beach on the weekend she arrived. Anything you'd like is fine with me, she told him. Not wanting to leave anything to chance, she started looking at hotels, wanting a back-up plan just in case.

"There's no telling how this will play out," Brett said one evening as she explained her doubts.

"I don't know if he'll plan something or not. I just think it's smarter to have something booked in case it all falls through. Honestly, who's to say he even shows up at the airport at all?"

"I can't speak for him because I don't know the man, but any guy that keeps in contact for three years isn't going to leave you stranded. If he does, you can always call me and I'll pick you up," he offered.

"I can't ask you to do that."

"Look, just take my number with you and that way you have it, but I bet you any money he'll be waiting anxiously to see you. From what you've told me, he's been a good friend for years, so obviously he cares."

"You're right, I'm sorry I'm all over the place, wondering about everything. I just want to be sure, that's all." She agreed to take his number along and after she hung up, she researched hotels from the list Brett gave her.

--Jade wrote:

I don't want to interfere with your life...the last thing I want is take away an income you need. I can find a hotel and share time when you fit me into your schedule. I'll be a spectator and simply watch at a distance. Even dancing, I could find my way and be a tourist enjoying the atmosphere. I'll strike up conversations with others as I watch you dance on your home turf. I just want to see your life and look you eye to eye again.

We talk of big dreams, but the likelihood is one in a million and with time, life changes so many things. Ya never know where we'll be a year or two from now. Who knows what tomorrow brings?

I don't want you to fuss. I can even stay just the one day as I originally planned. I'll adjust to whatever you decide. Time doing whatever you please is fine...whether riding a roller coaster, lounging at a beach, whatever. Please don't feel you have to make excessive plans around me, I can take care of myself. It might even be easier for you if I just happen along at various events. Think on it, I can handle whatever you wish.

Have a great day,
J

"I see your hamster just hasn't stopped, has it?" was Brady's first comment when she answered the phone the next evening. "I told ya, don't you worry about any part of my schedule."

"I don't want my coming there to..."

"Hush! I told ya I got it all figured out." He cut her off.

"But I found a hotel with an awesome weekly rate. I know you said you may want to go away, but it's cheaper to book this place for seven days than for five."

"Which hotel is it?"

"The Grand in Manassas, it's got a kitchenette and that way I can go about my day without all the restaurant expense. It even has a pool and a bar to keep me entertained. I might as well soak up some sun." The hotel was conveniently located near a train station so that she could escape if needed.

"I know that hotel, it's just off the highway, but it's a bit far away from Fairfax. There's shopping right around there and it's close to restaurants. How much is it?"

"It's regular $117.00 per night, but if I prepay for seven days, it goes down to $59.99." Jade was happy with the price; the hotels were too expensive closer to where he lived.

"That is a good deal! If you book it and we go away for the weekend, it's still cheaper than just the five nights. We could even leave some of your bags there until we get back."

If he doesn't show, I'd have a pool and I'll book a rental car to get around. "Should I book it then? That way if you end up busy with stuff, I'll have everything I need close at hand."

"You can book it, but I won't end up busy. Do you think I'd let ya come out all this way and not have a plan?"

"Just covering the bases, ya know. Who's to say something doesn't come up to side-track you?"

"There will be nothing to side-track me. The only thing to do that is a Canadian." He laughed heartily.

"Now wait just a minute! If anything, you've side-tracked me several times." She chuckled, but hoped he'd get the drift.

"We shall see. I didn't get your itinerary so what time does your flight arrive?"

"I land at four in the afternoon, so around four thirty by the time I'm out of the airport. I'll send you a copy of it by email."

"That is the busiest time of the day. It'll probably take us an hour to get out to Manassas."

"Should take a cab to the hotel?" she asked, thinking it would eliminate anyone needing to be at the airport and she'd be in charge.

"Absolutely not, do you know how expensive that would be? I'll be there when you land," Brady said firmly.

"On the map, the hotel is twenty miles away, if that."

"Uh huh, that would be twenty minutes in no traffic. You're coming to the big city now and the line-ups here get crazy," Brady teased.

"I'm renting a car so I can venture out shopping and drive into Washington."

"You won't want to drive to D.C.-it'll be easier to take the train."

"What do ya mean? I can drive."

"Hush, never you mind, shut off that hamster of yours," Brady joked, playfully taking charge.

"But…"

"Shhh!" he interrupted.

"Okay, okay."

"Glad to hear it," he said with a smirk in his voice. "You'll be on American ground, so I'll worry about stuff."

"You do realize we'll be doing things the Canadian way this time, right?"

"Nuh uh, American soil, American rules, just how it is, Sunshine."

"Well, Buttercup, since you don't come up to Canada to visit and probably never will, this time it's my way. You haven't seen me in two years and I'm not that shy woman ya met the first time."

"Ya think so? I do believe that will all change once you step off the plane, oh brave one."

"You watch me, I's way smarter. I know way more this time than last. I think you'll be impressed with how in control I'll be."

"We shall see," he said in a sarcastic way. "Just so you know I planned everything ahead of time because the week before you get here, I have to help move my grandfather to an assisted living place. I'm flying out to Wyoming on Sunday and will be back Tuesday."

"Brady, your family comes first so if this is a bad time, I can change my plan and simply visit with Nicki and Sarah."

"Don't you dare," he warned. "It's been hard with Gramps not being the same man I grew up with, so I need a break. It's funny, but I remember so many things like when I was a boy, I used to follow him around on the ranch and watch everything he did. I even bagged my first deer with him. Now he doesn't even recognize me, it's awful. I'll just go help to get it done, but I made sure to be back in plenty of time. I think I'm due to enjoy a bit of life and could use having my best friend around."

"Okay then. Will I get to go with you if you have to work at night? I'd really like to see you in action. Maybe we can even go to your favorite dance hall and I can watch you dance."

"Of course you can, but I can just imagine it. No yelling at the umpire," Brady said with a chuckle.

"Well what fun is that? I gotta give you a bit of a hard time, don't I?"

"Here it comes. I can see ya now standing up and hollering at my calls or at the bar I'll be on the dance floor and see the men flocking all over you. Some vacation I'll have!" They both laughed.

After they hung up, she hoped seeing his grandfather would be a wake-up call to find happiness. Life creeps up unexpectedly. What happened in a blink of an eye with her dad could happen again, and smiling every day is what really mattered.

As the days flew, she tried to gain more information as Ann, only to find Brady rarely on the computer. Leaving several messages, Ann received only one response saying he needed to deal with a family issue then his profile was gone, deleted from the site. Not having the luxury of poking and prodding, Jade was on her own.

When the countdown to her trip finished, she felt a peace settle over her. This was a long time coming and tomorrow she'd be stepping on a plane. These past months talking with Brady eased into a comfortable calm. With only one day separating them, there was no crazy rush of excitement like the first time. Instead, there was a sadness he wasn't privy to and she kept her cards close to her chest. Her flight would leave at six in the morning and she took the evening before to pack, needing to be at the airport two hours beforehand. Both suitcases stood at the door when her phone rang.

"You all ready, Sunshine?" The excitement in his voice was clear and she could almost envision his smile.

"Yep, are you excited? At this time tomorrow we'll be sitting having dinner."

"Yes I am! But with two layovers, it'll be ten hours for you to get here."

"I'll sleep on the planes."

"Oh, your hamster will be too excited, so you'll probably be dead tired by the time you land."

"Actually I don't think I'll have much of a problem. You'd be surprised at how calm, cool and collected I am."

"Can you text me to let me know you're on schedule? I'll keep circling the airport until I know you're here. Do you want me to meet you by the baggage or outside?"

"I'll meet you outside; it'll save you having to park."

With everything set, the only unknown was seeing Brady. Playing out different scenarios in her head, she decided that she'd deal with whatever reality happened.

And When

Explosions of the Heart

Chapter Twenty-seven

Jade woke hearing the landing announcement on the second leg of her journey. Next would be the flight that would take her into Dulles. After thirty minutes going through customs, she sat at a little restaurant next to her gate and ordered a sandwich and a drink. Within two hours she'd see him, she sent the text letting him know everything was on schedule. His "Woo hoo, text me when ya land" came a minute later. As she sipped her drink, a group of business men sat next to her discussing the day's meeting and how they couldn't wait to get home to Virginia. One gentleman said hello and she passed the time in conversation with them all. Hearing their familiar southern accents, she couldn't help but smile.

Jade touched up her make-up on the last leg, wondering if Brady would see right through her. The compact mirror showed a much wiser woman, someone he wasn't expecting. With the captain's landing announcement, she tucked away her belongings and looked out at the expanse of Virginia, which seemed to go on forever, stretching as far as she could see.

With her carry-on in hand, she followed the crowd, taking in the architectural beauty of the building along the way. This was the airport the world's elite traveled to and from. It showed with polished floors and brilliantly sculpted ceilings through a maze of brightly lit tunnels.
The luggage area boasted sixty carousels and asking a porter, she was sent the wrong way and forced to back track, delaying her. After she found her bags she texted Brady.

Walking out of the airport, Jade was instantly hit by the incredible heat and humidity. Placing her luggage on the curb, she checked her phone, not seeing a word. Twenty minutes later, she decided he'd left her high and dry and began to dial Brett's number when a familiar car appeared. Looking up, he exited his car and swiftly put her suitcases in the trunk then opened the passenger door.

"How come you didn't text me you were here?" He asked as he got into the driver's seat.

"I did!" Jade showed him the phone, proving she'd done so twenty minutes ago.

Picking up his phone, a message had just arrived. "Wow, twenty minutes, you must be roaming."

"Well, Buttercup, I'm here," she smiled and he leaned over to peck her on the cheek.

"Did you have a good flight?"

"It was long, but I managed to get some sleep."

"I was gonna say you don't look tired at all." He gave her a sideways smile as he drove out of the busy airport area.

"It's really beautiful here, not what I pictured at all." Pristine buildings, trees, shopping malls and…the traffic! "I can't believe the amount of cars on the road ahead, there's taillights for miles."

"I told ya it gets crazy here, but I'm going to take a back way to avoid all this." He turned to look into the next lane and shifted to an off ramp. "What did you picture Virginia as?"

"I thought it'd be more cement and not so many trees. Man, it's hot here though," she said as she took off her lined jacket. Wearing a short black skirt and shirt, sensible flat patent leather shoes for walking, the printed jacked and matching handbag finished the look. The forecast on her weather channel had told her to dress in lightweight clothing.

"You look wonderful, Hon," Brady said with a smile, his eyes hidden by his sunglasses.

"How was your day, were you able to get everything done since you had to leave early to get me?"

"Do you not think I would? I knew what time you landed and actually got here around four. I knew you'd be awhile getting your bags, so I circled a few times before I saw ya just standing there. I was like, why didn't she text me she was waiting?" He snickered. "But I could feel it when ya landed. I instinctively knew the Canadian was here."

"I bet that radar of yours went off."

"Uh-huh…it was like the hairs on the back of my neck stood straight up." He lifted his hand to the back of his neck as if to smooth them down. "Yep, da Canadian's landed." He laughed and she gestured to poke him in the eyes.

An hour later they pulled into Manassas. The hotel was off the highway on a side road, next to restaurants and gas stations. Brady pulled into the driveway and stopped at the front door, telling her to check in. Going through to the reception area, she saw the clerk off to the left and a comfortable seating area with couches and TV on the right, tastefully decorated in creams and blues. Through the glass doors at the far side of the room, the green blue water of the pool danced with glimmering sunlight.

"Room 216 around the back corner," she announced as she got back into his car.

They parked then stepped through a single door into a small patio area which serviced several rooms and a stairway that lead to the second and third level. Her room was average with a king- size bed, TV, easy chair and desk.

"This isn't too bad," she said as she laid her cases in the corner and checked the kitchenette. "It's not the Ritz, but it'll do." She turned to see Brady switching the air conditioning on full and remove his sunglasses.

"I guess it's alright, at least it looks clean," he said as grabbed the remote and sat in the easy chair.

Jade settled backwards on the bed facing the TV, with a pillow tucked under her chin. Soon after, Brady grabbed the remaining pillows and went to lie next to her.

"It sure is good to look into your eyes again." She took him in. His eyes still sparkled, his hair had a few more greys, but he looked great and there was never a more attractive man. "So Buttercup, what's the plan? You said I didn't have to worry about anything." She watched a hesitation pass over his face.

"I wasn't able to get away this weekend so I need to work a bit. Don't worry though, it won't be for long."

"Whatever, I'm here to see my best friend. Am I going to be able to watch?" An uncomfortable look danced across his expression.

"I don't think that would be a good idea, Hon. Lots of people know me," he replied softly.

"I'll go shopping or up to Washington. Brett said he'd take me there." She had expected he'd change things, even planned for it. The fact he didn't leave her standing at the airport was enough for now.

Suddenly she saw a flare of playfulness in his eyes and in one swift movement he jumped to straddle her with one leg on either side of her thighs. The rematch from two years ago, she rolled him off as their laughter started.

"Come on Sunshine! I thought you've been working out?" His words were broken as he struggled to keep her in place. She got out of every hold by twisting, turning and bucking until finally he held her down with the sheer weight of his body.

"Sure…pick on the girl who traveled ten hours and has been up since two in the morning!" She tried to appeal to his sense of fair play.

"Uh huh, blame the lack of sleep," Brady said with a big smile, his eyes victorious at besting her.

Her legs were beneath the bulk of him lying across her. His upper body pinned her chest and left arm. Holding her right hand around the back of her head, with his left he tickled her. There was no way out, Jade gave him the win.

With her submission, he moved his weight off, keeping his legs with hers as he did two years ago, winding them together. Fingers laced gently through the hand behind her head, they stared at each other. The hilarity and fun changed.

He's so perfect, she thought. His hair tousled, hazel sparkling eyes, she felt his legs move along hers slowly. Unable to resist, she raised her head to let their lips touch. Her heart swelled and broke in the same moment. There'd be no future…no hope…no forever.

Crushing her mouth with a need held onto for much too long, his tongue was almost brutal in its force. Winding his arm around her back, his chest pushed down against hers. Through his ragged breaths she heard his moans as she touched the silk of his hair, her fingers remembering its feel. Breathless, Brady pulled back.

"You are so fucking beautiful," he whispered. His mouth barely touched her lips, moving from side to side with tenderness, as if deciding if he should kiss her. Lifting himself further, his fingers gently moved a strand of hair from her face. As his eyes captured hers, she could see a struggle within and she remained perfectly still under his scrutiny. Is he afraid? Is he unsure? Figure it out, Brady, her mind demanded.

His fingers weaved through the back of her hair and pulled her upwards to meet his mouth. As he was kissing her deeply, a slow invasion of her senses started as her pulse matched his thrusting tongue. He breathed deeply and when he groaned again, abruptly he broke contact and sat back to straddle her legs watching her. His fingers roughly ran through his hair, his gaze never wavered, their eyes still locked.

She moved her hands slowly up his chest then down to his sides. Taking hold of the bottom of his shirt, she pulled it up over his head. Half sitting, her fingers traveled from his shoulders down his arms then back to his chest. Lost in the beauty of him, he shivered at her touch and she glanced to see his eyes close. Sliding her right hand down his abdomen, she unbuttoned, then loosened the zipper of his jeans. Opening his eyes, a smoldering gleam appeared as she reached inside to feel him. The hardness of him between her fingers, she stroked him gently, watching his lip quiver as he moved forward ever so slowly to kiss her.

Forcing her hand from its exploration, he pulled her shirt over her head then reached behind to unhook her bra. Gently pushing her onto her back, he brought the straps forward from her shoulders and put the garment aside. His hands moved to her breasts, his thumbs grazed their hardened tips. Wanting no barrier between them, she pushed downwards at either side of his waistband and he stood to remove them then he pulled her skirt and panties off. Jade felt completely beautiful as he looked down at her from the side of the bed with warmth and desire.

"You are so fucking perfect," he said as he slowly crawled on top, his arms supported him at either side of her. Lowering his head, his tongue slowly swirled around a nipple as he positioned himself between her legs. She needed him like the very air she breathed, her hand reached down to guide him.

"Shhh," he whispered barely audibly, then kissed her.

"I…can't…wait," she pleaded softly in between their kissing, her fingers splayed on his back, her body arched towards him. "Please…don't make me wait."

Brady slowly entered her then remained still as a shiver started from her core. She'd waited for this moment much too long. When her lids fluttered open again, their eyes locked and the connection passed between them, it was undeniable. His mouth found hers and he kissed her until she moaned softly from the intensity. As he started to move, the trembling in his body matched the electric current running through hers. Unable to control it any longer, her body shook from within and his mouth muffled the sound of her pleasure as he thrust deeply a final time and held her tight, finding his own release.

What both had craved for years, took only minutes to fulfill. As Brady's body quivered in the aftermath he gently caressed her face. His gaze intent, taking in every line, every freckle, he kissed the tip of her nose and softly brushed her lips. Rolling to his side with his arm around her, he cradled her to him as their breathing slowed. His hand roamed gently over her body, his leg over hers, keeping her still. Supporting his head with one hand, his eyes followed his fingers and when she reached for him, he placed her hand at her side.

"Relax," he whispered with his lips at her temple.

Fingers drifted lightly over her chest then continued downward to slowly stroke between her legs. Her eyes fluttered at the reaction as her muscles began to spasm.

"Enjoy," he whispered.

She watched him until she couldn't focus. Seeing his eyes dance with desire, she closed hers in sheer delight. "You're so incredible," he voiced softly as her body arched and she gasped for breath. Lost in ecstasy, he whispered loving words against her skin. Her brain, a mix of sensations and thoughts jumbled together. Is this love? I've never…. With her nerves sizzling, she thought she'd die from pleasure.

He refused to let her touch him until her body shook repeatedly, almost violently. Only then did Brady roll onto his back and bring her on top of him. Her quivering body pushed beyond anything she'd ever known, wanted nothing more than to feel him. She heard his deep groan as she joined them and his tender words escaped as she moved. Her body followed its own rhythm, guided by pulses within, his hips moved to meet her frantic pace. Grabbing her hair to bring her mouth to his, his tongue out of control, he held her tight and thrust upward until he groaned in release.

On his chest listening to his uneven breathing and rapid heartbeat, embraced tightly in his arms, when he eased she moved to his side to let her racing pulse slow. He wrapped himself around her then covered both of them with a blanket crumpled from the side of the bed. They lay silent for some time.

"You're incredible," Jade whispered, the backs of her quivering thighs nestled against the front of his.

And When

"You're the crazy one, you do this to me," he whispered. She felt his smile as the hand that slowly stroked her side, squeezed her ribs playfully.

"Nuh-uh, you started this, you're the crazy one."

Had they never met she'd not be in her current predicament. She had got on the plane this morning knowing this would be the last time she'd ever feel this. Lying safely in the circle of his arms now, she realized how horribly hard this was. It sounded so rational only hours ago. If I truly love him, I have to let him find happiness and forsake my own. His body like a glove with hers, he wound his legs through hers to get even closer.

Why? A single silent tear slid down her face and she turned her face into the pillow to wipe it away. I need to stop that or he'll know something's wrong, she lectured. Clearing her mind, she tried to memorize the feel of his arms, wanting to soak up enough to last forever.

An hour had passed when her stomach growled, bringing her back to reality and they giggled at the noise. "Umm Buttercup, can we get something to eat? I haven't had anything but a sandwich today and it seems I'm ravenous."

"Me too," he said, smiling against her skin. "Seems the Canadian causes quite the appetite," he said kissing her shoulder as his hand squeezed her thigh. "What do you feel like eating?" He nuzzled the side of her neck.

"Do they make a good steak down here?"

"Mmm...I could definitely go for a steak."

In the shower, Jade was careful to not wet her hair or it'd be another hour before she'd be ready. She toweled off and left the bathroom to dress. It was almost 8:00 p.m. Holy crap, we spent hours love-making, no wonder I'm famished, she thought. Hearing the shower start, she stepped outside to have a cigarette in the incredible heat of the night air.

From her perch on the stairs that led to the second level, she could see the illuminated patio where five men were at one picnic table drinking. They glanced when they heard her come out and she could hear their mumbled voices in the distance. A strange noise caught her attention from a tree in the courtyard only steps away. Not the chirping of a bird, it was a long, winding sound a child's wind-up toy would make. It lasted several seconds and was like nothing she'd ever heard. I'm in Virginia and from the stories Brady told me, there are many weird creatures around, she thought. He often said that he'd have to get rid of the snakes and critters on their ranch or she'd never come outside with him. She recalled the picture of a furry creature he'd sent, a fuzzy, gray/brown animal much larger than a rat, but smaller than a cat. He took a picture and captioned it, "Look what I got!"

Another time, while talking on the phone late at night, Brady was attacked by bats as he stood trying to capture an image of one of them diving at him. They had laughed hysterically that night as he gave the play-by-play. "'Okay…here he comes…shoot, missed him.'" It went on for an hour, both making fun of the situation.

The worst memory was when he went to borrow a friend's boat and trailer. He called that night as usual and throughout the conversation she teased him as he tried to fix the wiring in the dark. Making fun of his predicament, she jabbed at him as he fumbled with a flashlight, screwdriver and electrical tape as she pictured it all in her head.

"Oh my God!" he suddenly said. There was dead silence. Being on a phone 2000 miles away she couldn't imagine what made him react like that; she'd never heard that tone from him.

"What's wrong, what-oh my God?"

"Shh!"

In the tense couple moments before he spoke, Jade was actually afraid, feeling the hairs stand up on the back of her neck.

"What the hell is that?" he whispered very softly into the phone, like he was afraid whatever it was would hear him. She could hear his breathing change as he went on very quietly. "There is something at the edge of the road staring at me," he whispered as if he was holding his breath as he spoke. "Oh my God," he paused. "The eyes are gleaming red."

His tone scared the living daylights out of her and Jade held her breath as she waited to hear from him again, afraid to make a noise.

"I'm outta here!" His last words, she heard him running to get into his vehicle, hearing the actual foot-falls, the door slam and engine start. The gravel flew as he was hauling ass out of the area.

"Hon, you okay?" Anxious, she couldn't wait any longer.

"Oh my God, I have no idea what that was!" His breath was unsteady. "I am scared to death!" he admitted in a rush of words. "I think it was the devil or something staring at me. I've never been so scared in my life!" His words spilled from him in genuine fear.

"Maybe you should check it out? I mean if your friend lives there, maybe they're in danger!"

"Uh-uh! There is no way I'm ever going back there. I am not about to go back and check it out, who knows what the hell that was!" He began to chuckle in tense relief. "I'm putting as many miles between me and it as I can!"

He never did find out what it was, but that was the one time she'd heard him deathly scared. Staring up at the tree, she looked for the culprit who was making the noise when the door opened.

"There you are, are ya ready?" Brady appeared in the doorway looking as handsome as ever.

"Yep, just let me grab my key and we'll go." Stepping back into the room to retrieve what she needed, as the room locked behind them, she asked Brady about the noise.

"That's a cicada," he said as if she'd know what that meant.

"Sure is a noisy thing."

"Yep, he's calling out for a mate," he continued to describe a large bug the size of tree-roaches she'd seen in Texas, or June bugs back home.

"What restaurant do you want to eat at?"

"I don't know what restaurants you have. As long as it's a steak with a baked potato, I'm good. I'm so hungry I could eat a horse."

They left the parking lot and headed out on the freeway to the next town. Strange to be sitting next to him two years later, she'd always dreamt of being here under much different circumstances. Never mind, I'm on holidays and going to enjoy every moment, she lectured herself as she took in the city lights. Glancing to her left, she saw the pool hall he told Ann in an instant message that he frequented.

The music played softly in the background as she recalled their time shooting pool in Atlantic City. He won't take me any places he'd normally go. I can always venture out on my own if want to see them.

Seated at the comfortable booth across from one another, his eyes darted to check the room. Jade was ready with an imaginary story should someone walk up to their table. He's clueless I'm aware of his every move, she thought. Your eyes tell me lots, Hon. With your guard up, you're way more readable. She watched him closely. Deciding on a rib-eye, they spent a leisurely dinner talking and laughing.

Is this how he is on a date? She wondered. Careful to hide those thoughts, she couldn't help but imagine what would happen if she would've lived here all along. Would we have met? They say you meet the people in life you're supposed to and I feel like I've known him all my life, so why did fate bring us together? The thoughts danced as she ate her meal. It was the best steak she had ever tasted and when she was full, Brady joked that she still wasn't able to eat a full meal, half of it still on the plate.

"That's okay. I'll just ask them to box it and I can nuke it back at the hotel for another meal."

"You ready?" he asked after two hours at the restaurant, signaling for the check.

"You're in charge," Jade said as she took out her wallet only to meet with his frown telling her to put it away. They walked back to his car, arguing playfully about her wanting to pay her own way.

"Oh ya know!" he said. "You said I was in charge, so hush!" He smiled wickedly at her, making her eat her own words.

They pulled into the hotel and wandered to the vending machine to purchase a soft drink. The abandoned pool sparkled, the lights from within were beautiful and calming. It'd been a long day for them both and once in the room they relaxed, watching television. Jade lay on her stomach with a pillow propped under her head, Brady had a pillow on her back where he rested over her. It was only midnight, but the day of travel had caught up with her. Both completely relaxed, his hands lulled her by rubbing her back with a comfortable silence between them. It feels so good. He's always touching me. I wonder if he would be like this if we lived together? Would we curl on the couch after a long day's work, just happy to spend time?

"Tomorrow can we pick up a rental car and can I get a U.S. cell phone?" She turned her head to look at him. "Plus, I'd like to get a case of bottled water for the room."

"I figure we'll get that all done tomorrow morning. I have to be at work from four until nine, so I'll need to leave here around three." Brady divulged the plan as his hands continued their relaxing journey.

Jade turned her head back to the TV, sad she wouldn't have more time. "What time do you need to go on Sunday?"

"I have to leave at eleven in the morning until about nine." When he admitted he'd be gone the whole day, his hand stopped moving as if waiting for her reaction.

"And Monday you're back to work." She didn't want him to see the disappointment she felt and kept her eyes on the television.

At the end of the program, she went to her suitcase to grab the supplies to get ready for bed and headed to the bathroom. His teasing her over the years about her lingerie, this was the opportunity to wear it, a surprise he wouldn't expect.

Brushing her hair, she took one last look in the mirror satisfied with her reflection. I'm going to burn this image in your brain, she thought. Opening the door, she walked into the room to find Brady in bed with the TV's glare the only light. Walking to her side of the bed, she heard his intake of breath.

"Wow!" he whispered in the semi-darkness and he flipped the covers back immediately.

She kneeled over his legs, giving him a full visual. His hands circled her waist and began to stroke her sides. With his eyes changing to a smolder, he stared at her then moved to run through her long silky hair. "You are incredible." She watched him gulp hard.

"I thought you'd like this. I figured you didn't get a chance to see me all girly last time."

"No I didn't." His eyes darkened and a playful smile appeared as he reached one finger to trace the lace at the top of her breasts. "You do realize that it's not going to stay on long," he said with chuckle.

"Really," she said with a sarcastic smile. Aha, don't tell me you're not fussy, clearly you like this kinda stuff, she silently praised herself. And you said I was too shy. Hmph, I'm not done yet.

"Wow," was his last whispered word that night.

And When

Comfortable in Virginia

Chapter Twenty-eight

Lying on her stomach, Jade's eyes fluttered open as fingers applied a gentle pressure across her back and warm lips grazed her skin. A leg roamed along her calves, his thigh stroking hers. What a wonderful way to wake, she moaned in appreciation. Folding her arms beneath the pillow, the kneading changed into feathery wisps across her skin. Lord, he's making me crazy and I'm not even fully awake, she thought.

His leg nudged her thighs apart while fingers slid between to stroke her. Her abdomen tightened and short breaths escaped from her lips. As he moved his hand in circular motions, the tingling ceased and a fire started. Grasping the top of the mattress, she rose to her elbows and closed her eyes as electricity ran through her. Biting her bottom lip, "Oh God," she gasped when every nerve ending danced. "Brady," she whispered in a desperate plea.

Settling his body between her legs, his chest molded to her back, fingers grazed her neck as he moved her hair to the side. Hot breaths against the nape of her neck caused shivers, his hand moved to push between the bed and her hip to continue the assault on her clitoris. Raising her hips, wanting, needing him, he brought her body to orgasm as he pushed inside of her from behind. A throaty grumble reached her ears as he nuzzled along her shoulder blade.

"Morning to you too," she curled at his side afterwards. "Can you wake me up for the next twenty years?"

"Only twenty, I was thinking longer." With eyes closed relaxed in the aftermath, his soft smile was of complete contentment.

Wrapped together like a puzzle, each part fitting perfectly, he held her close after spending the morning in their intimate cocoon. Imagine what would happen if I wore lingerie every night, she smiled as she replayed last night in her head. I teased him relentlessly and kept him at bay, stopping his hands. We giggled like teenagers as I made him crazy. He could've taken control at any time, but allowed me to play, even wanted me to, until I pushed him too far. Then he was fierce and wild, I've never felt so desirable. This morning he is so loving and gentle, we'd have an amazing sex life, she grinned for a moment then stopped. There is no together, quit dreaming, she thought.

"I guess I should phone about the car rental. We are picking it up today, right?" She glanced to see him nod in agreement then she reached for her phone.

"What do you mean you close in twenty minutes? It's only 11:40," she said after a minute's conversation and looked over at Brady. He's so relaxed, but if we don't do this…she debated. "Yes, please reserve a mid-size for me and we'll be right down." Giving the clerk her name, they quickly dressed and rushed out the door. Pulling the visor mirror down, she applied make-up and ran her fingers through her hair.

"You don't even need any of that," Brady glanced at her. "You're beautiful in the morning and I kinda like the messy hair." He winked at her and reached to the back of her head.

Getting the rental, wanting to be at the wheel to get familiar with the area, Jade drove and they dropped his car off back at the hotel. Brady treated her to biscuits and gravy, something she'd craved since she used the last package of the mix he'd sent her. Then at the mall, she bought a pay-as-you go cell phone and supplies for the room.

"What's the plan, Buttercup, what do you want to do now?" Starting the car, she hoped he'd show her some of the sights.

"Let's get this stuff back to the room and I'll set up your phone. I brought my laptop so you can let your family know you're safe and sound with me."

In the room, she quietly packed away the supplies while Brady set up his laptop. After a quick email to her family she headed for a shower. After she finished, she dressed in a jean skirt and top then sat on the bed watching him fight with her phone.

"I guess me being here kinda makes things awkward for you, huh?" she asked. His eyes had constantly darted around as they walked around the mall, she didn't know how to feel about that. Angry, sad, a multitude of emotions played.

"Nope, it's not awkward. I'm not worried."

"Since you have to work later, do you want to stay here and relax?" She said then waited. Watch, he'll stay where no one can see him, I bet.

"I don't think we have much time for anything else. Here you go, I got it working." He handed her the phone. "I'm going for a shower." He kissed her on the way to the bathroom.

Sending text messages to Vicki and Sandy to let them know all was well, she lay on the bed mulling things over. He had insisted I stay a week, why did he push for the added time if he's afraid to be seen with me? The disappointment surged.

"That feels better," he said coming out wrapped in a towel.

"Hon," she started.

"Oh boy, okay let's hear it!" He smiled down at her as he towel-dried his hair.

"Wouldn't it have been better if I only stayed here the one day like I planned?"

"No!" His quick, harsh response caught her off guard. "Why would ya say that?"

"I didn't want to make you uncomfortable being here and now that I know I won't get to see any part of your life, why would ya want me here for a week?"

"Are you sorry you came?" He looked hurt.

"No, you don't seem okay with me being here." She watched mixed emotions play over his face then he came to lie next to her. Inches apart, they stared at each other.

"Do you think I'm not okay with seeing you?" He reached to stroke her hair and push it behind her ear.

"I think part of you is glad I'm here and the other part is wishing I wasn't."

"Ah, Hon…" He looked away momentarily then back. "It would've been easier if we were able to go away, but don't for one second think that I don't want you here. I want you to stay even longer. I feel bad I have to leave ya alone while I work. Honestly, you've made me very happy by coming."

"You just seem so tense when we're out and I hate that me being here does that. I guess when we discussed things, you said you were comfortable with me seeing your life and now that I'm here, you're not." I'd stay in the background and with my own car, I could go to and from without anyone thinking differently, she thought. He needs to trust me, but he doesn't.

"This is just harder than I thought. Many people know me. If it weren't for the money, there is no way I'd be working while you're here. Come here." His arms wrapped around her. "I don't want you to feel I'm not happy, I've looked forward to this for so long." He kissed her with tenderness.

At three o'clock, he stopped at the threshold to look back at her under the sheets from their afternoon. His expression said there was no place he'd rather be and he regretted having to go. When the door closed, she lay back. He invested years and at any time could've disappeared, yet never did, why? The little things he sent like the gravy mix, cards, even the stamps when I needed postage, he was always there and my phone never stopped ringing. How am I going to tone this down to friendship?

"God, if you're listening, can you help me?" she whispered to the empty room. "I thought this would go so differently. I mean, come on…can ya make this any more difficult? Why do ya let people meet when things won't work?" She waited for an answer and not getting one, she got up to shower again, deciding to spend her day shopping.

After using the lobby computer to find the stores she wanted, on her way out, she ran into a gentleman leaving at the same time. The older man wasn't paying attention and nearly knocked her over.

"Oh, I'm so sorry," he said as she held the door open for him. "I should be holding the door for you ma'am," his voice sounded flustered.

"Nah, I'm Canadian, we women do for ourselves." She smiled at him as he walked through ahead of her.

"Canada? Where ya'll from?"

"I live above Minnesota."

"Wow, that's cold up there, what brings you to Manassas?"

"I'm on vacation."

"Well, my name is Chuck." He stretched out his hand. "I'm mighty pleased to meet you."

Shaking it, she introduced herself.

"It's getting to the point I don't know how to treat women! My wife divorced me because I work on the road. You see, I'm from Nebraska, but my work drags me all over the place and I guess I'm getting too old to know how to treat a woman no more. It used to be you held the door open, be polite, courteous and things worked out. I just don't know how to be." Chuck finished as tears started to come down his face.

She was used to people pouring out their lives in an instant, but this came far more quickly. "Ah Chuck, I'm sorry to hear you're having difficulties with things. It must be hard to rebuild, especially with working away from home." She watched his shoulders slump and knew he was about to completely fall apart. "What do you do that takes you on the road?"

"I'm a line guy and we go where the money is. We've been up here for the past three months and we'll be here another three," he proudly stated.

"What's a line guy?"

"We hook up the electricity and run the wiring. We work mainly on new construction, but at times we do a lot of fixing old."

"Do you work for the government?"

"No we work for a private company. We were in South Carolina before here."

"Well, Chuck, that's exciting! You get to see different parts of the country and your company pays for your hotels. I bet you meet many people on your travels." Jade put a brighter spin on the life he'd just told her about.

"I guess that's one way to look at it, but the downside is you never get to settle down no place. It gets hard on a person to be alone all the time."

She definitely saw the downside, but didn't want to leave him distraught as a fresh bunch of tears began.

"I'm so sorry miss. I guess you caught me on a bad day when I'm missing my grandchildren and home," Chuck continued as he wiped away the evidence of his sorrow.

"Ah, Chuck, please don't apologize for being honest. Sometimes life throws us something really hard to deal with and it takes time to think of it in a new way. The way I see it, you're just having a moment. Certainly being here for three months you've ventured out. I bet you've met some ladies that would be more than happy to go out to dinner or a movie?" She could tell he was thinking about someone.

"There was one lady a couple weeks ago. I met her right here and we hit it off real well. I asked if she'd go out with me and she agreed. I gave her my number, but she never called."

"Well now, I can see a problem with the way you operate. You should've asked for her number, that way you're in charge. You gotta take the reins!" Jade smiled playfully.

"Aren't you a breath of fresh air," he said then broke out in laughter. "Maybe we could sit sometime and you can update this old guy on how to be single."

"I'll be here for a week, so I'm sure you'll see me about the place when I'm not out shopping or visiting. We'll get you all up to speed on date life, how's that?"

"I sure would appreciate that ma'am. You're a special lady and I want to thank you for giving some of your time to this old coot." He grabbed her hand as if to shake it then wrapped her in a bear hug.

"You're very welcome. Well I'd best be off, it's time to shop. You know us ladies."

Getting into the rental car, she put in a disk she'd brought and let the music blast through the speakers. It was 104 degrees and she rolled down the windows wanting to enjoy the fresh air and not succumb to the air conditioning. Jade reviewed her printed map one last time then set the car in motion. She'd avoid the freeways and duck around using the side roads until she got more familiar with the area.

Stopping at three stores, she bought several items then headed back to the hotel. It was near six o'clock and when she had talked to Brett earlier, they had arranged dinner at seven. They'd meet in the lobby then go to the restaurant. Placing her new found treasures in her suitcase, she picked up the phone to touch base with Sarah and Nicki.

"Hello from Virginia! What ya doing, girly?" she responded to Nicki's hello.

"You know, shopping, cleaning, laundry, the usual. How are things?" Nicki asked.

"So far he picked me up at the airport and we got settled in the hotel then went out for dinner. Today I did some shopping and running around."

"And," Nicki prodded.

"We get along great."

"And, what about the rest of it, come on is the spark still there?"

"Unfortunately, it's even stronger than before," Jade said quietly.

"Unfortunately, it's a good thing, isn't it?"

"My life sucks! I meet the most perfect man and I can never be with him. I come here being all brave to say goodbye to the dreams, thinking we probably won't feel a darn thing and oh man, the chemistry is off the charts. So how the heck am I gonna say goodbye to 'one day's'?" Jade said with humor in her tone, hiding the sorrow inside.

"Don't say goodbye then, problem solved."

"Sometimes I think maybe one day it'll change and then I think what if it doesn't? This is just crazy, why did we meet?"

"I know Babe, it ain't easy. I honestly don't know what to say. I don't think I'd know what to do if it were me."

They discussed their upcoming time together. On Friday, Jade would hop a train to Atlantic City to stay at Nicki's for a few days. Setting up the plan, the next call to Sarah in Jersey was much the same, except Sarah wanted the happily ever after.

"Come on now! Maybe you don't say one way or the other and just wait and see what happens in the future. Maybe seeing you, he'll realize just how good things could be. You never know, maybe life will change and it all works out."

"Part of me wants to believe and the other is afraid to. Seeing him online again, I just don't know if he'll be around when 'one day' comes. Virginia is filled with beautiful women. I looked around as I shopped today. Why did he pick me when he could have any one of these women right in his back yard? Look at him trying to meet Ann, he has no clue it's me. If he's looking already, he'll simply find what he wants elsewhere." Two peas in a pod, yet one pea lived 2000 miles away and in a messed-up situation.

"Baby, you are one of a kind and don't you think for one second that he doesn't know that. All you can do is to wait and see what happens. I still believe in fairy tales."

Sarah's optimism made Jade smile as she got ready for dinner. After checking the mirror she went to the lobby and looked forward to meeting Brett, to hear his take on this whole crazy mess.

"Jade?" The tall, blonde, techno-wizard said with a smile ear to ear as he walked in the front door.

"It's nice to finally meet you." She stood to greet him.

He wrapped her in a hug and his sharp Georgian southern accent greeted her as it had on the phone. "Hiya, Hon, ya'll look so pretty," he said in an exaggerated drawl.

"Hey, Brett, you're pretty darn handsome yourself."

They took seats in the empty restaurant and there wasn't any subject they didn't touch on. From computer trends, phone apps, dating, relationships, writing, to deep philosophical discussions and how each viewed life. In person, she could watch Brett's enthusiastic, energetic personality. When he asked how things were with Brady, he listened intently and he was impressed with how he was treating her.

He asked her to see his apartment in person since he'd sent pictures after re-decorating and they agreed to make time on Thursday. Losing track of time, at eight-thirty he left in a rush to meet his movie date. It was still early and Jade didn't feel like hanging around the room. Not familiar enough with the area to venture out, she mixed a drink and walked to sit by the pool. As she passed a picnic table, Chuck called out to her from the group of men.

"Hey there, Canada, come join us."

Looking at the five faces that turned towards her 'Why not?' she thought. Quick introductions were made as a younger man slid over to make room for her. They asked about Canada and it became a hilarious learning of cultural differences. The blue-collar men were from different states and they'd been drinking since they got off work. Attempting to be gentlemen, they apologized every time one slipped up with a profanity. As a few more came out of their rooms to join the table, the apologizing seemed to dominate the conversations.

"Excuse me ma'am", "pardon me ma'am." Arguments ensued between them. "Ya don't be saying that with a lady here. Excuse him ma'am, his momma didn't raise him right." The offender would apologize on top of the apology.

I feel like I'm in a "Who's on first" skit, she thought. After her drink, she excused herself to return to the room. It was almost 10:30 and Brady would be back soon. Having been in the heat all day, she showered and changed into comfortable clothes.

"Hiya, Hon, how was work?" she asked, taking in the sight of one tired Brady who was sweat-covered. Pulling the easy chair to the edge of the bed, he removed his shoes and put his feet on the edge of the bed.

"It was okay, I'm hot though." He gave her a slight grin.

"Yes, you are," she said with a playful wink. If only he knew how sexy he was right now.

"I need a shower, that's why I'm not on the bed," he said. "How did it go meeting your friend, what's his name?"

"Brett, and he's just like I pictured him. Tall, handsome and full of energy, we had a great time." She described her day, ending with the men by the pool.

"Oh ya know, now everyone loves da Canadian! I leave ya alone for one day and suddenly you have all these men talking to ya."

"It was harmless fun. Honestly though, I think one of those guys was eyeing me up. I can't remember his name, but he was overly polite and always staring."

"Uh huh, I bet more than one was eyeing you up." He frowned.

"Did you get some dinner, have you eaten anything?"

"Nope, nothing yet and I'm hungry!"

"Do you want me to run through a drive-thru and pick up something? You could grab a shower and eat when you're done." Jade had driven by several restaurants today and could easily run out.

"You'd do that? I'm not gonna let you run all over for me."

Obviously he wasn't used to someone putting his needs first. Pulling open the dresser drawer, he grabbed the telephone book and flipped to the restaurant section. Placing an order, he laid money on the nightstand.

"So what did you all buy today?"

"I spent far too much money. I've only been here a day and if this keeps up, I'll be broke."

"Show me what you got."

"You want to see?" No man cares about clothes and shopping, it seemed odd.

"Come on now, show me," he coaxed, sounding interested.

"I hit a few good sales." She went to her suitcase then held up each item. "I bought this outfit." She unfolded the shirt and pants then pulled out shorts, a skirt, shoes and two more shirts and showed him.

"I really like that. That's sharp!" He said at his favorite.

"Then I bought a bunch of girly stuff, you know bras and underwear," Jade said as she walked back to the bed.

"Well?" Brady raised his eyebrow.

"Well what?"

"I want to see them, ya know."

Back at her suitcase, she pulled out the bag that contained her treasures and lifted each matching set.

"Wow, I like that purple one with the bow on the side," he said with a mischievous glint in his eye.

"It is cute, but I like this set the best." Jade slowly unbuttoned her shirt to show him the pink and orange bra.

"Wow! Now that is sexy!" He whistled.

She daringly slid her waistband down to reveal the matching pink and orange lace.

"Ya killing me, ya know." He smiled and ran his hand through his hair, shakily.

"You're tired. I think you should relax for tonight, young man. Remember you're forty-three, ya don't have the stamina of a young fella no more!" She walked past and swayed to avoid him trying to smack her butt.

Guess he proved me wrong about the stamina thing, she thought curled next to him later that night. Her body exhausted from his ardent attention. For hours they laughed and then the moments they were so close, it felt like time stopped. Falling asleep, everything was right in her world.

Jade opened her eyes to hear Brady's deep even breathing. Let him sleep, she thought. He has to work all day and he only needed to leave at eleven. I'll wake him just before since we stayed up late. Only a sliver of sunlight where the curtains met said it was morning. She slipped from the bed and after her shower, dressed then sat in the easy chair watching him. He's totally relaxed, lost in his dreams. He's so cute. His tousled hair, the way he grasps his pillow, I could see this every day of my life, the thoughts played and a sadness washed over her. With only five days left, how do I let him go? She stared at his face which took on a boyish look. Sleep is the one place he finds absolute peace, she smiled.

"What are you doing?" his mumbled voice startled her.

"Umm..." Feeling suddenly caught like a child stealing candy, she stumbled.

His eyes blinked opened to look at her. "And why are you dressed?" He rolled to his side.

"I knew you had to leave, so sleep to your heart's content. You'll be putting in a long day and then have to go back to normal life."

"Nuh-uh," he mumbled sleepily. Pulling down her side of the blankets, he tapped the bed.

"You want me to come back to bed?" she stammered.

"Uh-huh and I don't think you need them clothes," his playful tone and crooked morning smile were boyishly sexy.

Jade undressed and crawled next to him.

"That's better," Brady said in a husky voice, burying his face in the mass of her hair, his hand traveled down her sides and back up. "This is how to wake up, I could get used to this." He tickled her side playfully for a moment and she squirmed. Clamping his legs around her, he began to knead her thigh then moved up to her chest. Hearing his husky breath, his body came awake fully as he spooned her.

"I want you," he grumbled as his hand slid down her abdomen.

She reached behind to touch him and heard his husky groan in appreciation. "You're going to be late if you keep this up," she whispered then giggled at the unintended pun.

He chuckled. "I have no intention of keeping that up. You do that to me. Work or the beautiful Canadian, it's an easy choice."

Taking his time, he held her as he made her body quiver repeatedly. The most giving lover, his breath quickened with hers when the spasms wracked her body as if he could feel what he did to her. At quarter after ten they quickly dressed, neither wanted to leave the bed.

"We'll go here for breakfast. I have to eat something before I leave, I'm starved! You make me so damn hungry!"

And When

Wet In Washington

Chapter Twenty-nine

For the third day in a row the temperatures soared and Jade spent that Sunday stopping at various shops, outlets and points of interest, taking pictures as reminders of her time. Brady had given her his GPS Saturday, but he grabbed the device on his way out this morning. Having stuck to main drags to avoid getting lost, by mid-afternoon she headed back, wanting to cool down by taking a long leisurely swim, then darken her tan.

Getting back to the hotel, the pool area was filled with a crowd. Stopping to take in the scene, it was clear Chuck's company was hosting a party for the workers. There must have been fifty men. This is crazy, she thought. She ducked into her room until a knock came at her door.

"I seen ya sneaking to your room and I figured I'd bring you one of these and see if ya wanted to come out for a bit," a young man from the night before asked as he held out a beer.

"That was nice of you," Jade said. "I think it's a private party though."

"Oh come on, just for a bit?" He smiled, still holding the beer towards her.

"Just for a little while." She took the beer he offered and they walked to the picnic tables.

"This here is Jade, she's from Canada," he said in a thick Alabama drawl. She shook the outstretched hands and returned the nods of those standing further away. A man stood from the table to offer his seat.

"That's okay, I don't mind standing, I won't be here long." This is awkward-I should've said "no thanks," she thought.

"I insist ya sit! I was going to go with the crazy bunch," he said as he pointed to the three men standing on the other side of the patio waiting for him.

As she sat down, the crew divulged a bit of hotel gossip.

"We was thinking you was one of them other girls. Then Mike here told us you was from Canada so we figured you wasn't like them." The remark came from a man across the table who was eyeing her up and down.

"Excuse me, which other girls?"

"You know them girls ya see here, the ones for us." His eyes spoke volumes and Jade looked from face to face at the table. Holy crap! She thought.

"Yeah, the blonde up there," another man said, pointing towards the balcony above her room. "And that one yonder in the pool," he drawled, pointing at a brunette surrounded by several men.

"There's one more dark-haired one around, but I don't see 'em right now, she must be busy." A different man finished then winked.

"I'm just a tourist on vacation, definitely not for hire." She smiled uneasily.

"I was about to offer you five hundred," said a man around forty years old with shoulder-length hair who stood at the left side of the table.

"I'm flattered that you think I could charge and if I ever do get into that business, I'm gonna charge by the pound, so I'd be way too expensive." Her nervous smart-ass remark caught many off guard and they howled with laughter.

"Okay, I'll give you a thousand," the man continued, serious with the offer.

The table hushed and all eyes were back on her. "I don't think a thousand covers the by-the -pound price. I guess I'm just a tourist."

The man sitting next to her put his arm around her. "I like your fiery tongue. You're okay in my books." The rest of the crew laughed and raised their beers, toasting her.

The conversation stayed on the prostitutes and some revealed how they all enjoyed the hired help. Most admitted they'd bought the women's services and her stomach turned at the idea.

"How can you pass the same women around?" she asked, not able to hide her discomfort.

The man who offered her money explained. "Well when ya get to live this kind of life, it solves the problem while being on the road. So you see why it's worth paying a lot of money to have one that no one else touched." His wink left her uneasy.

The man sitting across from her starting speaking about the knives he carried. Somewhat drunk, he bragged how he almost cut his roommate's throat when he woke him out of a dead sleep. Describing his skill with the tool, he admitted he had three on him and offered to show her the blades as proof.

"I've had a long day and I think I'll go relax and watch some TV, but thanks for inviting me."
She stood and politely smiled. Back in her room, she locked the slide bolt on the door behind her. "That was weird," she said out loud as she settled in the chair. After dinner, she phoned Sarah and Nicki to catch up and when Brady called on his dinner break, she recounted the event.

"Wow, a thousand dollars! You got offered money? Ya know! I leave ya for a day and you're already getting offers." He chuckled uneasily.

"It would pay for the trip, Hon!" She threw back at him. "There was a guy here who was half looped and wanted to show me his knives. He is scary enough, never mind his knife fetish."

"Most southern men carry knives so that doesn't surprise me. To know they're passing around prostitutes, that is something I never expected. I bet that's what was going on last night. Didn't you hear that argument at three in the morning?"

"I didn't hear anything."

"You were sound asleep and I was afraid it would wake you so I left the bed to look out the window to see a man with a blonde woman on the second floor in the heat of an argument. I thought it was kind of strange they were arguing about money at that hour."

"Great hotel I picked, huh? I bolted the door just in case they get really drunk out there tonight. I mean they came to my door to invite me so they know where I live. One guy wants to buy me and the other wants to show me his knives, all the while prostitutes earn their money with them all. It's like watching a bad movie, a B-rated one."

"I think you better stay in and make sure you keep that door bolted. I hope nothing happens because I'd hate to have to explain this all to mom." He started chuckling. "Hello mom, well I'm sending ya daughter home. Yep, seems she sold herself to a group of men and it didn't turn out so good."

Both in hysterics, they talked until he finished his break, then said goodnight.

Waking the next morning to a beep, she glanced to see it was past nine and her phone signaled she received a text. Brady had sent three messages. The first, 'G*ood morning Sunshine!*', then repeated with a question mark, and the last 'A*re you okay?*' Quickly she sent a response since he was probably worried after yesterday.

Missing the sleepless nights, Brady style, Jade pulled the covers up, disgruntled, then had just turned on her side to take her medication when her phone beeped again. His message '*Whew, was worried!*'

After a shower, she had breakfast then printed a map on the hotel computer. Reviewing it in the car, she studied how to get to the specific store she wanted in Woodbridge, forty minutes away.
After several attempts over the next hour, she found herself in parking lot at the southern tip of Manassas. Completely overwhelmed, she sent a text to Brady, '*Am lost, Hon.*'

Immediately her phone rang. "What? Where are you?"

"I was heading to Woodbridge and I'm in a parking lot on Weems," she blurted out, her frustration evident in her tone.

"Why don't you use the GPS?"

"Well I would've, Buttercup, but it seems it's in your car at the moment since you grabbed it when you left yesterday."

"Shoot! I'm so sorry, I forgot about that. Hang on. Let me get a map up on the screen."

"I know I have to be on the other side of Sudley so I'm heading back while you get the map." Jade thought it would be best to head back to the major road to follow his directions.

"Hang on! What street are you at again?" She heard him typing on a keyboard.

"I just turned back onto Sudley and I'm turning left on Beauregard, trying to get out of all the traffic!" The steady stream of cars kept her from heading south so she went with the flow until she was able to get turned around. "Okay, I'm just passing Taylor and I'm pulled to the side. Man, these streets are small."

"Okay, okay, I got ya…let me figure out how to get you to the freeway. Why are you going to Woodbridge?"

"There's this shop I want to go to and....shoot, I gotta move, there are cars coming and no way for them to get around me, damn it!" She moved to the next street and turned left then pulled over. "K, I'm on battle now."

"Sunshine, I think you need to just stay put and not move until I figure this out. Just stop and stay there!"

"I would stay pulled over, but cars just keep coming and I'm blocking traffic. Shit, here comes more traffic."

The narrow streets didn't allow for cars to be on the side of the road. With barely room for traffic, she was forced to move as cars appeared from both directions, needing to get out of the way. "Okay, I'm on Ewell Street in someone's driveway."

Brady laughed. "Is there anybody home, because ya trespassing on private property."

"Oh ya know!" She heard his laughter increase. When he settled down to a smirk, he gave her concise directions which led her from Battle to Church, which became Center Street, then to the Prince William Parkway.

"I'll keep the map up and look forward to your next call from North Carolina," he teased.

As the freeway exit approached, the butterflies in her stomach started since multiple lanes led everywhere. She needed to head south and checked the odometer noting the mileage. Her next turn would be Minnieville Road sixteen miles away then another seventeen miles heading east. It was her first taste of the Virginia countryside as she took in the rolling hills and scenery. Finding Minnieville, she drove down a winding two lane road where the hills and corners revealed breathtaking views. This would be the perfect place to build a ranch and she imagined horseback riding through the area.

Arriving in Woodbridge, she pulled into the first parking lot, needing to look at the second map to guide her to the store location. Looking for Smoketown Road, her phone rang. "Are we there yet?" Brady chuckled into the phone. "I timed ya and figured out when you should arrive there. If not I's ready to send a posse to come get ya."

"Yep, I'm in Woodbridge. I'm just trying to find where the store is."

"What's the address, Hon, I'll lead ya there. I's here for you."

"I'll find it, it's around here someplace."

"When ya done shopping and ready to leave there, text me. There is a faster way to get home and I can get you on the Prince William and get you to turn off at 66 which will take you right back to the hotel."

Isn't that sweet, he's looking out for me, she thought with a smile. Nah, he probably doesn't want me to end up in North Carolina.

Finding the store, she spent several hours shopping. Careful to head back before the rush hour began, Jade called Brady to receive detailed directions, making the ride back much simpler. When I66 came into view she followed exactly what he'd told her.

Before dropping her purchases in her room, she peaked at the pool area to find it deserted. Quickly changing, she spent the rest of the afternoon swimming and deepening her tan. Brady was supposed to leave work early, but a text said it wasn't to be. When the workers started to appear after their workday, Jade slipped back to her room, not wanting to be in open view. The next morning as she finished her make-up, a text interrupted, asking her to open her door. Dressed in blue jeans and muscle shirt, Brady stood with a smile on his face.

"You ready to see Washington?"

"Huh, I thought you had to work today?"

"Nope, I took the day to be with you, unless you don't want to go with me to Washington," Brady teased.

"Are you sure? I mean Brett said he'd take me."

"Nope, you want to see Washington and I'm taking ya!"

"Really?" she said, unable to hide her excitement. "You're sure? I mean we could laze around the pool instead and give you time off."

"Nope, da Canadian wants the White House, so get your stuff and let's go."

In shorts and black shirt, she wondered if she'd be cool enough for the intense heat expected today. Wearing sneakers for comfort, she grabbed her purse, camera and they were out the door. At a metro station they parked to ride into Washington and Jade got a bird's eye view of Virginia as the train followed its route. Mainly above ground, it gave her the opportunity to see cities along the way as Brady explained the many different lines; green, orange, red, yellow, all serviced different states leading to Washington. Arriving at Metro Center, they disembarked and climbed the stairs.

The heat was incredible and not used to it, she quickly found a vendor to purchase bottled water. It was 110 degrees and the cement only radiated the sun.

Brady walked to the information board, asking what she'd like to see. "The White House, Smithsonian, Washington Monument and the Library of Congress, especially the Library of Congress since copies of my books are behind the walls."

As Brady studied the board, Jade took in the large grass area lined with tall trees that separated Jefferson and Madison, the two streets in this tourist's haven. The Washington Monument was just west and she turned to capture a picture. Looking east, the buildings often seen on her TV screen back home, the United States Congress loomed. The street was a constant hub of traffic with tour buses and cars. Sidewalks were jam-packed with a steady crowd. As they began walking east, she marveled at the architecture of the buildings. Some had stood here for a hundred years, while others were marvelous new creations like the Ripley Garden building, a massive cylinder shape. She snapped photos while trying to keep up with Brady.

Crossing Seventh Street with the many pedestrians, they entered the National Air and Space Museum, the air conditioning a welcome relief. Looking at the exhibits, Jade thought of her dad and how he would've loved this place. It was Brady's first choice and not on her list. Small and full-sized airplanes, from the old to the new technology of the stealth were displayed. Even the Wright Brothers' airplane sat in a room all on its own, marking the beginning of flight.

Leaving the building, they walked across the grassy area to the Smithsonian National Museum of History. As they passed the Art museum, Jade thought that given the opportunity, she would've loved to walk through.

This heat is unbearable, she thought as they waited in line at the museum entrance. Brady had already mentioned her bright red face, but once inside, the cool air gave her the break she needed. After walking through, Brady guided her to the most impressive display of all, the Hope Diamond.

Walking up to the square glass display, she waited while each tourist took their turn then stepped closer to view the incredible vision. The bluish black rock rested on its white revolving pedestal.

"Hon, I think this would make a great souvenir for my visit, can you get it for me?"

"I'll get right on that." He grinned mischievously. "Tell ya what, why don't ya just go ahead and take it. I bet you look real pretty in an orange jumpsuit and hey, you'd become a resident!" He poked her in the ribs. "Mom, your daughter is becoming a U.S. citizen!"

Stepping back into the heat, he turned to ask what she'd like to see next.

"It's getting too hot for me." Jade wiped her sweat covered brow. "Maybe we can just see the White House?" she asked warily. "I can't take this much longer, we've only been here two hours and I'm nauseas."

"I was gonna say you're looking red again. Okay, let's go then we can head back."

He led the way back to the metro and after the short ride they emerged on a busy downtown street surrounded by cement buildings and offices. It was cooler, but Jade marveled at how men breezed by in three piece suits, looking dapper and untouched by the humidity. They passed a small park with sprinklers watering the grass, the mist a welcoming coolness. The entrance blocked with large cement pillars prevented anyone from driving through without checking with a guard. As they approached Pennsylvania Avenue, the White House came into view.

"It looks bigger on TV!" she remarked with a smile. "I thought it would be this huge massive building."

"Way back I suppose it would have been considered big," Brady replied.

She saw his frown. He went out of his way to do this with me when he knew full well Brett was willing to bring me here, she thought. "Well, Hon, let's head back." He seemed to relax. They made their way back to the station and waited for the train underground, protected from the heat, Brady sat alongside her.

"Are you okay, you look awfully red in the face," he said with a smile.

"I'm just too hot. We're not used to this kind of heat in Canada."

"It usually isn't this hot here. We haven't seen temperatures like this in ten years. You picked a heck of a week." He poked her in her ribs.

"I must look a mess!" Jade ran her fingers through her sweaty hair to push it in place.

"You look just fine, you're always beautiful."

When the metro arrived the doors opened and a rush of heat greeted them. They settled into a seat side by side. I think I'm going to barf, she thought. After three stops, they were asked to move to another car since the air conditioning had stopped in their current one. Far more comfortable in the next, they spent the rest of the ride in comfort. Arriving in Vienna where they parked, they saw gray storm clouds roll in as they stepped onto the platform.

"Do you want these as a souvenir of our day?" He handed her two tokens.

"Thanks, Hon."

Leaving the building, they were met with the beginning trickles of rain and barely made it to the car when the fury of the sky opened up with rain in sheets. Starting the car, the wipers couldn't keep up with the blast of water from the heavens.

"Holy cow," Brady remarked. "One more second and we'd both be drenched. Not that I'm saying that would be a bad thing." He winked at her. Jade held her breath as he maneuvered into the freeway traffic. She couldn't see the hood of the car, let alone anything in front of them.

"You hungry?" he asked and glanced to see her nod. "What would you like to eat?"

"Whatever you choose is fine. I haven't eaten today, but I'm not all that hungry." It'd been a mistake and her stomach rolled, thinking of food.

"Should've eaten, no wonder you're not feeling well," he scolded.

In the buffet-style restaurant they each filled plates and settled into one of the tables. She finished as Brady went up for a second helping. Back at the hotel, they spent the next couple hours enjoying time until Brady needed to leave for his evening job. Tomorrow she'd spend time with Brett and see his fancy apartment.

And When

New Ways to Deal

Chapter Thirty

Jade sat in Sarah's passenger seat on the drive back to the airport. The two weeks had passed far too fast and she was heading home. She had a tearful departure in Virginia when Brady picked her up to drive her to the station. Before leaving, Chuck appeared at her door as she was busily putting her suitcases together. On Thursday, she had chatted with him by the pool and he wanted to say goodbye. She introduced Brady, who watched Chuck hug and thank her for her help.

"Do you know how special this woman is? She's one of a kind." Chuck shook his hand.

"That she is," Brady replied.

Arriving, they had a half hour to wait for the train that would take her to see her friends.
The Manassas train station was right out of a history book, an original building from 1914, painted a rustic red. The clay roof and the wooden overhang held by large wooden pillars displayed an old state flag proudly at each top.

Jade walked around the platform thinking, while Brady lounged on the bench. Since he arrived this morning, he seems relaxed, she thought. Maybe he's grateful I'm on my way and he doesn't have to make time for me. Last night he squeezed me in after work when we went for an ice cream.

"Are you happy you'll have your life back to normal after I'm gone?" she asked, hoping to hear he'd miss her.

"Define normal." He smirked at her and a sad expression appeared in his eyes.

Not wanting to force words he didn't feel, she tried another way to see what he was thinking. "I wish I lived here, I'm going to miss spending time with you, ya know?"

"Would be nice, wouldn't it? But you have your life back home."

"I could definitely live here. It's beautiful, warm and friendly, maybe one day when I'm rich and famous."

"If you're rich and famous, don't you think you'd want to live in Hawaii or Florida, why would you pick Virginia?"

It's obvious why I'd pick here, she thought and turned to look the other way. If he doesn't feel the same, there is no point in me explaining it. The train whistled in the distance, a signal she'd soon be gone. Careful to hide her face as a tear escaped, she knew that the time had come. From the end of the platform she watched the train pull in. I wonder if I'll ever see him again, the thought danced through her mind. Her plan was to get back home and focus on her writing. First I'll have to stop loving him, but who knows what tomorrow brings, right?

When the train stopped, she stood in line to board with her bags at her side and Brady stood watching a few feet away. She turned to look at him then quickly away as sadness enveloped her. When the last person boarded, she turned to find him right by her side. Looking up into his eyes her tears started. Just say it, damn it! Tell me you don't want me to leave and I'll not give up. Say you love me. Say something, Brady! Do you still want a life one day? Who am I to you? He looked at her as she searched his eyes, her heart crumbling inside.

"Ah, Sunshine," he said then wrapped her in his arms for a brief moment. There were no words of feelings. No "I'll miss you's." Not even "I wish you didn't have to go."

"All aboard," the man hollered from the train steps looking directly at her.

She pecked him on the lips, then stumbled at what to say. "Try to be happy and smile more in life, Hon."

The conductor signaled her and she grabbed both suitcases. With a tearful look back she climbed the stairs. Settled into a seat against the window, the tears rolled down her face. He stood on the other side of the glass watching with concern. She mouthed the words "Goodbye," then turned her head not able to look at him. When her tears subsided, she moved to the dining car and thought about spending time with her friends, needing to get rid of the sadness.

After a week of fun with Nicki and Sarah, it was time to head back home, having enjoyed her time. As they drove to the airport, Jade's phone rang to find Brady on the line.

"Hey you," he said, sounding upset. "We gotta talk!"

That was never a good start. "What's wrong?"

"Well my phone is being watched at work again and they're looking into the calls to Canada." His voice sounded panicked. He had texted a few times and called her U.S. phone twice since she left Virginia.

"Your phones been calling me for how many years, what's really going on Brady, what are you trying to say?"

"I'm not saying anything. I just wanted to tell you we got problems."

"Look Brady, if you don't want to talk to me anymore you should just come out and say it." Jade turned to see Sarah's concern. Her son looked back at her with a sad expression from the back seat.

"I'm not saying that! I'm just telling you I don't know why this is happening and thought maybe since you were here something started again. I won't be able to call you for a while until this settles down."

"Ya know, this just doesn't make sense! So you lied to me when you said they knew about me and this is the truth? Here we go again with bullshit. What if I need to get hold of you, let's say I'm pregnant, what then, Buttercup? I can't believe you'd do this!" She felt the fury inside. Having to say goodbye to the feelings he'd built over the years was hard enough, but his saying there'll be no communication at all was too much.

"Do ya think you are?" he asked.

"Do I think I'm what?"

"Pregnant?"

"No! That was just to show how little you think of me. Why you'd do this when I'm on my way to the airport is just wrong. I didn't tell anyone I was there, so if your work is up your ass, you must've said something. Jesus, Brady, if you don't want me around then so be it, you do what you gotta do!" She hung up on him.

Explaining the call to Sarah, neither could see any other reason for what Brady had said other than to blow her off. Tired of his games, she sat in the airport boarding area waiting for her plane after hugging her friend goodbye.

I should've spent only the one day, but no, he begged me for more time and for what? Why did I bother? Staying a week didn't answer a damn thing. To hear he wants to stop the friendship completely, after all he put me through, I'm not worth anything? Not even friends? I blew a fuse with the pregnant line, but it proves my point, he doesn't care. Her head swam with thoughts.

"What?" she asked, answering her phone seeing Brady's number on call display.

"Look, I will find a way to contact you. I know you're upset and rightfully so, but I promise I will call you, okay?"

"Don't worry about it, Brady. I'm okay with it all. It's just another blow I have to take at your hands and this is the final one." She felt the tears run down her face and looked around to see several people watching her. "I'm tired of not knowing what the hell you're thinking. If I'm not worth holding onto in life then let me go." Her voice raised and a man smiled at her a seat away with pity in his eyes.

"Aw Hon, I'm not saying I don't want you in my life, I'm just saying I have to find a new way. I promise I'll call!" His voice sounded strained.

"If you really wanted to keep me, you'd buy your own damn cell phone and tell me what the hell the truth is. To call me when I'm sitting in a busy airport to make me cry is just…..whatever! I have to go…my plane is boarding."

"Text me and let me know you got home safe."

"What do you care?"

"Don't say that, because it's not true! You mean a lot to me. Text me so I don't have to worry. I can't tell you what's happening, because I don't know and need some time to figure it out."

"I have to go." Jade stood to get in line with the boarding passengers.

"Promise me you'll text me, Hon."

"Fine," she said then hung up.

Arriving home at two in the morning, she shut her cell phone off, then curled into her bed. There are questions again and I'm so tired of asking them. I spent years trying to figure him out. This trip was to end things on my terms and just when I resolved it all, he throws another soap opera. I guess I'm losing my best friend. She couldn't even cry anymore. Drained, she fell asleep.

And When

The next morning she woke to a ringing phone.

"So how was the trip?" Lisa asked excitedly.

"It was great!" Jade said and described most of the trip, leaving out the details of Brady. Their conversation would be cut short by her beeping line. "Can I call you back, that's probably Mom checking on me too." They said goodbye and Jade switched to the call waiting.

"Hello?"

"Hey, why didn't you text?"

"It makes no difference."

"What do you mean no difference? It makes a difference to me."

"Look Brady, I don't know what's going on. We spent a great week together and the next thing I know I'm being fed some line that doesn't make sense. I came down to say goodbye kinda, thinking we'd still be friends, but you're ending the friendship and I don't know what to say any more."

"I'm not saying the friendship is ending. What do you mean you came to say goodbye? I kinda thought something was up, but I figured it was just me," he said, shocked by the news.

"This craziness has to stop, it's too hard. With you constantly talking about 'one day's' and the ranch, flirting…it's hard to not know what you really feel. You never once opened up or said any words. It's a constant guessing game of who I am to you. You've got a mixed-up life, Brady, and I can't give my all to someone who will never do the same. I came to let go of the dream of ever being together, but I thought we'd still be friends."

She heard his long exhausted sigh. "Look, I'm going through something. I know ya not gonna understand, but I need some time to sort it out. It has nothing to do with you. I need you to trust me, because I do need you in my life. It may take a while to figure stuff out, but I promise we'll talk all about it. Please don't give up on me."

"Why do you even tell me things like that? You know my hamster won't stop until it knows what the hell is going on. Why don't you just tell me? You ask me to trust you, but you certainly don't trust me, do ya?"

"It's a long story and I can't go into it all right now, but I promise I will."

"I don't get it! You've been in my life for years. I didn't force you to stay. Not once did I demand anything from you. I asked for common courtesy and truth. Now you're telling me you will call me someday and you don't trust enough to tell me? You are the most infuriating man. If you leave, that's your decision."

What can I do, hold a gun to his head? I want to interrogate him and strap him to a lie detector just to make him stop these games, she thought.

"I promise I will fix this all."

"After all the crap you put me through, I can't believe this." She hung up the phone, not knowing if it would ever ring again. Follow the plan! Carry on with life. You can learn to live without his support, she lectured herself.

She opened two emails from her agent, Dennis, who had received two contract offers for her series. He knew she'd been out of town and asked her to call the second she landed. Reading the email filled with hope was what she needed. Listening carefully to the publishing offers, each would give a small advance for the first volume and wanted the rights to the others. Not happy with negotiating all volumes, Dennis felt they should offer the first volume and then wait to see the outcome.

It came down to who would launch her series more successfully. As they spoke, Jade went to the publisher's websites and although Dennis favored the larger of the two, she liked the marketing advantage the other offered. Both reputable choices, he suggested she hire a publicist to help with the promotional side.

Asking him to forward both contracts before agreeing to either, the next day she spoke with Linda and discussed the options with her family. The consensus was the smaller firm. Having a full-time job she'd need all the extra help she could get. Signing the contract, volume one was handed over and Jade started writing a novel.

Within two weeks she started receiving daily emails from editors, marketing people with changes needed and the endless work started. The marketing department wanted to hype her work and prepare for the planned release date of next August. With the promotional side already underway, the cover displayed on their website as a "coming soon" feature.

Jade spent every free minute doing whatever they asked. Nothing was going to stop her from achieving the dream. In November when her phone rang, "Jade speaking," she answered, expecting it would be about the book as usual.

And When

"Hey, Sunshine," Brady's voice came across the line.

It'd been three months since she heard from him. "Hey," she answered.

"I wanted to check on you. I've been worried about you."

"I'm keeping busy. Have you worked through whatever the big mystery is?" She bit her tongue in telling him her big news. If her life was about to take a new direction, she didn't want a leaning post that moved.

"No, I'm still going through things, but I just needed to hear your voice. I wanted to see what you've been up to and how you've been."

"Work, home, writing…the usual," Jade said then heard his long exhale, the line silent with neither talking. I used to look forward to his voice, she thought.

"I know this is hard on you, I can hear you're still hurt, but I promise this will all change soon and we'll get back to normal."

"It is what it is, whether it's hard on me or not. I'm done believing in someone who doesn't believe in me. Working things out over the past years means little, because here we are right back at the start when I thought I proved you could tell me anything."

"I'm so sorry for all this. Things are coming to a head and I'm trying to get a handle on it. I can't even explain it to myself, never mind to someone else."

"Whatever," she said. This call brought the sadness she didn't have time for and their conversation ended moments later. The uncomfortable pauses replaced the laughter they had once shared. Not being able to tell him her news killed her. He'd always been her biggest supporter.

The world went by in a blur as she worked day and night, a constant learning process and a to-do list that kept her occupied. Change this, fix that, open a bank account for book royalties, talk to an accountant and if she had any free time, she wrote as a way to help her not think.

The book was a love story, a failed one based on the world of online. Her cousin Jacquie suggested it and thought it would resonate with many. With Nicki's man never coming through and the many stories of the pain people suffered it gave her more than enough material to craft a story. At night the pages flowed from her fingertips, the anger and sorrow spurred her on as she created a world of date site nightmares. After five months, the manuscript was finished, having exorcised the pain within.

And When

Getting to the Bottom

Chapter Thirty-one

"I know you're surprised to hear from me," Brady started the conversation in early May. "I know you've talked to Val. I just want to say I'm sorry," he said in a rush of words, his tone breathless.

"Val?" she asked.

"The woman I got mixed up with last spring, she said she called you."

"What? I think you'd better explain." Her anger growled. It's been six months, for fuck sakes, and I was doing just fine. I knew it! Just when everything is going right finally, damn him!

"I swear my life is a twisted mess and I tried to keep you out of it. That's why I wasn't calling. I tried to keep you safe, but with her talking to you, it seems you're going to be dragged into this."

"I want answers and you're going to give them to me!" Jade's anger unleashed. "How many are there, how many?" She yelled into the phone.

He took a deep breath. "I spoke to several on the net and met a few, but not as many as you think."

"I want to know when and where, how long ago, how many. I want details, you hear me!"

"You were the first and I never even thought about anyone else. When it all fell apart with us, I was afraid I'd lose you. Then as things got back to how we used to be, I felt even lonelier. You are so far away and I figured I'd try to find what we shared. The same way you did before. I met the first lady and I didn't feel the connection, so I kept looking. I'd meet them face to face, but it just didn't feel the same. Honestly, nothing happened until Val." He paused for a moment.

"She was in the same boat as me and it just sorta happened. I didn't plan for it, but one night suddenly she was grabbing me and I didn't stop her. I don't know why. I didn't feel anything for her and she said it was just sex since her husband hadn't touched her in years. We got together a couple times, but it felt forced, robotic in a way. When I told her I didn't want to any more she demanded I leave my family."

"Jesus Christ, Brady!"

"I know! I stopped seeing her, but she threatened to tell people. It took months talking and she'd text or send emails constantly. When I told her she made me feel empty inside, she disappeared. I thought she finally got the message. Then somehow she knew I was talking to you last summer, don't ask me how, but she did and it started again. By then you were already coming here and when you were here, I caught her following me a couple of times and had to shake her off. She's made my life a living hell ever since. Honestly, I didn't want to bring you into this, but she said she talked to you."

"Why would you let me walk into this? How could you put me in this situation? You should've told me before I came down there and I wouldn't have come."

"You won't believe this, but it's the complete truth…I wanted to see you. As selfish as that sounds, you are the only one I've kept in my life. I love you and needed to see you. God, I've missed talking to you over the months. I kept my distance and thought I could handle this, but it's only gotten worse. She's out to destroy me." He inhaled then continued. "The day you left, she went to my work and started causing trouble. I got hauled in and questioned since she'd been writing the head of security and telling them all kinds of shit about me. That's why they asked about your number. I'm about to lose my job, my family and I just don't know what to do. I'm in the biggest mess and it's all my own doing." Brady sounded as if he'd cry.

"I want everything. Her name, email and address, something's not right with this. I haven't talked to anyone, so there's a lie right there. I'm getting a feeling someone's not the only fucking liar in Virginia. Tell me every detail right from the start."

"I met Val in a chat room. I found out later she was stalking me right after our first lunch. Nothing had even happened between us. We were only friends and met for dinner or lunch to talk about our troubles at home and I thought I was helping her. She told me all about her husband and how he beat her and I felt sorry for her. But she has pictures of every woman I met. She photographed every single one! Snapping a picture of us having dinner or drinks. Even pictures of women I work with or talked to in the parking lot. She followed me for months and knew where I'd be and when. She had copies of every email. Private conversations and some were racy, but I'd never even been with any of them, it was just all talk. She printed everything and gave me a copy and told me she was going to ruin me if I didn't leave my family."

"How could she get all your private emails? That's impossible. Are you sure you were talking to different women or did Val make up different profiles?"

"Huh?"

"I have to tell you the truth. I did the exact same thing last year."

"What do you mean you did the exact same thing?"

"Remember Ann? That was me. I'm not proud of it, but I wanted the truth. When you denied playing online and outright lied to me, I created Ann. You flirted with her and wanted to meet. That's when I decided to say goodbye since you obviously were looking for someone."

"I felt something wasn't right about her. It was just when this all started with Val and I made up a whole bunch of stuff, trying to figure out who Ann was. I thought it was one of Val's friends trying to pump me for information." He chuckled. "Sunshine, I can't believe you did that. You simply amaze me sometimes. I was looking over my shoulder the whole time you were here because all this shit was going on. At least I know that was you, but the women from a few of those emails I did meet. It wasn't Val."

"What the hell did you get yourself into?" Jade debated for a moment. "I'll try to help you figure this out, but I need to know everything that happens from now on, every detail."

For the next two weeks he filled her in nightly by phone, trying to keep their conversations private, yet Val knew every time he spoke with her, or anyone. Jade got him to send phony emails to fake addresses she created and after each, he received a text from Val asking why he was talking to that person. How does she do it? Jade researched using her computer, finding sites for cell phone tapping. As she read, she learned that for anyone with a Blackberry, everything would be accessible. The culprit needed only a moment alone with a phone to infiltrate. No password needed. After questioning Brady thoroughly if he'd left his phone unattended, Jade told him what she discovered. If he'd replace his SIM card, Val would no longer know his whereabouts. Jade almost laughed at how easily she'd figured this out. Brady lived with this terror for months, some computer genius he is, she thought.

He was too afraid to tell work his phone may have been tapped so Jade guided him to a computer site about tracking attempts. He sat in his car using both hands typing on his laptop and placed his phone on the dash using the speaker. In the midst of talking, suddenly she heard a female's voice.

"What do you think you're doing?" a woman screeched.

"I'm looking at options to deal with you!"

Jade sat deathly silent, afraid to make a noise, fearing she'd be discovered. She heard the rustle of him closing the laptop or putting it aside.

"I can't believe you! You lie to people and you won't talk to me anymore? You'd better watch your step, you fucking asshole," the woman ranted.

"You're sick in the head, ya know that? My work is onto you and if you keep it up I'm going to charge you! Quit following me and messing with me or I'll go to your husband and end this sick game."

"You started this and you think you can leave? Nice fucking try, I don't think so. You live in your big fancy house and think nothing of hurting people. My husband knows everything so your threats are empty!"

"You're lying…your husband don't know shit!" Brady's voice shook.

"You're an asshole! You have a week to fix this the way it should be or you'll regret it!"

"You're nuts! You need fucking help. Stay away from me or I will go to the cops and have you arrested. Leave me alone and you can stay out of jail," Brady yelled back.

"Like I'm scared, you're gonna regret this for the rest of your life."

"I already regret it. I regret meeting you. Regret knowing you and I if I ever hear from you again, prepare to go to jail."

Jade wanted to yell out and tell him to get away from the psycho. Val was unstable, but up until now Brady hesitated to believe it. Crazy doesn't shake your hand and introduce itself, she told him several times.

She heard foot-steps and a voice calling him filthy names in the distance. A car engine started and tires peeled away in haste. Brady exhaled and then she heard the car door open and close. Within seconds the line went dead. At least she finally knew the truth. Hearing Val's voice confirmed this was real.

A few minutes later Brady called back. "I'm sick to my stomach. What the hell am I gonna do?"

"Go to the cops Brady, do you see how totally nuts she is?"

"Look, I'll call you tomorrow. I'm about to be sick."

The next night she spoke with Brady and repeatedly told him to file charges. Brady believed his threat would end this, ashamed to ever have gotten mixed up with Val. He struggled to come to terms with his life being threatened by someone he chose to cheat with.

Three months later she heard from him again when her phone rang late one Thursday night.

"Jade, I just want you to listen." He took a deep breath. "Even if I live to be a hundred, I don't think I can ever express how sorry I am for hurting you. I don't care about what I've done to anyone else as much as I care about what I did to you. I'm sorry I ever lied to you, sorry about all of it. I know it doesn't help anything and I wouldn't blame you if you hate me for the rest of your days, it's what I deserve. I need you to know that you are the last one I ever wanted to hurt." His tone scared her. "I don't deserve someone like you and I don't know why I did this. I have no excuse or explanation. I'm lost and don't know anything anymore, I'm about at the point where I can't go on no more."

"What's going on?" Jade asked in a hushed tone, scared of his mindset.

"I needed to talk to you, needed to hear your voice again. I feel so horrible and understand how much pain I caused you. I never intended to hurt you, please believe that. I understand the hurt you feel." A long pause before he continued. "Sunshine…I don't know what to say or how to make it up to you, you were right about it all, everything."

She could hear the tears that slid down his face, his voice shaken. "Where are you?" she asked softly.

"I'm lying in a hotel room. Val did it. I've lost my job, my wife, my kids, you, I've lost everything. I tried to explain to work that she was crazy. They interrogated me and Jenny, then all the people who know me. She sent a copy of things I kept in my phone for work right to security and added a bunch of stuff that was never even on my phone, but no one believed me."

Shocked it'd gone that far, she remained silent, not knowing what to say.

"She told everyone who knows me I wrecked her life. Said I left her pregnant, can you believe it? I haven't been with her since last March, over a year ago so the dates don't even add up. She'd have the kid by now if that were the truth, but no one believes a damn word I say. She's five months pregnant and changed all the timelines. Two months ago she demanded twenty-five thousand dollars or she'd make sure I lost everything. I didn't have that kind of money and I told her to fuck herself. Now, I have nothing."

"I don't think you'll ever figure out why you ended up here until you look inside. If you love your wife, then fight to get your life back. The paternity test can be court ordered and that will show Jenny the truth. I know it could take her years to trust in you, or maybe she doesn't want to and you go your different ways, but you are a father to those two boys, don't you ever think they don't need you. You've got to be there for them. That's what matters. Nothing else is important but being a dad to them no matter how this all plays out." Jade was afraid he was thinking of ending things.

"You're incredible, ya know. Here I've put you through hell and you're worried about me." She heard a shaky laugh come through his sadness. "What did I ever do to deserve you?"

"Well it sure wasn't a bunch of good deeds." Jade heard his chuckle. "What I feel is par for the course, but you brought something good to my life when I needed someone."

"Yeah, I brought you a bunch of misery and pain."

"You brought me reality-some of it's not so good, mind ya." She chuckled to lighten his mood hearing him chuckle. "But you were there through the worst time in my life and taught me how to feel again, how to love. You gave me that." Of course it was only to be ripped it into shreds, the hurt went so deep, she thought. I finally understand what it means to lose my heart. Follow who you are Jade, be true to yourself and thank him for touching your life, the right thing is always the hardest, she lectured herself.

"Brady, you said I was your first, maybe meeting me made you end up here." If she'd told his wife years ago, maybe this would've never happened. She struggled so long with the right thing. Maybe she'd been wrong?

"None of this is your fault, Hon. I did this all, everything." His voice filled with pain.

She heard him sobbing quietly and it ripped at her heart to hear him this way. "Maybe I wrecked ya," she whispered.

"How did you wreck me?" he whispered back.

"Maybe ya tried to replace da Canadian since I was the first and that's why none of the other one's worked out. I's kinda irreplaceable, Hon," she said and heard a soft chuckle then a long exhausted breath.

"That you are Hon. I do believe there will never…be anyone like you. I've never talked to someone…as long as I have you…you're the only one." He sounded half asleep. "You know…I wish I met you…we'd…be together…I care for..."

"Sleep on things, Handsome. You sound like you've been through the wringer. Tomorrow when you wake up, go hug your boys, they need you." She whispered into the phone, a gentle reminder not to do anything stupid.

"I am…oh so…tired, Hon. Don't…think I've…ever been this…way. I will hug…promise. Sleep…well…Beau..." His voice soft, he was almost asleep.

"Night, Buttercup, love you," she whispered softly. She listened to hear his deep breaths and hung up, scared. What if he took pills? Shit, I don't know what to do. Do I phone his home and tell Jenny or wait until tomorrow and check on him?

For the next two months she sent emails, texts and even tried to call, but Brady was gone. No explanation, nothing. Checking the Virginia obituaries, she feared the worst, but didn't find his name anywhere. He'd simply vanished. She was tempted to phone his family, but what if he was just tired that night? They'd sure as hell be angry to learn of another woman in his life. Being 2000 miles away left her helpless.

And When

The Hopes of Future

Chapter Thirty-two

After four years of pain-staking work, Jade began traveling the U.S. to promote her second novel. The first was quickly picked up by a publisher after the tremendous success of her series. She was an established author with her series topping the charts two years ago. Six months after the first volume launched with sales through the roof, the publisher quickly negotiated a substantial advance for the rest. Having gone through publishing the first, the remaining volumes were a breeze and after trademarking the character, a merchandise line started.

She spent the next year writing more volumes and now fourteen lined the store bookshelves. She couldn't help but pause at the bookstore to see her work displayed. She took a break from the series, and when her first novel hit the shelves running, she was kept busy as it jumped up the charts. After a year of promotional tours, she started the sequel and this tour was to promote it.

After hiring Diane, her publicist, Jade found things easier to manage. When the tour for her first novel started, she quit her full-time job and the jumble of dates, times and places became a big mess. She hired Diane halfway through, needing a professional and she'd been on board for two years.

Jacquie became her full-time personal assistant to keep her organized with a never-ending list of demands on her time. Catapulted into a new arena, it was a daunting schedule of meetings, negotiations, decisions and travel. She'd lived in more hotel rooms the past three years than anything else. Selling her little house, she rented an apartment, not having the time to maintain things anymore. With the first novel hitting best-seller status, the movie rights were negotiated and soon she'd see her work on the big screen.

Life changed completely in ways she never expected. Even her love had life kicked in a year ago. She had met Derek, a PR manager for a magazine in New York. He joined a session where she was being photographed for an article. Being man stupid as ever, she had no clue he was interested until flowers showed up at her hotel room with a note asking her to dinner. It'd been a long time since she even thought about going there again. It took years to get over the pain of Brady and the nightmares still came on occasion.

Derek, was tall, dark haired, and with a career in the public relations, he was away on business much of the time. It was an easy fit since time together was limited, giving her space to get to know him. They liked many of the same things, but a few big differences still loomed.

Both independent, at first he said he shared her dream of a horse ranch. Born and raised in Texas, he moved to the big city in his twenties and never looked back. He viewed it as a vacation home and that was a sore spot for her, but they were working on it. Jade took up riding and tried to spark his interest, but Derek conveniently was always unavailable.

It took her months of repeated effort to not feel bow-legged or to walk crooked after saddle time. It was a way to test if the dream still existed since childhood wishes sometimes fizzled with adulthood. With her first time back on a horse she was hooked, the beauty and strength of the animal still captivated her. When Jade traveled she'd scout areas for the ranch. Derek would join her on occasion, but it was usually Jacquie who tagged along for the rides through the countryside looking at properties. It was the life she never believed would happen, the very goal she had reached for, but it was hard to get used to. Her name appeared here and there as gossip spilled about her and Derek's relationship. His job saw their image in the papers on the odd occasion, which Jade didn't enjoy. They'd broken up and gotten back together so many times according to the rumor mill, that it was a shock when he announced their engagement two months ago.

He surprised her during one of her speaking engagements, when he posed the question from the audience during the question and answer segment. The room silenced after he stepped to the microphone and asked "Will you marry me?" Caught off guard Jade looked to Jacquie sitting in the front row, then back up at Derek, standing several feet behind her.

"Umm…that's not a question about writing," she stuttered and put her hands on her hips in a playful manner to hear laughter in the room. He's waiting, but what to say? "Are ya sure ya want to marry someone who spends most of her time behind a keyboard? Have ya thought about that?" She posed back to him, trying to find the answer, stalling for time.

"I think that would be the perfect marriage. I'll build matching offices in the house facing each other so we share time." Derek's humor played back and the audience howled.

"Geez, how does a girl say no to matching offices?" she said in jest.

The audience cheered in response and he jumped up on stage to slip the ring over her finger. I didn't say yes, she thought and felt panicked.

Confused, she didn't move as he kissed her in front of everyone. It'd been an unconventional proposal and they'd only known each other ten months. After discussing it in private, he agreed to a long engagement before heading to any altar. At that time her life was taking off in new directions and she needed to be sure about him. He was happy with her saying "yes" and would wait until she was ready.

"So what's my schedule?" Jade looked to Jacquie on the flight from California to Texas for the next set of book signings.

"We stop in Houston on the 6th at two locations, then San Antonio on the 8th and 9th at three then off to Dallas on the 10th for two and Garland on the 11th for the last stop. We fly off to New Orleans on the 17th then Florida on the 25th. I'm not giving you those dates until we're on our way." Jacquie knew she could only handle the here and now. "Is Derek still coming to meet you in Texas?"

"He said he would. There's an old ranch near Garland that I spotted and want to check out. Here." Jade passed her the write-up. "It doesn't look like much, but it has the riding arena and the stables are ready to go, but the house would be a tear-down." Jade had seen many different places over the past while and none fit her dream. I want to stand on the site and know this is where I want to be and I'll keep looking until I find it, she had told Jacquie at the last place.

"Once we're done in Garland, I think I'll book off a couple days and go visit my brother in Mission."

"Sounds good to me, you deserve a break. This schedule is getting to us I think," Jade said, realizing how much she relied on Jacquie. They'd been on the road for three months already and the excitement of the tour was wearing thin.

"By the way, the studio called again wanting you to look at a re-write of the script. They want your approval to change things in scene 141," Jacquie told her.

"Oh ya know! Ya think they'd just be able to do it. Why can't they just decide how to present it?" To have to keep going over it was like never closing the door on the memory. The hurt faded with time, but it never disappeared. She'd lost her best friend, no rhyme or reason and had to silently accept he was gone from the face of the earth.

It was bad enough that at signings she'd hear how fans suffered hurts, both men and women who had their lives torn up by people on the Net. Jade knew that pain all too well. Her books stemmed from the online world, she crafted the novels by encompassing many people's experiences. Being the go-to person for years, she'd seen the pain it left behind. Money, love, lust, it was a big game for some out there and it left casualties every day.

"When we get to the hotel, remind me and I'll look at the changes they want me to approve," she said, looking over at Jacquie to see that worried expression. She had watched what Jade went through for years after Brady's last phone call. Listened to her every nightmare and dealt with the tears that fell when the memories haunted her.

On the last leg in Garland, Jade, Jacquie and Diane, sat at the table in the center of the B & N bookstore in Fire Mill mall, tired from the past week's hectic pace. When they arrived at eleven this morning, they were ushered in through the back entrance to avoid the crowd in the front. Like every other signing, Jade greeted the crowd with a question/answer period about the new book and after a half hour, they took seats as she signed her name repeatedly into every book cover.

It was wonderful to meet the fans and most asked when the next book was coming. Jade diverted the conversations to the task at hand, not wanting to ever promise another sequel. It was time to forget about online. This novel had carried on with the nightmare stories of heartbreak and uncertainty, but she needed to find a new subject, this one emotionally drained her.

It was easy to get tied up with each individual, but as always Diane kept the line moving. Jade got better with speeding the process at every signing not wanting to leave any person standing when the time ran out. It was after four p.m. and they'd been here a half hour longer than originally planned, but she'd gotten to them all, the store almost empty with only a few shoppers milling about in the aisles.

"So I guess you're outta here for a couple days, did you call Dan to let him know you're coming down?" She turned to Jacquie who sat sipping a coffee as Jade stood to stretch her legs.

"I told him I'd be driving and I'd be there at around ten. I guess I should let him know this ran late and I'll see him later." As Jacquie dialed her cell to contact her brother, Jade turned to Diane, who'd fly back to her office in New York for the next six days to be with family and then meet them in New Orleans for the next round.

"I want to start promoting the movie end of things as soon as I get the studio's permission. I've prepared a press release that I want to show you."

Diane said as she rifled through her briefcase to retrieve the sheet. She grumbled about the studio's caution in not revealing the information before their stamp of approval, clearly frustrated with having to wait.

"Excuse me. Sunshine, can you sign this to Brady?" Her breath caught and a heartbeat sounded in her ears. Jade glanced to see Jacquie's shocked expression, her cell phone motionless in the air. Feeling her knees begin to tremble, afraid to turn around, she held her breath, feeling about to collapse. Slowly she turned to meet the dazzling hazel gleam she'd never forgotten.

The End

Wendiann

I was raised in a small Canadian town, in an average middle-class family. Living an ordinary life, I've married, divorced, dated, loved, lost, struggled, worked, succeeded and failed. I am blessed with friends and family who patiently let me find my footing as I spent endless hours in front of the computer following my inner voice.

Discovering my newfound love of writing quite by accident in 2009, I sat at my computer following a new idea. The '*Sit N Do Nothing-Hamster Series*' was the first project and it took three years to complete the workbook series of self-discovery. I created it with the hope that people share tidbits about their lives for now and generations to come.

Finding my inner voice, I tried my hand at fiction. '*And When*' was written from September 2010–January 2011. '*Now What* the sequel, was started in July 2011 and nearing completion.

I hope to keep creating forever and encourage anyone who ever thought to try something new, to follow your inner voice and enjoy every moment. You never know what lies around the corner when you dare to dream.